Pathways in Geography Series

The National Council for Geographic Education

THE PATHWAYS IN GEOGRAPHY SERIES has been created by the Special Publications Editorial Board of the National Council for Geographic Education to support the teaching and learning of themes, concepts, and skills in geography at all levels of instruction.

DATE DUE

Demco, Inc. 38-293

nguage
s

ehl

PATHWAYS

PATHWAYS IN GEOGRAPHY Series Title No. 1

The Language of Maps

For information about this title or about the series:
National Council for Geographic Education
16A Leonard Hall, Indiana University of Pennsylvania
Indiana, PA 15705

ISBN 0-9627379-3-3

Printed in the United States of America.

THE LANGUAGE OF MAPS

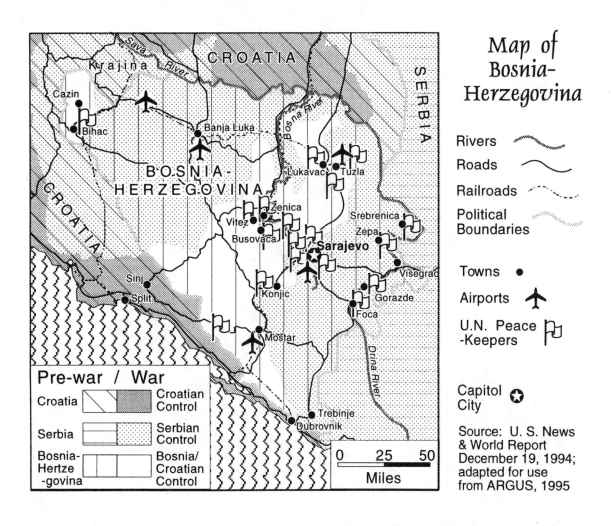

Map of
Bosnia-
Herzegovina

Rivers
Roads
Railroads
Political
Boundaries

Towns •
Airports ✈
U.N. Peace
-Keepers

Capitol
City ✪

Source: U. S. News
& World Report
December 19, 1994;
adapted for use
from ARGUS, 1995

**STUDENT MATERIALS
GEOGRAPHY 1-1501**

SPRING 1996

GERSMEHL

STUDENT MANUAL

THE LANGUAGE OF MAPS

Phil Gersmehl
Department of Geography
University of Minnesota
Minneapolis, MN 55455

with many contributions
from many people, including:

Greg Chu
Phil Porter
Sona Andrews
Dwight Brown
Richard Skaggs
Carol Gersmehl
John Fraser Hart
Joseph Schwartzberg
Margaret Rasmussen
Catherine Lockwood
Althea Willette
Eric Anderson
Phil Heywood
Cary Komoto
Clay Mering
Todd Henry

and, especially,
Jim Young

TABLE OF CONTENTS

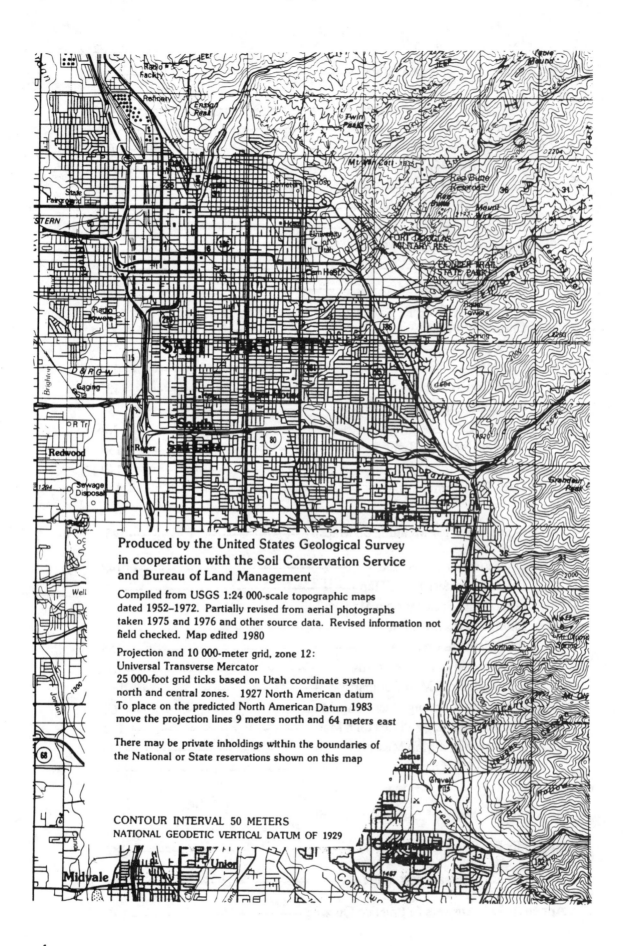

Produced by the United States Geological Survey
in cooperation with the Soil Conservation Service
and Bureau of Land Management

Compiled from USGS 1:24 000-scale topographic maps
dated 1952–1972. Partially revised from aerial photographs
taken 1975 and 1976 and other source data. Revised information not
field checked. Map edited 1980

Projection and 10 000-meter grid, zone 12:
Universal Transverse Mercator
25 000-foot grid ticks based on Utah coordinate system
north and central zones.   1927 North American datum
To place on the predicted North American Datum 1983
move the projection lines 9 meters north and 64 meters east

There may be private inholdings within the boundaries of
the National or State reservations shown on this map

CONTOUR INTERVAL 50 METERS
NATIONAL GEODETIC VERTICAL DATUM OF 1929

PART 1
COMMUNICATING BASIC SPATIAL CONCEPTS

Imagine trying to read a book by looking at one randomly chosen letter at a time. It would soon become obvious that individual sensory impressions do not convey much meaning all by themselves. For example, the single letter "G" has a wide range of possible meanings, which become clear only when we learn what letters go before and after it. "CUGDH" is a meaningless string of letters to most people, but "LIGHT" does mean something to people who speak English. Its message is still ambiguous, however; notice what happens to the meaning of "light" when surrounded by other letters: flash*light*, de*light*, s*light*, en*light*en, *light*er, *light*ning, and *light*weight. This is a mighty important idea, even though it may seem almost too obvious: the meaning of a letter or word in a language like English depends on its position in the *sequence* of letters or words around it.

Like a spoken or written language, a map consists of individual symbols that show their full meaning only when they are seen in the context of all the other symbols around them. The symbols on a map can be described as "letters" or "words," but the analogy with a spoken language is not quite accurate, because the map symbols are related to each other in *two-dimensional space* rather than in *one-dimensional sequence*. The "grammar" of a map is therefore not the same as that of a spoken language. The rules of the language of maps have some special traits that help a map do what it is supposed to do, namely to show the arrangement of (and connections among) things in space.

To make things even more complicated (but realistic), we must keep in mind that the language of maps, like any spoken or written language, is a human invention, the result of many people thinking their own distinctive ideas in dissimilar places at separate times. As a result, different kinds of maps, like different spoken languages, may use different "letters" and "words" to say the same thing. The maps below are the products of two ancient groups of seafaring people, who independently developed some unique ways of navigating across the ocean and communicating ideas about location on it.

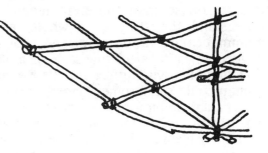

Part of an ancient Polynesian stick-map

The sticks represent wave angles and star positions, two key elements in their successful navigation system.

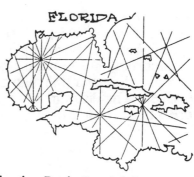

Part of a medieval Portolano chart

The lines represent shorelines and compass directions, key elements in an alternative navigation system.

INTRODUCTION -- THE ELEMENTS OF A LANGUAGE

The language of maps, like other languages, has elements that we might reasonably describe as *vocabulary* and *grammar* -- things that seem to act like the nouns, verbs, adjectives, paragraphs, and tenses in a spoken or written language. A map communicates through graphic symbols, whether on a printed page or a television screen. (Right at the start, we should admit that the phrase "language of maps" is a convenient expression, but it has a lot of conceptual problems. For example, maps do not have a single coherent set of symbols; as you have already seen, "the" language of maps can have many different ways of expressing the same idea, and some of those alternatives may be mutually contradictory, like different dialects of a spoken language.)

Reading a map is in many ways like reading a written story. There are *characters* (the houses, roads, crimes, and other things depicted by the map symbols), and they have *traits* (*Victorian* house, *interstate* highway, *violent* crime), which are important to the narrative. The story has a *setting* -- it occurs in a specific place (Milwaukee, New England, Asia) and usually at a specific time (1987, the Middle Ages, Pleistocene). There are *relationships* and *interaction* among the characters (area X is *close to* place Y, regions P and Q have a paved road *between* them, city A is *upstream from* factory B).

As with a written story, the reader must have a prior knowledge of most of the technical aspects (the symbolic vocabulary and the structural grammar) of the language used in order to understand the story. Even so, each reader will see something different in the story, because the unique perspective and experience of each individual will color the meanings of the words for that person and thus influence the way in which the story is read.

We should not carry the analogy with a written story too far, because the symbols in a written language occur in a one-dimensional sequence, and there is a conventional way to read them -- a reader of a page in English will start at the top of the page and read each line from left to right. A map reader, by contrast, can start anywhere in two-dimensional space, and there are no clear rules that specify the order or speed in which that space should be explored.

Learning a different language can be frustrating, because the learner must operate on so many different mental levels at the same time. You want to understand the story as a whole, and yet you find yourself struggling with grammatical details or the meanings of individual words. It can be irritating to get bogged down in calculating scale or looking up the definition of a new symbol, but that kind of "trivia" turns out to be essential if we are to figure out how a given kind of map could serve some "higher" purpose, such as to persuade someone to accept a particular opinion or to support a given policy. When the details of this language get frustrating, it may help to remember that a newspaper picture can say something even to an illiterate person, but most of the message is visible only to the person who knows how to read the caption and the accompanying story.

Finally, we should emphasize that the process of communication is <u>not</u> a one-way pipeline, through which a "sender" transmits a "message" to a "receiver." On the contrary, both the cartographer (the "author" of the map) and the map reader have an important effect on the kind and amount of information that can be gained from a map. Moreover, the map dialect and production technology can also shape the message. The diagram and text on the next page show one way of looking at the process of communication.

A GRAPHIC MODEL
OF THE PROCESS
OF COMMUNICATION

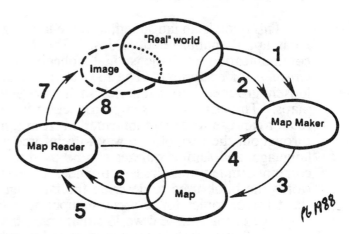

COMMUNICATION PATHWAYS

1) **Sampling.** The map maker goes to the "real" world and gets some information from it. The nature of that sample depends on the purpose for the map and the skill of the map maker, but no amount of technical graphic wizardry can cover for bad information-gathering.

2) **Sensing.** The real world also "sends" a message to the map maker, in the form of some unsolicited sensory impressions -- like answers to questions that were not asked. Even though they were not consciously sought, these impressions may affect some of the decisions made by the map maker.

3) **Symbolizing.** The map maker "encodes" the information into map symbols and places those symbols on the physical object (the map) that is the focus of our attention in this book. This step almost always involves some modification or simplification of the data.

4) **Considering.** The appearance of the map may affect how the map maker thinks about the world and thus may lead that individual to make some changes in the map. Indeed, many geographers make maps just for themselves, to help interpret some information they have just obtained.

5) **Searching.** A map reader goes to a map in order to answer some question. This question may be precise and sophisticated ("How many young steelworkers live in Democratic voting precincts west of Cicero Avenue?") or extremely naive and vague ("What does this blue area mean?")

6) **Transmitting.** Like the real world, a map also sends some visual impressions that are strong enough to be noticed even though they were not specifically sought. A person should neither exaggerate nor minimize the persuasive ability of a printed map.

7) **Interpreting.** The map reader takes some ideas from the map, combines them with prior knowledge, and uses that combination to form an image of the real world. This image rarely is the same as the one the map maker had. Indeed, some people try to describe "communication error" in terms of the differences between the map maker's and map reader's images.

8) **Reconsidering.** The map-derived image now stands "between" the map reader and the "real" world, and it may alter how the map reader sees the world. When you stop to think about it, isn't that the main reason for communication: to change what or how someone thinks?

A MAP OF THIS BOOK

This book is an introduction to the language(s) that people use to express ideas about spatial relationships. The first part of the book is about the communication of basic spatial concepts -- ideas like *location, distance, direction,* or *enclosure.* The next chapters describe various kinds of maps, loosely grouped into categories such as *reference, topographic,* and *thematic* maps. The last section is an introduction to some analytical tools that a map reader can use to extract information from a map. *Practice pages,* scattered throughout the text, offer a way to reinforce your grasp of the details of the language, and sample quizzes can be used to check your understanding. A combined index and glossary provides a review of some of the specialized words the book used to describe the language of maps. Finally, there is a short list of topics for *projects,* independent investigations that employ the language of maps in real-world situations. If you are taking a formal course on the subject, your instructor may assign a blend of tests and projects in order to evaluate your mastery of the language.

We have deliberately structured the book so that the individual parts can be "covered" in any order. If more than a casual acquaintance with another topic is needed to understand a given idea, we put a cross-reference into the text. Part 1 (basic spatial ideas) provides a logical foundation for the course, but knowing all of the optional ways of expressing the fundamental spatial concepts is not absolutely essential to understanding the rest of the book. You could skim Part 1, go on to the rest of the book, and return for a more detailed look if you need some of that information for a project. Part 2 (the shape of the land) is a sequence of ideas that build on each other; a person needs to know how a map shows elevation and slope before trying to draw a side profile of the land or plan a route through rugged terrain. Parts 3 (topographic map features) and 4 (thematic map types) are organized like a "gallery," with self-contained "rooms" that you can browse through in any order. The first five chapters of Part 5 (searching for meaning) are more like part 2, in that each chapter adds detail to a single basic idea. The analytical tools are presented in "cookbook" fashion, so that you can do some rather sophisticated map analysis with little time spent in building a mathematical foundation. The chapter on distortion is, in many ways, a summary of the rest of the book; it looks at ways in which a map message can get confused.

Over the years, we have tested most of the chapters individually with a large number of students, who have been more than willing to tell us where a particular idea could be explained in a better way. We welcome additional suggestions for improvement; please send your ideas to this address:

Phil Gersmehl
Department of Geography
University of Minnesota
Minneapolis, MN 55455

A final word: the book uses a variety of maps as illustrations, but you should feel free to substitute maps that cover specific areas of interest to you. We have tried to write the text so that it can be used with different examples. Our students are almost all Americans, and therefore most of the examples in the text are maps they are likely to encounter here. The accompanying worksheets and handouts are designed to be flexible; the teachers' guide provides suggestions for substituting maps of other topics or areas.

COMMUNICATING THE IDEA OF LOCATION

The *position* of an object in space is its most fundamental spatial attribute. Unfortunately, a close look at the concept of *location* reveals an occasionally frustrating fact: it is difficult to express the idea of position without using the related ideas of distance and direction (which deal with the relative position of two objects). And it is just as difficult to describe distance or direction without using positional words. At a very basic level, the communication of spatial ideas seems to rely on a kind of circular logic. It is not surprising, therefore, to find that different people at different times have developed different ways to communicate the concept of position.

The first step in learning how to interpret a map is to become familiar with its "vocabulary" and "grammar" of position -- the "words" and "sentences" that it uses in order to say where things are. In everyday life, you are likely to encounter at least six different ways of describing position:

1) **Egocentric location** -- Young children view the world only in relation to their own bodies. In this worldview, things that are out of sight literally do not exist. This mode of organizing space remains quite useful as we grow older, even though we learn more abstract ways of describing places and things that are not visible at a given time. Our verbal language has a rich variety of words to deal with space that is organized around a central person. Consider, for example, the complex use of body orientation and perspective in this statement: "I left the shovel behind you; look over your right shoulder, just beyond the third rosebush." People also unwittingly use this locational language every time they turn a map so that it points in the direction they are facing.

2) **Landmark location** (neighbors) -- One way to communicate the location of something that is not visible from where you stand is to describe some landmarks near it: "It's under the maple tree by the library." This system works fairly well, but only if two conditions are satisfied: there must be a suitable landmark near the object of interest, and both the speaker and the listener must know where that landmark is. In practice, the landmark system begins to break down as soon as there are two or more libraries, trees, etc. Assigning proper names to landmarks (e.g. Wilson Library) can help, but that solution does not negate the fact that a comprehensive system of landmark location demands an enormous amount of basically trivial knowledge: the locations of a large number of landmarks.

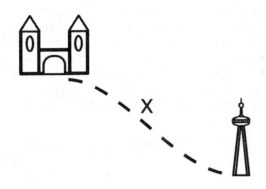

3) **Line-of-sight location** (route) -- This method may have evolved as a way to solve the problem of not being able to keep track of a huge number of landmarks. The key to line-of-sight location is to use a restricted set of prominent landmarks as reference points. These in turn allow people to describe the locations of new objects in terms of their position along a line between two major landmarks: "It's about one-third of the way from the Student Union to the Tate statue." A variant of this system is to specify a landmark and a route: "Go ten minutes east on highway 46 from the old water tower."

4) **Network location** (address) -- An existing network of roads or trails can provide another way to specify the location of an object: "It's near the intersection of Main and Oak Streets." This system works best when the basic arrangement of roads has a clear pattern (e.g. when 351 North 12th Street is between 3rd and 4th Avenues on the street that is 12 blocks east of the town center). Unfortunately, the answer to the key question, "What is a clear road pattern?" depends largely on experience; Americans find square grids fairly easy to understand because most of us were taught how to use them in elementary school.

5) **Enclosure location** (jurisdiction or ownership) -- It is also possible to specify a location in terms of the area that surrounds it: "You'll find it in the maple forest" or "It's in the east half of Hospital Complex." In geometric terms, an *area* is basically the two-dimensional counterpart of a landmark (a non-dimensional point) or a route (a one-dimensional line). The areal method of location is widely used in the rural Midwest and the Great Plains, because the original Public Land Survey divided the land there into square "Townships" that contained 36 "Sections," each supposedly one mile square. The 640 acres in each section, in turn, were divided into sixteen square "Forties." "They're out on the lower forty fixing fence" thus describes the location of two farmers in terms of an enclosing area small enough that you should be able to see them as soon as you are also inside it. (Pages 38-41 have more on this survey system, which is very important in specifying the locations and sizes of real estate.)

Maple forest

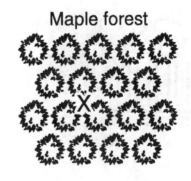

Hospital complex

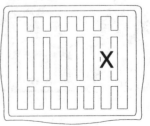

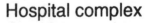

6) **Coordinate location** (abstract grid) -- The most abstract and yet potentially most precise way to communicate the location of an object is to describe it in terms of its position on a set of mathematical coordinates superimposed on the landscape. There are three different grid systems that are in common use in our culture:

a) *Polar coordinates* form a circular grid, on which a given position can be described in terms of its direction and distance from an arbitrary point at the center of the grid (e.g. an airport control tower or a navigation beacon).

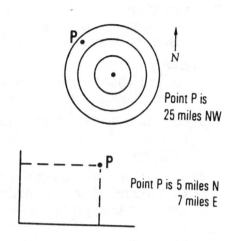

Point P is
25 miles NW

b) *Orthogonal coordinates* form a rectangular grid, on which a position is described in terms of its distances from two arbitrarily established reference lines that cross each other at right angles.

Point P is 5 miles N
7 miles E

c) *Spherical coordinates* are like a blend of polar and rectangular grids. Near the Equator, the latitude-longitude grid system of the earth looks like a set of orthogonal coordinates. Near the north and south poles, it is (not surprisingly) polar. In the middle latitudes, the two systems compromise in a way that allows us to express locations on the curved surface of the earth (see also Page 25, The Global Grid).

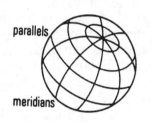

parallels

meridians

REPRISE -- AN INEVITABLE CIRCULARITY

The category of basic spatial concepts includes position, direction, distance, and enclosure. In this book, we discuss them in separate chapters, as if they were logically separate, yet all of our ways of communicating the idea of position seem to rely on an understanding of one or more of the other basic concepts. This apparent circularity in our logic will not go away. The next few chapters deal with ways of communicating the ideas of direction, distance, and area, and it will become all too obvious that all of those vocabularies take the idea of position for granted.

A crash program to "improve the language of maps" will not solve this logical dilemma. In fact, we should probably take comfort in the fact that it underlies all forms of communication -- at some level, we all combine our own experience and the words of others in order to give meaning to what are no more than arbitrary symbols. The resulting language becomes useful as a way of communicating ideas only to the extent that other people share the same set of arbitrary associations of "words" with "meanings." Here, the logical circularity becomes even more acute, because we really have no way of knowing exactly what idea a given person associates with a given word.. All is not hopeless, however: we still can watch whether someone who asks for directions actually gets to the destination.

LOCATION -- PRACTICE

There are four levels of competence in the mastery of any language. In order of increasing sophistication, these are:

1) *identification* -- can you tell what language is being spoken? Can you recognize the characteristic patterns of symbols that are part of the essence of a given language?

2) *comprehension* -- can you comprehend a sentence in the language? Can you tell what combinations of symbols carry a message and which ones are meaningless in a given language?

3) *expression* -- can you say something clearly in the language? Can you choose symbols that express exactly what you want to say in a given language?

4) *translation* -- can you translate ideas from one language to another? Can you recognize the subtle nuances that require you to reformulate an idea into an appropriate idiom rather than merely recode the words into a given language? (You may have heard of the preacher whose sermon quotation, "The Spirit is willing, but the Flesh is weak," was literally translated into Russian as "The vodka is strong, but the meat has spoiled.")

You should learn to be comfortable (at all four levels) with several different "vocabularies" of location before going on with the rest of this book. Using the map on the next page and working with a partner, practice using different combinations of seven locational languages (egocentric, landmark, route, network, enclosure. and polar and rectangular coordinate systems). Describe the location of any of the map points A through Z in terms of its relationship to the figure of a person, its proximity to a mapped landmark, position on a line of sight, street address, enclosure within a marked area or legal jurisdiction, direction and distance from the Control Tower, or distances from the labelled Baselines. Then, give your locational description to your partner, who should decode your message, try to figure out which of the lettered places you were describing, recode it into another language, and give that message back to you to decode and check.

For example, you could express the position of place S as "The place that is about 800 meters north of the Airport Control Tower." Your partner would then interpret that phrase, recognize it as a form of polar coordinate location, decide what place you are describing, and translate its location into a different language: for example, "It is near coordinate 6C, about three centimeters to the right of Westline and six centimeters up from Baseline." Your partner should then give the new message back to you, and you should decode it to check whether it is still talking about place S.

CAUTION: our experience with many students over the years seems to indicate that most people <u>do</u> need to practice this process of translation in order to achieve fluency in the languages of position. The vocabulary of position is important for almost all of the advanced skills in map reading and interpretation. If you can invent another way to accomplish this objective, fine, but we must remind you that we do have our institutional ways of finding out whether you have achieved all four levels of mastery!

TRANSLATING THE LANGUAGES OF POSITION

Place	First description of its location	Second description of its location	Check
1	next to control tower	at 2t/Ct	✔
2			
3			
4			
5			
6			
7			
8			

COMMUNICATING THE IDEA OF DISTANCE

The second fundamental spatial concept is *distance*, defined as the amount of space between two locations. As in the case of location, the basic idea of distance is usually expressed in terms of some other basic ideas, and therefore it can be communicated in a variety of different ways:

1) **Physical objects.** The space between two locations can be estimated by noting the number of objects of a known size that can be put between them. The handiest measuring devices for this purpose are parts of the human body -- guess where people got the original idea for the distance unit that the English call the "foot?" Other physical distance measurements, now more or less obsolete, include the *span* (the width of an outstretched hand, or about nine inches), the *cubit* (the distance from elbow to fingertip, about 18 inches), and the *pace* (the length of two steps, about five feet).

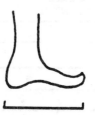

2) **Arbitrary standards.** The wide range of shoe sizes in the human population illustrates an obvious problem with the first definition of the foot. To solve that problem, a new distance unit, the *meter*, was defined as one ten-millionth of the distance from the equator to the north pole. Unfortunately, a permanent metal reference meter was made and adopted as the official standard before the earth was measured accurately, and therefore the official meter is not exactly as long as it was supposed to be. Other arbitrary standards include the *nautical mile*, the *league*, and the 66-foot *surveyors' chain* with its 4 *rods* (each 16.5 feet or about five meters long) and 100 *links* (each about eight inches long).

3) **Angular displacement.** One can also communicate the distance to a specified location in terms of the *sight lines* (directions!) from two places with known positions. This method relies on well-tested rules of plane geometry, and it can be a useful practical tool. For example, to measure the distance across a stream without getting your feet wet, you could:

1) sight a prominent object on the far side of the stream,

2) walk along the stream at right angles (a square corner, or 90 degrees) to your first sight line,

3) count your paces as you walk, and

4) continue in a straight line until you can sight back to the same object at exactly a 45 degree angle away from the first place (a piece of paper folded diagonally can make an acceptable sighting device).

5) Since the two legs of a 45° right triangle are equal, the distance across the stream (A) is equal to the length of your path (B).

This *baseline-and-angle* method works as long as there is enough space on your side of the stream for a baseline of adequate length. Alternatively, you might memorize the angle and length relationships for a number of common triangles and use the one that seems most appropriate:

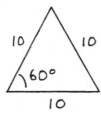

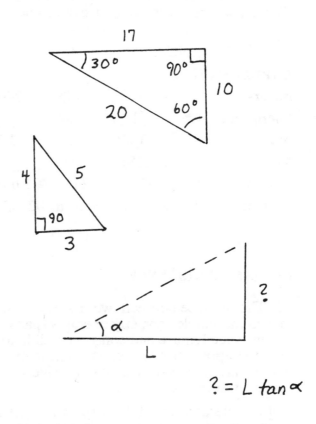

The next step is to use a sighting device and *trigonometric* table. As long as the first sight line and the baseline meet at right angles, the distance across the stream is always equal to the length of the baseline times the *tangent* of the sighting angle. A surveyor's transit, laser range-finder, or satellite transponder can improve the accuracy of the distance measurement, but the basic principle remains the same: you can always figure distance if you know two angles and a distance or two distances and an angle.

$$? = L \tan \alpha$$

4) **Time equivalents.** Another way to express the distance between two places is to figure the amount of time necessary to go from one to the other at some standard speed: "It's about a three-hour walk from here." To translate a time-distance expression into traditional distance-terms, use this formula: $d = r * t$ (*distance* equals the average *rate* of speed, usually expressed as a distance per unit of time (e.g. 30 miles per hour), multiplied by the amount of elapsed *time* (expressed in the same units)). A nation-wide speed limit for auto travel has made this method useful in describing distances between towns, at least in uncongested areas; two hours at 50 miles per hour is about 100 miles. A variant of the time-distance idea is the measurement of driving distance in terms of gallons of fuel or six-packs of liquid refreshment.

5) **The one constant.** Einstein's theories of relativity have pointed out that our yardsticks and other units for measuring distance can all change their lengths, depending on our velocity and where we are in the universe; the only invariant is the speed of light in a vacuum. This fact has been used to develop some extremely precise methods of measuring distance. These measuring devices depend on the fact that each different kind of radiant energy (orange light, blue light, heat, radio waves, X-rays, etc.) has a unique wavelength (think of it as the length of a single step) and frequency (number of steps per unit of time). When multiplied together, wavelength and frequency always equal the constant speed of light.

DISTANCE -- PRACTICE

Fill in the blanks on this table of six different distances. Use the ones that are already filled in as guides to show you how to convert from one measurement system to another -- for example, distance B tells you that one kilometer is a thousand meters and a mile is about 1.6 kilometers. By the time you are done, each distance will be expressed in five different ways.

DISTANCE:	A	B	C	D	E	F
EXPRESSION						
meters	1000	1609	2400	___	___	___
kilometers	1	1.6	___	___	___	.025
miles	0.62	1	1.5	___	17	___
feet	3281	5280	___	23,000	___	83
time at 30 mph	75 sec	2 min	3 min+	___	___	___

(hint: 30 miles per hour is equal to 1/2 mile per minute)

ROAD-MAP DISTANCE

The distance between two places is a more complicated idea in the real world than in the simple geometry of empty space. Factors such as route alignment, road quality, speed limits, and congestion all help make "actual" distance greater or less than the apparent distance on a flat map. Partly in response to this situation, a typical state highway map may provide one or more of several different ways to figure distance:

- a verbal statement of the map scale ("one inch represents 26 miles"). This allows you to use a ruler (or your thumb, hand, or outstretched fingers, if you know their lengths) to estimate the distance between two places.

- a line with marks that represent distances on the map. This allows you to "measure" a map distance with your fingers or other tool and compare it with the marked line.

- a grid to help locate places. On one city map, for example, "Frogtown - C4" says to look for the town in the fourth row from the top and the C column (the third from the left edge). If the grid sectors are squares 20 miles on a side, a place in sector C8 would be about 80 miles from Frogtown.

- a distance table ("triangle"). This table allows you to look in the *row* that is labeled by one city and the *column* that is headed by another to find a number that indicates the distance between them.

- small numbers next to highways. These show the distance between towns, intersections, asterisks, or arrows; check the map legend to see what endpoints are used. CAUTION: Some maps may use several different kinds of endpoint symbols with numbers of different sizes or colors; make sure you use the right ones.

- a simplified map with straight lines between major cities. Numbers next to those lines show distances and/or travel times.

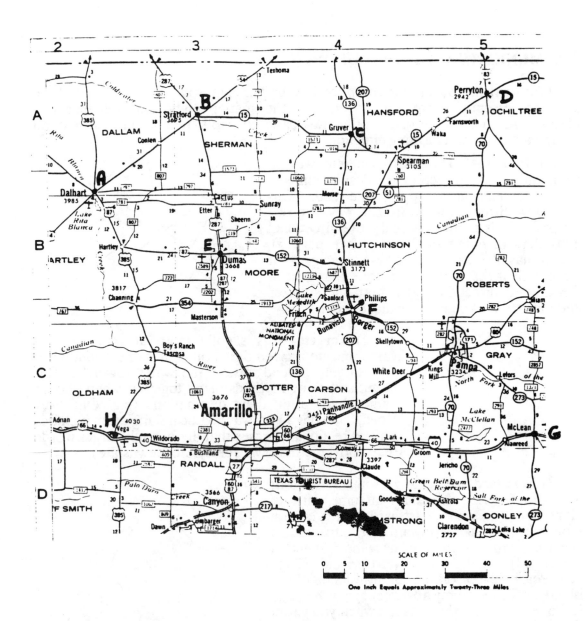

SAMPLE QUIZ QUESTIONS -- DISTANCE

You will be given a portion of a highway map.

_____ 1) Print the straight-line distance (nearest mile) between point *B* and point *D* on the highway map.

_____ 2) Print the highway distance (nearest mile) between point *A* and point *H* on the map.

_____ 3) Print the shortest highway distance (nearest mile) between point *A* and point *C* on the map.

_____ 4) Print the amount of time (within ten minutes) it would take to go from point *A* to *B* at a speed of *40* miles per hour.

_____ 5) Print the name of the town that is closest to *the center* of grid sector *D4* of the map.

_____ 6) Print the designation for the sector that contains the point marked *B*.

COMMUNICATING THE IDEA OF DIRECTION

Direction, like *location* and *distance*, is a fundamental spatial concept. All three ideas are essential if we want to describe the spatial relationship between two places. As in the case of the other two basic concepts, people have developed many ways of communicating direction:

1) **Routes** -- The most concrete way to communicate the direction to a destination is to put the traveler on the appropriate road: "This is Willow Street; follow it that way for two blocks." This method is really the directional equivalent of *landmark location* (see page 5), and it has the same basic disadvantage -- it works only if there really is a street that goes in the desired direction <u>and</u> if both the speaker and the listener know where that street is.

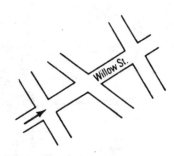

2) **Targets** -- A slightly more abstract way to communicate a given direction is to name a landmark as a target: "Head toward the water tower." The target and route methods blend together when people name roads after their destinations (e.g. Old Fort Road, San Diego Freeway). Local slang often includes some directional phrases that are actually target words (e.g. upriver, crosstown, Jerseyside, downstate).

3) **Standard targets** -- Hawaiians use four words to describe directions in some parts of Honolulu: *mauka* (toward the central mountain), *makai* (toward the surrounding ocean), *Koko* (toward a hill near the east end of the island), and *Ewa* (toward an old village near Pearl Harbor on the southwest side of the island). "To get to my apartment from here, go Koko on Dole and then Mauka when you get to Palolo Valley." This system makes sense in a place where some roads and bus routes go all the way around the island and thus technically go in every compass direction at least part of the time.

Koko, then Mauka

4) **Sun and star sightings** -- Most children know how to find Polaris (the "North Star"), and nearly everyone associates sunrise with east and sunset with west. Some cultures, however, have developed a more complex system of astronomical direction finding: "Go three fingers to the right of where Vega rises in October." This system works best in deserts and on oceans, where clouds and trees do not interfere with seeing the sky. Though it sounds primitive, we should remember that people used this technique to cross the Pacific Ocean long before compasses were invented.

5) **Clock numerals** -- Fans of old war movies will recognize the way pilots warned each other about enemy planes: they used an *egocentric* language that has an imaginary clock face, with a 12 straight ahead of the plane, a 3 to the right, a 7 almost straight back over the left shoulder of the pilot, and so on. A full sentence in this direction-language might say something like "You have bogeys at four o'clock high." The clock language is crude but quick, and speed is an big advantage when pilots are flying in tight formation and a delay can be fatal.

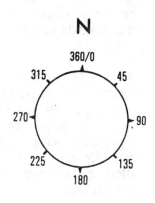

6) **Compass points** -- Sailors developed a numerical system that resembles a clock, but it has a big difference. The nautical compass has 32 points instead of 12, a minor improvement in precision, but it also has a fixed north, a major change in logic. A *reading* of 16 on the nautical compass always means south, regardless of what direction a ship is going. However, a *change* of a specified number of points can occur from any direction: "Bring her around 8 points to starboard" is a command to turn right and head southeast (12 points on the compass) if you had been going northeast (4 points).

7) **Azimuth degrees** -- The point system has been largely abandoned in favor of a 360-degree *compass circle*, also with zero to the north and numbered toward the right (like a clock that has 360 hours). An azimuth of 119 is thus about one-third of a full circle clockwise from north. Translated into other languages, that would be a bit less than 11 points to an ancient mariner, or about 1 o'clock to a pilot going east. On a circle the size of the earth, a degree is about 70 miles long. Each degree can be subdivided into sixty *minutes*; a minute, in turn, has sixty *seconds*. Degrees, minutes, and seconds are also used to specify location on the global *latitude-longitude* grid (which is not the first time the same word has been used to mean different things (pages 25-29 deal with the global grid).

8) **Mils and Grads** -- We inherited the 360-degree circle from the ancient Sumerians, who lived in what became Babylon, Persia, and now Iraq. These people had a sophisticated number system based entirely on sixes. The *grad* (an angular unit that is 1/400 of a circle) is an attempt to "metricate" the 360-degree circle by putting an even hundred units in each *quadrant*. The process of subdividing a circle may have reached a practical limit with the *mil*, which is 1/6400 of a full circle. Mils and grads, like degrees, are numbered clockwise from north; west is therefore 300 grads or 4800 mils. Frankly, we doubt whether you will ever see a grad, and the only place where you are likely to encounter a mil is on a detailed topographic map, where the precision of that unit is useful in specifying the small annual change in the magnetic declination for a local area (see the caution about magnetic compasses on the next page).

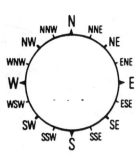

9) **Cardinal directions** -- The four basic directional names (north, east, south, and west) can be combined to specify a large number of in-between directions such as *northeast* (4 points or 45 degrees), *east-southeast* (10 points or 112-1/2 degrees), or *southwest-by-west* (one point to the west of southwest, or 236-1/4 degrees). It should be easy to see how lawyers could get quite wealthy sorting out problems that occur if someone accidentally miscopies a named direction on a property deed.

10) **Surveyor's bearings** -- Many property descriptions are written using a directional system with four 90-degree scales that go away from two different zero points, one north and one south. Thus, the phrase S30°E in a property deed means a line that goes 30 degrees to the east of due south (this would be an azimuth of 150 degrees). The bearing system has one big advantage over other directional vocabularies: a *backsight* (the direction exactly opposite to a specified direction) is easy to calculate (the backsight of S30°E is N30°W). This feature is useful for a surveyor, because one way to check a survey for accuracy is to run it backwards and see if you wind up where you started.

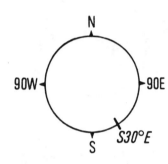

CAUTION: *True* north (toward the north pole) and *magnetic* north (the direction a compass needle points) are rarely the same, because the magnetic north pole is in northern Canada, a long way from the north pole. Written or spoken expressions of compass points, mils, grads, azimuths, bearings, or cardinal directions thus should be prefaced with "magnetic" or "true" in order to make sure that the hearer knows what reference system is being used. The amount of deviation from true north is called the *magnetic declination*, and it varies from place to place and changes through time.

A set of connected arrows is the standard way to indicate the *grid north* (GN), the orientation of the local UTM grid (see page 33) and the magnetic declination (MN) in the area shown by a map. In this example from Colorado, a magnetic compass would show a reading of 77 degrees when the "true" azimuth was actually 90 degrees. Many pages have been written to explain how to adjust for magnetic declination, but for a typical hiker the solution is simple: just draw lines on the map at the proper angle to represent magnetic north, and do all of your compass sightings with respect to those lines -- after all, "true north" is just as arbitrary and therefore no more "true" than any other way of expressing direction. Be warned, however: magnetic declination changes through time, and a conscientious map-maker will indicate the rate of change somewhere on the map, so the reader can adjust if necessary.

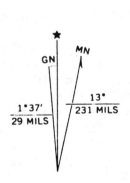

DIRECTION -- PRACTICE

Fill in the blanks on this table of different ways to express five different directions. As in the case of the distance practice on page 12, you should use the filled-in examples as guides in formulating your own rules for translation (e.g. "multiply points by 200 to get mils").

DIRECTION EXPRESSION	A	B	C	D	E
Cardinal name	east	southwest	_____	east northeast	_____
Points	8	_____	28	_____	14
Azimuth degrees	_____	225	315	_____	_____
Mils	1600	4000	_____	_____	2800
Bearing	N90°E	S45°W	_____	N67°E	_____
Backsight	S90°W	_____	S45°E	S67°W	_____

SAMPLE QUIZ QUESTIONS -- DIRECTION

You will be given part of a 1:24,000 topographic map.

_____ 1) Print the true azimuth (within 10 degrees) that corresponds to the cardinal direction *north-northeast*.

_____ 2) Print the true azimuth (within 10 degrees) of a straight sight from point *B* to point *C* on the topographic map.

_____ 3) Print the magnetic compass reading (within 2 degrees) that corresponds to a true azimuth of *120* degrees on this map.

_____ 4) Print the magnetic compass reading (within 10 degrees) of a straight sight from point *C* to point *E* on the map.

_____ 5) Print the letter of the point on this map that is at a true azimuth of *115* degrees from point *F*.

_____ 6) Print the letter of the map point from which you would see point *A* at a magnetic compass reading of *263* degrees.

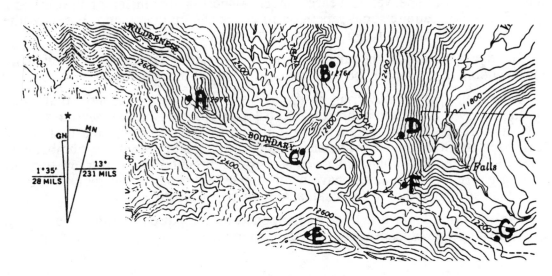

A CASE OF MISDIRECTION

A Trans-Pacific flight, at night, is as effective as an isolation tank in blotting out the world. The cabin lights are dim, and the pastel-colored ceiling hides the sky. The window is a scratched and dusty filter, between you and the view outside. The sea is dark and featureless, far below. At the margins of your sight, the humid air blurs the horizon. The vibration of the engines is steady, easy to ignore, but loud enough to muffle conversation. All in all, it would be a great time to sleep.

But in the cockpit of the plane, sleep is the ultimate mistake. Boring as it may be for the passengers, a Trans-Pacific airline flight is not an automatic point-and-go operation. Here, the fundamental circularity of our spatial language is not just an academic observation. The black ocean has no landmarks to tell you where you are, and both speed and direction are hard to measure in the absence of clear knowledge of position.

Take a piece of string and stretch it from Detroit to Tokyo on a globe. It starts out going northwest, crosses Lake Superior, and enters Canada. By the time it reaches Alaska, it is heading almost due west, and when it reaches Japan, its flight path is toward the southwest. It seems strange, but it's true: the pilot must continually change the compass direction of the plane in order to keep it on a reasonably direct line to its destination. In other words, to stay on a "straight" line, the plane must frequently appear to "turn" to the left on its compass. The big question, of course, is trying to decide *when* it should be traveling in a particular compass direction (and, by extension, when and how the pilot should change its compass direction).

One could answer that question with nothing more than a string on a globe. In the real world, however, the navigator must also deal with the wind, which can alter both the direction and the speed of the plane. If you knew the speed and direction of the wind, the relationship between the plane and the air would be a solvable problem. Unfortunately, the wind is not the same from place to place, or from minute to minute, or even from one layer to another in the air. Its effects on the position, speed, and direction of the plane, therefore, cannot be predicted very accurately.

For that reason, the navigator is forced to rely on indirect ways of determining position, speed, and direction. And that, inevitably, means a lot of numbers, on the cockpit dials, on the radio, on the maps, on the route log, and in the whispered conversations with the pilot. Ninety-nine-point-nine percent of the time, those numbers get from speaker to hearer intact, a successful transfer of information. Failsafe systems require some repetition to check the numbers, and therefore the chance of error is much smaller than one in a thousand.

In other words, amid the millions of numbers typed or spoken on a given night, it is inevitable that some will be read or heard wrong at some time.

Now look again at the string on the globe; a plane trying to follow that route would pass over Alaska on a direct route to Japan. But it is not allowed to go that way; it must stay south of Kamchatka, the cold and barren peninsula that would have been its first contact with Asia. And, on one fateful night, a number was misread (or ignored), a plane followed a compass direction that was a few degrees to the right of where it should have been, a missile locked on the radar image of that plane as it passed over Kamchatka, and many people died.

We still don't know exactly what happened on the Korean airliner, but we do know the language of maps is complex enough to allow fatal misunderstandings.

AREA AND VOLUME

The amount of space occupied by something is the last of the basic spatial concepts we need to consider before going on to analyze real maps of the really complex world. *Area* is the two-dimensional equivalent of distance; *volume* is a related three-dimensional idea. For the moment, we will consider area and volume together, because they are hard to tell apart on a typical map. A landscape feature such as a lake is actually a three-dimensional volume, but all we can depict on a flat sheet of paper is the area it covers. To show the depth of the water, we must add some kind of abstract symbol like a *hachure* or *contour line*, which is the subject of part 2 of this book.

To communicate the surface area of a map feature like a lake, a map-maker can use any one of several alternative methods:

1) **Comparison** is a handy way to estimate the size of an area on a map -- just compare the area with the map image of something whose size you already know. A simple visual comparison can eliminate the need to deal with the complexities of scale and distortion (to be described in detail later). Your efficiency in doing this kind of area estimation depends on how many sizes of things you know. For this reason, it may be useful to spend some time going through memories, books, and atlases, consciously trying to learn the sizes of things that may appear on maps and thus offer clues about scale. The sizes you should learn can range from the simple and standard (a United States football field is 160 by 360 feet, including end zones, and therefore it is slightly larger than half a hectare or 1-1/3 acre) all the way to the subtle and specific (the length of a city block in downtown Chicago is 1/8 mile (1/5 kilometer); the average spacing of the sand hills in west-central Nebraska is slightly more than one mile; the "bottom" of Idaho is 300 miles (500 kilometers) "wide").

2) **Geometric formulas** can be useful if you are able to simplify a shape on a map so that it resembles a regular geometric figure:

rectangle --
    length times width

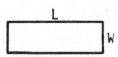

trapezoid --
    1/2 (top plus bottom) times height

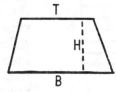

right triangle --
    1/2 leg times leg

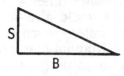

hexagon --
    2.6 times side times side

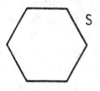

other triangle --
    1/2 base times height

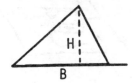

circle --
    3.14 times radius times radius

3) A **square grid** or **dot grid** can help you estimate the area of an irregular shape on a map. Place a piece of transparent graph paper on top of the shape whose area you want to measure. Count all of the squares that are more than halfway inside the shape. Then, figure out how large the graph-paper squares are at the scale of the map (or, if you think ahead, you could find or make graph paper that was of just the right size so that each square on the graph paper would be the exact size of some easy-to-remember area on the map).

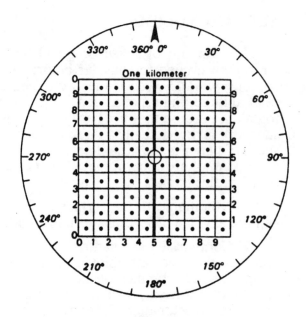

Your set of class materials includes a plastic *roamer* like the one drawn here. When used with a standard 1:24,000 topographic map, the big square in the roamer is one kilometer on a side, and each tiny square is exactly one hectare (an area 100 meters by 100 meters, or 10,000 square meters). Other ways of using a grid to figure the size of an area: count graph line intersections within it, or put a dot in the middle of each graph square and count dots within the area.

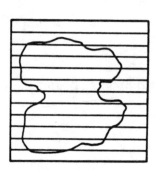

4) **Line lengths** offer another way to figure area. Draw a reasonably large number of equally-spaced parallel lines across the shape whose area you want to determine. Take a ruler and measure the length of each line within the shape. Add the total length of the lines and multiply by the map distance between the lines; the result is a good estimate of the area. For example, suppose you had a map with a scale of 1:250,000 (one inch equals about 4 miles, a very commonly used scale). If you drew lines one fourth of an inch apart across a shape on that map, those lines would be exactly one mile apart in the real world.

If you then measured a total of 18.5 inches of lines within a given shape, that would be the equivalent of 74 miles of real-world distance (18.5 inches times 4 miles per inch). Laying all of these "slices" of the shape end-to-end would give you a new shape that measured 74 miles by one mile, or 74 square miles, which is a good estimate of the area of the shape you wanted to measure. Manual line-measuring is usually slower than dot-counting, but a computer is easier to program as a line measurer, and therefore this method is used far mor often than one might think.

5) A **planimeter** is a mechanical device that allows a person to trace around a shape on a map and then read its area from a dial (or, in more expensive but much more versatile versions, see it displayed on a computer terminal or display screen).

SCALE

There are exceptions (a map of the AIDS virus, for example) but most maps are *reduced representations*, physically smaller than the real world. The degree of reduction is an important factor in determining how much detail a map can show and how much area it can cover (and still fit in a automobile glove compartment, desk drawer, computer monitor, or projection screen). The *scale* of a map is the degree to which it reduces (or enlarges) the real world; scale can be communicated to a map reader in many different ways:

1) **pictorial symbols** -- A map may depict an object of known size, such as a house or football field, which the reader can compare with other distances on the map. This method is like landmark location; it works only if the reader really knows the real size of the object <u>and</u> if the relative sizes of things on the map are correct. Unfortunately, when a map is greatly reduced from a large area, it simply cannot show small things like roads or houses at their proportional sizes. Direct visual comparison may still work if the reader is familiar with the sizes of larger things (e.g. a county or state).

2) **labelled features** -- Highway maps often have numbers that show the road distance between marked places; these can remind readers of the scale of the map. It works fairly well, as long as people remember what units of distance the numbers represent; many Americans, however, get confused when they try to use Canadian or European maps, which show distances in kilometers rather than miles.

3) a *scaled line* that shows one or more distances. This line allows a map reader to use a finger, ruler, or piece of paper to measure a map distance and translate it into a real-world distance.

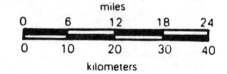

4) a *verbal expression*, such as "one inch equals two miles." This kind of scale works much better in the metric system, in which different distance units are exact multiples of ten.

5) a *representative fraction* (RF scale) that shows how many units of real-world distance are represented by one unit on the map. An RF scale of 1:1000 means that one unit of measurement on the map depicts 1000 of the same units in the real world. RF scales are not tied to any single unit of measurement -- they work equally well for centimeters, inches, paces, miles, kilometers, leagues, thumbwidths, or cubits.

CAUTION 1. The earth surface is curved, and any attempt to map it on flat paper will cause some distortion. Scale variation from place to place on a map becomes more likely as the area of the map increases. See the section on map projections (page 30) for more information on this kind of distortion.

CAUTION 2. Verbal and RF scales are valid only for the original drafting of a map; they go wrong whenever a map is reduced or enlarged from its original size. A pictorial, label, or line scale, by contrast, will change along with the map and thus remain accurate.

TOPOGRAPHIC MAP SCALES

This page has fragments of three topographic maps of the area around the Minneapolis-St. Paul airport at three different scales. The map on the right has a scale of 1:250,000; the one at the bottom has a scale of 1:24,000; and the map just below this paragraph is from the new 1:100,000 series. The other two maps in the lower right-hand column are photographic enlargements of the 1:250,000 map, with its scale changed to match the topomaps in the left column. Note the differences in detail shown on (and area covered by) the three map scales.

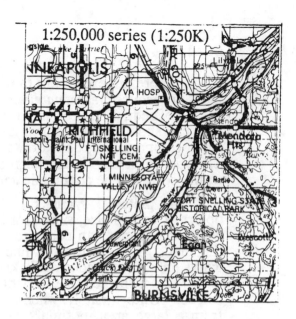

1:250,000 series (1:250K)

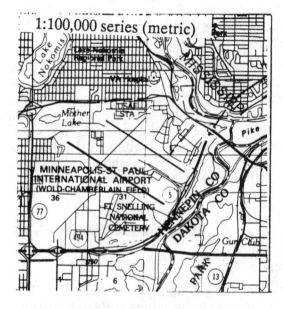

1:100,000 series (metric)

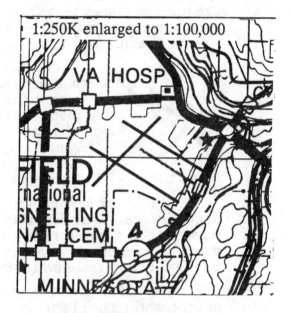

1:250K enlarged to 1:100,000

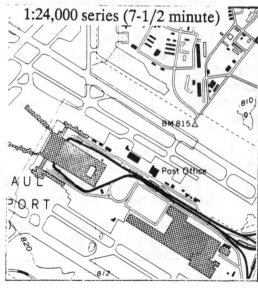

1:24,000 series (7-1/2 minute)

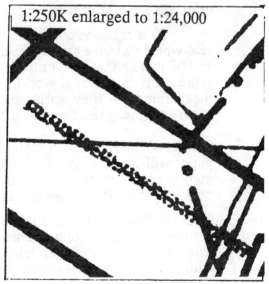

1:250K enlarged to 1:24,000

DETERMINING THE SCALE OF AN UNLABELLED MAP

Occasionally, you may encounter a map that has no clear statement of its scale printed on it (e.g. when only a portion of a map is printed and the scale was omitted). To determine the scale of such a map:

1) Select two clearly marked map positions with known spacing in the real world (e.g. two towns a known distance apart, a road or other line whose length can be measured on another map, or the edge of a Public Land Survey *section*, which is supposed to be a mile square (see page 38)).

2) Measure the distance between the two locations on the map with the unknown scale, and express that measurement in terms of some convenient units of length.

3) Determine the real-world distance between the places, in whatever distance units are appropriate.

4) Translate the real-world distance into the same units of length as your measured map distance. Do not be surprised if this turns out to be a very large number.

5) Form a ratio by writing the map distance (from step 2) in the numerator and the real-world distance (from step 4) in the denominator of a fraction.

6) Divide the ratio, so that you get a fraction with 1 in its numerator; this is the representative fraction (RF scale) of the unknown map.

7) Depending on your purpose, you may convert this representative fraction into a verbal expression.

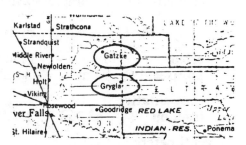

Gatzke to Grygla is about 9 millimeters (use ruler)

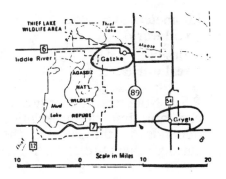

Gatzke to Grygla is about 12 miles (use map scale)

12 miles is slightly more than 19 million millimeters

9 / 19,300,000

Map scale is therefore about 1:2 million

1 inch on map is about 34 miles

SCALE CHANGING. At times, a map must be enlarged or reduced in order to fit a page or to allow easy comparison with another map. Scale can be changed manually by drawing a square grid over the map and copying each segment onto another grid whose lines are spaced an appropriate distance farther apart or closer together. Other (easier but more costly) techniques for changing map scale include copy machines, optical projectors, process cameras, or computer programs. To communicate the desired scale change to someone (e.g. a printer or programmer), you should specify the final size as a percent of the original -- "Enlarge this map to 300%" means "Make it three times as big as it is now. Reducing a 1:20,000 scale map to 50% of its original size will change its RF scale to 1:40,000.

SCALE CONVERSION - PRACTICE

A person who is fluent in the language of maps can convert from one scale to another (at least approximately) without too much conscious thought. Some of this ability consists of simply memorizing the traits of some common map scales. Fill in the blanks on this table of six maps, each representing a widely used scale.

MAP	A	B	C	D	E	F
verbal phrase	1 inch = 1 mile	1 inch = 4 miles	4 cm = 1 km	____	____	____
representative fraction	1: 63,360	1: 250,000	1: 25,000	1: 1,000,000	____	____
centimeters on map	10	____	5	14	50	____
inches on map	4	8	2	____	20	4
kilometers in real world	6.3	____	____	____	1.92	____
miles in real world	4	32	____	____	____	112

P.S. Note that the ratios of centimeters-to-inches and kilometers-to-miles are constant, but the translation of centimeters-to-kilometers and inches-to-miles depends on the scale of the map. Incidentally, now do you see why most cartographers prefer metric units for map construction?

SAMPLE QUIZ QUESTIONS -- SCALE AND AREA

_____ 1) Print the representative fraction (RF) scale of a map with a verbal scale of *one inch equals six miles.*

_____ 2) Print the real distance (within 100 meters) shown by a line *24 millimeters* long on a map with a RF scale of 1:*40,000.*

_____ 3) Print the real area (nearest square kilometer) represented by a square centimeter on a map with an RF scale of 1:*320,000.*

_____ 4) Print the real distance (within one mile) from point *B* to point *B* on the left-hand map below.

_____ 5) Print the RF-scale (within ten percent) of the right-hand map below; use the left-hand map for comparison.

_____ 6) Print the real distance (within ten percent) represented by a map distance of *3 centimeters* on the right-hand map below.

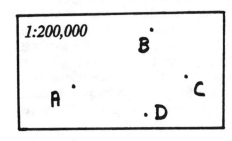

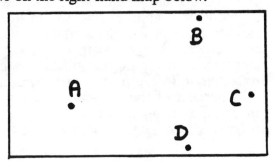

THE GLOBAL GRID

A book on map interpretation should have a separate section on global location, because the earth is a sphere (roughly), while the polar and rectangular grid systems described on page 7 are both drawn on flat paper. One obvious trait of a sphere is the lack of an obvious beginning or end: it has no place on its surface that stands out as an obvious origin for a geometric grid. Fortunately for map makers, the earth is always spinning, and its mass is so great that the spin is exceedingly regular (it does wobble a bit, but the wobble takes about 23,000 years, long enough that you do not need to worry about it for the midterm exam).

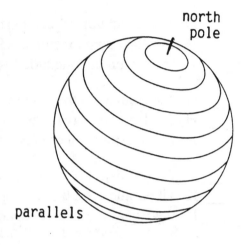

north
pole

parallels

The axis of the earth's rotation provides two fixed points (the North and South Poles) for us to use in creating a location system. We could have decided to call the North Pole "zero" and measured distances away from it (like they do at an airport control tower). This might make some abstract mathematical sense, but it would be a practical nuisance because the Polar region is unoccupied and not important economically. People a long time ago decided to draw a line around the earth halfway between the poles, call that line the *Equator*, and use it as the zero line of a global coordinate system. In this system, the *latitude* of a place is defined as the angular distance of the place north or south of the Equator. One degree of latitude is about 70 miles; a place at 30°N is therefore about 2100 miles from the Equator. For greater precision, a degree can be divided into 60 *minutes*, and each minute has 60 *seconds*.

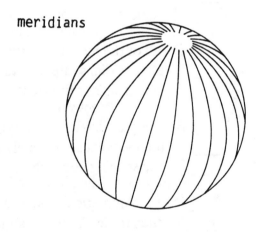

meridians

East-west measurements are more complicated, because every line that goes north-south from pole to pole is of equal length. Thus there is no north-south line like the equator, uniquely placed, easy to locate, and clearly longer than all other lines of *longitude*.

At one time or another, many different lines were used as the zero longitude for maps. The resulting chaos led to a major international agreement to use the Greenwich Meridian (the longitude line that goes through an observatory near London) as the *Prime Meridian* or zero line of longitude. However, a few dozen countries still prefer to use some other meridian as their zero line.

To summarize -- *latitude* lines vary in length, run east-west, and are numbered in degrees and minutes north or south of the equator. *Longitude* lines are all of equal length, run north-south, and are numbered in degrees and minutes east or west of the Prime Meridian. Any location on the earth surface can be described precisely by noting its latitude and longitude: the Kentucky Derby takes place at a racetrack located at latitude 38°12'N and 85°46'W.

THE GLOBAL GRID -- PRACTICE

You probably know most of this already, but there may be a few facts worth checking. Find a globe, examine it carefully, use your plastic roamer (page 20) or a piece of string to measure whatever you think you should, and put a T in the space by each of the thirteen (13) <u>true</u> statements on the list below:

_____ A - the zero meridian runs almost directly through London

_____ B - the Equator runs through the northern third of Africa

_____ C - parallels of latitude are numbered in degrees north of the South Pole

_____ D - the maximum latitude north is 90 degrees

_____ E - the maximum longitude is 90 degrees east or west

_____ F - the maximum longitude line is also called the International Date Line

_____ G - the Equator is the longest line of latitude

_____ H - the Equator is twice as long as the Prime Meridian

_____ I - the Equator is much closer to the South Pole than to the North Pole

_____ J - all meridians are the same length

_____ K - all parallels are the same length

_____ L - the Equator crosses every one of the meridians about halfway
            between the North Pole and the South Pole

_____ M - more than half of Alaska is north of the Arctic Circle

_____ N - almost all of South America is east of the meridian that runs
            through Miami, Florida

_____ O - all of the meridians come together at the North Pole

_____ P - all meridians intersect the Equator at right angles

_____ Q - all meridians intersect the other parallels at angles
            between 45 and 85 degrees

_____ R - the parallels are evenly spaced on any one meridian

_____ S - the meridians are evenly spaced on any one parallel

_____ T - the spacing between meridians increases as you approach
            the North or South Pole

_____ U - the Antarctic Circle is about 76 degrees south of the Equator

_____ V - the Arctic Circle is about 23 degrees south of the North Pole

_____ W - the Tropic of Capricorn is about 23 degrees north of the Equator

_____ X - the 60th parallel is about half as long as the Equator

_____ Y - the 40th parallel is about three times as long as the 80th

_____ Z - the distance between meridians is half as great at 45 degrees of latitude
            as at the Equator

Now, go through the list and determine what you would need to change in order to make each false statement true. This may seem rather mechanical at this time, but a very clear understanding of the traits of the global grid is essential in order to recognize the kinds of distortion that can be caused by various ways of portraying this curved surface on flat paper.

NAVIGATION - LATITUDE

The spin of the earth around a fixed axis provided a basis for at least part of the art of navigation in the pre-radio era. The geometric relationship between the sun and the earth allows people to determine the latitude of a place by comparing two angles: the angle of the noon sun above the horizon at the place, and the angle up to noon sun at the equator on the same day. The difference that you obtain when you make that comparison is the same as the angular distance of the place from the equator, which (remember?) is the definition of latitude.

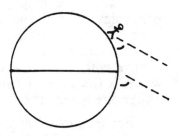

Your packet contains a transparent plastic half-circle about the same size as the one below. When used together, these two half-circles are a shortcut to help you solve some earth-sun problems. The printed half-circle shows the latitudes of places; the transparent one shows the angle of the sun down from overhead at noon. Put the plastic half-circle directly on top of the printed one and then turn the transparent one so that its zero line is at the latitude where the noon sun is directly overhead on the date of the problem (that information can be obtained from an *analemma*, a figure-8 diagram like the one below). The numbers on the transparent half-circle will then give you the noon sun angle, *down from overhead*, at any latitude on the solid printed circle. Remember that the angle of the noon sun above the horizon is equal to 90 degrees minus its angle down from overhead. And if you think that this information is meant only for navigators, think again -- the ability to predict sun angle can be very useful in designing solar collectors, orienting windows and furniture, choosing campsites, locating gardens, or landscaping a yard.

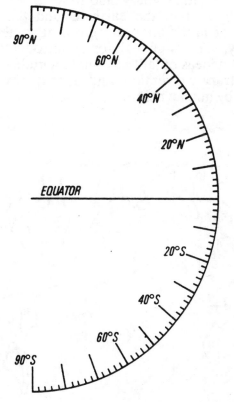

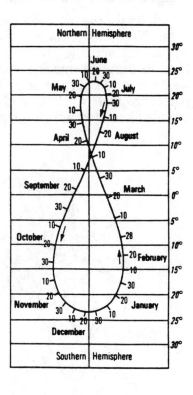

NAVIGATION - LONGITUDE

Finding the longitude of a place is another application of the same basic principles of earth/sun geometry. You need to compare some measure of local solar time with Universal Coordinated Time (the clock time at the zero meridian, near London). You could use sunrise or sunset, but the times of those events can change with latitude and season. Accuracy is better if you use local solar noon, which is the time of day when the sun reaches its highest point in the sky and is either directly overhead or due north or south of you.

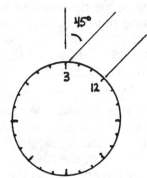

For example, suppose that you observed local solar noon at 3:00 p.m. UCT. The fact that it is mid-afternoon at the zero meridian means that the sun must have already passed London on its apparent trip from east to west around the earth. Therefore, you must be west of the zero meridian. Since the sun takes exactly 24 hours to make its complete 360-degree circuit, it must "travel" 15 degrees of longitude every hour. When you put those two ideas together, you get a longitude of 45 degrees west for your location.

It is important to use *solar* noon for these calculations, rather than local *clock* noon, because people have divided the globe into "time zones" that are only approximately 15 degrees of longitude wide and therefore not always exactly an hour apart. In theory, you could be off by as much as 7-1/2 degrees if you used clock time to figure longitude. In practice, however, the error can be much greater than that, because nearly all time-zone boundaries have been aligned to suit local economic and political conditions. Some places even insist on having local clock time that is several hours or fractions of an hour ahead or behind the sun, and things like "Daylight Savings Time" make the mess even messier.

A final note -- if you were really navigating, you would have to use Adjusted Solar Noon to allow for the elliptical orbit of the earth around the sun (the analemma actually provides that kind of information, too), but at some time we have to draw an imaginary line and say, "This is enough for an introductory book; we have made our major point about the ideas of latitude and longitude -- they are part universal principle and part arbitrary convention, and in that way they are exactly like any other language devised by human beings."

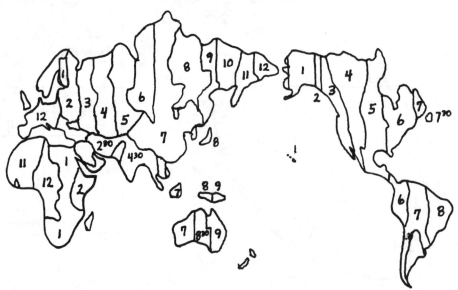

SUN ANGLES -- PRACTICE

Fill in the blanks on this table of observations of the noon sun at seven different locations. Use the analemma and sun angle diagrams on page 27 for background, and remember that the angle *down from directly overhead* is equal to 90 degrees minus the angle *up from the horizon*. If you get stumped trying to find the answer for one location, study the figures for other places for clues.

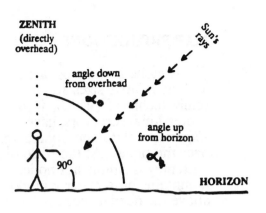

PLACE	1	2	3	4	5	6	7
Hemisphere	N	N	S	N	S	N	—
Latitude degrees	30	56	49	—	—	28	42
Date	Oct 24	July 4	Feb 12	Sep 23	Dec 1	—	Apr 23
Degrees up from horizon	—	—	—	70	—	52	—
Degrees down from zenith	43	—	—	—	63	—	30 north

SAMPLE QUIZ QUESTIONS -- GLOBAL LOCATION

Use a globe to answer these questions.

_____ 1) Print the name of the major city at 56^oN and $37^o\frac{1}{2}E$.

_____ 2) Print the latitude and longitude (within three degrees each) of *Sydney, Australia*.

_____ 3) Print the great-circle (shortest) distance (within 1000 kilometers) between $19^oN/98^oW$ and $39^oN/118^oE$.

_____ 4) Print the direction (within ten degrees from true north) of the <u>start</u> of a great-circle airline flight from *London, England,* to *Miami, Florida*.

_____ 5) Print the clock time (don't forget a.m. or p.m.) at *New York City* if the time is *6 p.m. at Tokyo, Japan*.

_____ 6) Print the longitude of the place where local solar noon occurs at *9 a.m.* Universal Coordinated Time.

_____ 7) Print the great circle distance (nearest 500 miles) from *Baghdad, Iraq, to Hanoi, Viet Nam*

_____ 8) Print the amount of time (within an hour) an airplane would take to fly at an average speed of 500 miles per hour on a great circle route from *New York* to *Rio de Janeiro, Brazil*

_____ 9) Print the angle of the noon sun above the southern horizon (within three degrees) at 45^oN latitude on *October 21*.

MAP PROJECTIONS

A globe is the most accurate way to communicate the shape of the earth and the relative sizes and positions of objects on its surface. If you want to get really technical (which, fortunately, only small number of people, such as professional surveyors, have to do every day), the earth is actually an irregular *ellipsoid*, a flattened sphere that is slightly bigger around the equator than over the poles. At the scale of a typical classroom globe, however, the polar flattening is simply not noticeable to the unaided eye. Moreover, the highest mountains on a classroom globe should be only a few tenths of a millimeter above the deepest oceans (in other words, practically imperceptible).

Although the globe is the best representation of the apparent shape of the earth, there are many disadvantages in using the "vocabulary" of a globe to communicate ideas about the earth. For one thing, you cannot see the entire surface at one time. You cannot afford a globe that is big enough to show the residential neighborhoods of a city or the hiking trails of the Grand Canyon. You cannot fold a globe and put it in the glove compartment of your car. And imagine how much room you would need to store an "atlas" of 250 detailed globes!

Because of these problems, map-makers usually try to transform the curved surface of the earth onto a flat piece of paper. These translations from the three-dimensional language of a sphere to the two-dimensional language of a plane are called "projections." It is not possible to design a projection that does not have some distortion of the "true" shapes or sizes of things. Over a small area, the distortion may not be very important, but over a large area the "errors of translation" may become large enough to interfere with the message that a map is trying to communicate. For this reason, map-makers have designed a variety of projections, which focus on preserving the relationships that are essential for a given purpose.

A skilled map reader is able to recognize the nature of the projection that was used to make a particular map; this information allows the reader to compensate for the distortion that may be caused by the projection. In order to make this adjustment, you must first be aware of the general spatial traits that may be distorted by a map projection:

Distance -- "Equidistant" projections try to be accurate in depicting distances away from a central point or line. In order to do this, they usually distort areas and directions.

Size -- "Equal-area" projections try to show the relative sizes of areas without distortion. In doing this, they usually mangle shapes, distances, and/or directions.

Shape -- "Equiangular" (or "conformal") projections try to show the general shapes of features, but they cannot do so without altering the relative sizes or locations of objects.

Direction -- some projections try to show compass directions accurately, but shapes, distances, and areas really get warped.

Everything -- Finally, some projections are best described as compromises, because they actually distort all spatial relationships, but they trade off size, shape, and direction in different parts of the map so that nothing is too severely distorted.

EXAMPLES OF DISSIMILAR MAP PROJECTIONS

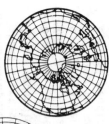

Orthographic

preserves the appearance of a globe
shows only half of the earth at a time
distorts shape and direction near edges
useful for magazine illustrations

Planar Equidistant

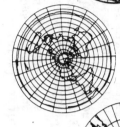

shows accurate distance from center
shows actual (not compass) direction
distorts area and shape near edges
useful for military and travel planning
(e.g. airport control towers)

Gnomonic

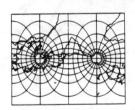

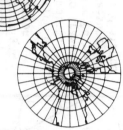

shows shortest paths as straight lines
shows only a small part of the earth
distorts shapes and areas severely
useful for air or sea navigation

Equatorial Cylindrical

made by fitting a cylinder around the globe
shows cardinal directions as straight lines
distorts area at top and bottom of map
fits neatly on a standard piece of paper
useful for navigation and climate analysis

Transverse cylindrical

made by fitting a cylinder along a meridian
very accurate for area near its central meridian
square grid is intuitively easy to use
serves as base fortopographic maps
widely used in military maps

Conic

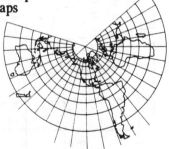

made by fitting a cone over part of the globe
depicts mid-latitude shapes and areas well
distorts direction toward sides of map
cannot show entire earth at one time
used for most United States maps

Mollweide (homolographic)

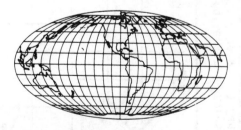

made by showing meridians as ellipses
has straight parallels like a cylindrical
has pleasing rounded (globe-like) shape
distorts shape and direction near corners
useful for simple maps of entire globe

Robinson

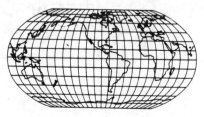

compromise between Mollweide and cylindrical
shows different areas in proper proportion
distorts shape and direction near edges
widely used in textbooks and magazines

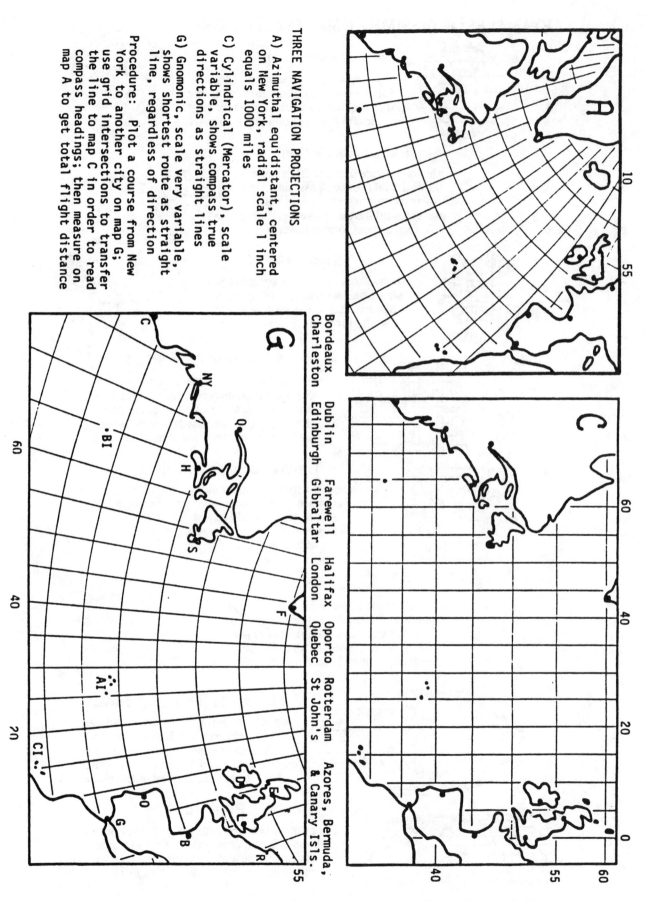

THREE NAVIGATION PROJECTIONS

A) Azimuthal equidistant, centered on New York, radial scale 1 inch equals 1000 miles

C) Cylindrical (Mercator), scale variable, shows compass true directions as straight lines

G) Gnomonic, scale very variable, shows shortest route as straight line, regardless of direction

Procedure: Plot a course from New York to another city on map G; use grid intersections to transfer the line to map C in order to read compass headings; then measure on map A to get total flight distance

Bordeaux Dublin Farewell Halifax Oporto Rotterdam Azores, Bermuda,
Charleston Edinburgh Gibraltar London Quebec St John's & Canary Isls.

THE UNIVERSAL TRANSVERSE MERCATOR GRID

The historical roots of the Universal Transverse Mercator (UTM) grid are fairly easy to trace -- military officers needed a flexible but accurate way to specify the locations of targets for their new long-range cannons and missiles. At first a classified secret, the UTM system has evolved to become a widely used method of precise locational description.

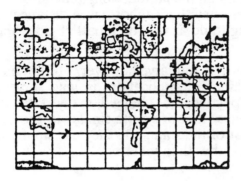

The name comes from the *Mercator projection*, an ancient method of translating the latitude and longitude grid of the globe onto a plane coordinate system (much like unwrapping the label on a tin can). The Mercator map is quite accurate right along the equator, where the coordinate grid of the paper cylinder actually touches the sphere. As you go north or south from the Equator, however, the Mercator projection begins to distort the sizes of things, and it really exaggerates area near the poles.

Despite these limitations, the Mercator projection was popular for world maps, especially in schools and newspapers (and with Pentagon planners, who found the hugely distorted Soviet Union was useful in maintaining popular support for defense spending during the Cold War era. Even though it has fallen out of favor for textbook and wall maps, the Mercator projection still has a very important use. Turning the cylindrical grid so that it stretches from Pole to Pole rather than east-west along the Equator will yield an accurate map of a thin strip of land and water along one meridian (longitude line). As you might expect from a Mercator-like projection, however, distortion becomes severe when you go more than a few degrees away from the *central meridian*.

For that reason, the people who designed the UTM grid first divide the entire globe into 60 separate *zones*. Each zone is exactly six degrees wide at the equator; the zones are numbered going east from the International Date Line in the Pacific Ocean. Seattle is in Zone 10, Minneapolis in Zone 15, Chicago in 16, Ney York in 18, and so on. What Zone contains Boston? Miami? Denver?

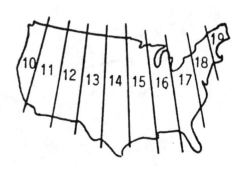

The Equator is designated as the UTM zero line for all places in the northern hemisphere. (The zero line for the southern hemisphere is an imaginary east-west line that is exactly ten million meters south of the equator.) The *UTM northing* of any place on earth is its distance north of its zero line, expressed in meters.

East-west measurements are a bit more tricky, because the earth surface is curved but the UTM uses a rectangular grid. An imaginary line, 500,000 meters west of the central meridian, acts as a reference line. It runs parallel to the central meridian and near the left-hand edge of the zone. The *false easting* of a place is its distance to the right of this reference line; it is called "false" because "to the right" on a square grid is not exactly "east" on a spherical surface.

A brief review: the UTM grid describes the location of a place in terms of its zone number and its distance in meters east of an arbitrary reference line and north of the Equator. You might wonder how this system can be any better than the "familiar" latitude-longitude grid you were wrestling with a few pages ago. The answer is simple -- the individual units of the UTM are perfectly square, whereas the area bounded by one degree of latitude and longitude can vary in shape and size, depending on where it is on the globe. Areas, distances, and directions are much easier to calculate on the UTM grid than on the latitude-longitude grid. Now recall the original purpose of the UTM -- an army that cannot figure distances and directions quickly and accurately is not going to do as well on a battlefield where a hidden enemy is "visible" only via a map.

These advantages are not restricted to the military, however. The simple square grid of the UTM lends itself to all kinds of applications in land surveying, forestry, highway construction, mineral prospecting, etc. Indeed, many states were already using "State Plane Coordinate Systems" that are quite similar to the UTM (they have false origins to the south and west of the state, and they use square grid cells, but most of them are calibrated in feet rather than meters).

THE THEOREM

The key to the usefulness of the UTM is the *Pythagorean Theorem*, the old Plane Geometry rule that says that the square of the length of the *hypotenuse* (the longest side) of a right triangle is equal to the *sum of the squares* of the other two shorter sides. Given this rule and the UTM coordinates of two places, it is easy (for a computer, anyway) to figure the distance between the places.

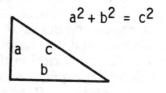

$$a^2 + b^2 = c^2$$

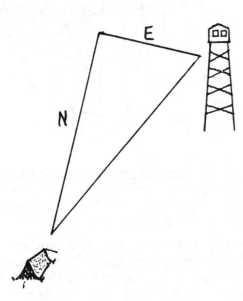

For example, suppose you were lying in a tent with UTM coordinates 687,221 meters East and 5,308,336 meters North, Zone 15 (the UTM numbers always go in "alphabetical" order, easting-northing-zone, and yes, the UTM system can be accurate enough to describe the location of something as small as a single tent). If the coordinates of a lookout tower were 687,398 meters East and 5,308,793 meters North, zone 15, the tower would be 177 meters "false" east of your tent (just subtract the eastings) and 457 meters "false" north. Its distance on a straight line would therefore be the square root of the sum of 177 squared and 457 squared (or 490 meters, according to my hand calculator; check it on yours). As distances increase, the problems with fitting a square grid to the curved earth increase, but at a human scale, the UTM is one of the most useful ways of specifying locations.

UTM COORDINATES -- PRACTICE

The plastic *roamer* (pictured on page 20) is a device to help someone measure lines, areas, directions, and UTM coordinates accurately and (with practice) quickly on a standard 1:24,000 topographic map. Just slide the roamer until the lower left corner of the square is directly on the junction of two one-kilometer UTM reference lines (shown either by a grid of thin lines or by tickmarks in the margins of the map). Then, read the roamer like a graph -- the numbers along the bottom of the square measure the UTM *easting* of the place in hundreds of meters from the north-south kilometer line. The numbers along the left and right edges show the UTM *northing*. For example, the coordinates of point A on the map below are about 342,200 m E and 5,727,750 m N. Use a ruler or your roamer to figure:

_____ 1) the easting of point B

_____ 2) the northing of point B

_____ 3) the easting of point C

_____ 4) the northing of point C

_____ 5) the distance in meters eastward from A to B

_____ 6) the distance in meters northward from A to B

_____ 7) the straight-line distance in meters from A to B

_____ 8) the distance in meters eastward from B to C

_____ 9) the meters northward from B to C (a negative number)

_____ 10) the straight-line distance in meters from B to C

BACKSIGHTING

Another use of the roamer (or any good compass) is to establish your position on a map by working backwards from sightlines toward prominent features. In some ways this is a review of concepts presented in the chapter on direction (page 17), but it is also an illustration of the way in which the UTM can allow a computer to solve both locational and directional problems at the same time. To find your position with the roamer:

1) Locate three prominent objects that are clearly visible from where you stand and can also be found on the map.

2) Sight toward those features and use your compass to determine their direction away from you.

3) Express those directions in degrees to the right of magnetic north.

4) Calculate *backsight* directions by subtracting/adding 180 degrees to those magnetic directions.

5) Look at the magnetic declination on your map and draw *magnetic north lines* directly on the map.

6) Place your roamer with its center at the location of one of the objects on the map.

7) Turn the roamer so that the zero points toward magnetic north.

8) Draw a *backsight line* in the appropriate direction away from the object.

9) Repeat steps 6 and 7 for the other two object(s).

10) If each step is done properly, all backsight lines should intersect at your location on the map. If not, check your work by including backsights from more objects until you get a better result.

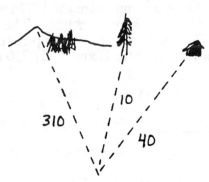

hill	130°	$(310 - 180)$
tree	190°	$(10 + 180)$
house	220°	$(40 + 180)$

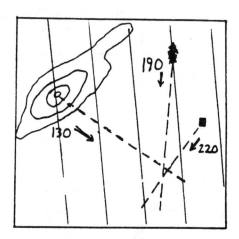

A computer can do all this in "mathematical space" by using trigonometry to transform each backsight direction into the equation that describes a line passing through the object. Solving the resulting set of *simultaneous liner equations* would yield the UTM coordinates of the point that lies on all of the lines.

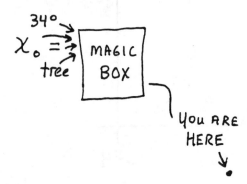

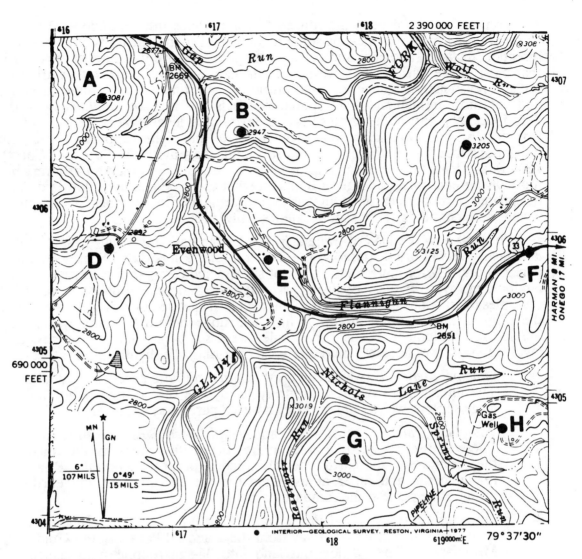

SAMPLE QUIZ QUESTIONS -- THE UTM GRID

You will be given part of a standard 1:24,000 topographic map.

_____ 1) Print the UTM easting (within 100 meters) of point *B*.

_____ 2) Print the letter of the map point that is nearest UTM coordinates *618,100* and *4,304,500*.

_____ 3) Print the UTM northing (within 200 meters) of the place (NOT lettered point) that is exactly halfway between point *F* and point *G*.

_____ 4) Print the UTM easting (within 100 meters) of the lettered point from where you would see point *C* on a magnetic compass reading of *66* degrees.

_____ 5) Print the UTM easting (within 500 meters) of the place (NOT a lettered point) from which point *B* is seen on a magnetic compass reading of *20* degrees and point *F* is at *70* degrees.

_____ 6) Print the UTM northing of that place (within 500 meters).

THE UNITED STATES PUBLIC LAND SURVEY

By now, you have been introduced to (or perhaps just reminded of) a wide variety of ways of communicating some fundamental spatial ideas, such as position, direction, distance, and enclosure. The main point of this entire Part of the book is that most of the basic spatial "words" in our map language(s) are rather arbitrary but still reasonably effective for most purposes. In some ways the most arbitrary and yet most influential of all spatial words is the idea of *landholding* -- the description of a part of the earth surface in terms of its legal owner (the party of the first part, who is beneficiary and recipient of all the rights, appurtenances, and obligations that accrue thereunto; and so on, all the way to the Supreme Court). As with any legal term, "ownership" is no more (and no less) than an arbitrary but mutually agreed-upon package of limits on what other people are allowed do in a designated part of the earth. Obviously, enforcement of those limits depends upon a clear understanding of the spatial extent of "my" property.

To show how the idea of ownership can be the basis for a full-fledged spatial language, we will briefly describe the United States Public Land Survey (see also pages 77 and 132 for more on the topic of surveys and ownership patterns). Many landholdings west of the Appalachians have sizes that are supposed to be exact multiples or fractions of forty acres. This regularity is one obvious consequence of the original Public Land Survey, which was done before the land was legally opened for settlement. The survey rules were set by an Act of Congress and involved five sets of lines and markers, each operating at a slightly different scale:

1) *Principal Meridians* (which run north-south) and *Base Lines* (east- west). The intersections of these arbitrary lines were the starting points for large surveys, which in many cases covered parts of several states.

2) *Standard Parallels* (east-west) and *Guide Meridians* (north-south). These lines are spaced 24 miles apart; they define areas within which the curvature of the earth is for all practical purposes ignored. Road realignments and other adjustments for the curvature of the earth usually take place at the standard parallels.

3) *Township* (east-west) and *Range* (north-south) *Lines*. These lines are spaced at 6-mile intervals away from the Standard Parallels and Guide Meridians. They divide the land into 36-square-mile units called *Townships* (which also serve as units of local government for some purposes, such as road-building, in some parts of the country).

4) *Section lines.* Spaced one mile apart, these lines divide a Township into 36 *Sections*, each nominally one mile square (but they often contain a few acres more or less, because a square grid does not fit the curved earth perfectly, and the surveyors were not always as sober as they should have been). Sections are numbered in a distinctive way, beginning in the upper right-hand corner of the township.

5) *Markers.* Surveyors put markers every half mile along the section lines, to help divide the sections into fractions. A *half-section* has an area of 320 acres; a *quarter* is supposed to be 160 acres. The "north half of the northeast quarter" contains 80 acres ("more or less"). The quarter-quarter section (40 acres) is the basic ownership unit; areas smaller that a *forty* are surveyed individually from the mile and half-mile markers.

The legal description of a tract of land should note the Meridian, Township, Range, Section, and fraction: e.g., the NE 1/4 of NE 1/4 of S32, T4S, R3E, Indian Meridian.

Several Scales of Land Division in the Public Land Survey

National scale -- 1:55,000,000

Principal Meridians and *Baselines* were arbitrarily established at the origin of each survey

County scale -- 1:400,000

Townships are numbered in *Ranges* east and west of the Principal Meridian and *Tiers* north and south of each survey Baseline

Town scale -- 1:32,000

Each Township is a nominal square, six miles on a side. The *Sections* are numbered in sequence from 1 to 36, beginning in the northeast corner of each Township

Farm scale -- 1:40,000

Each square-mile section is marked along the edges and can be subdivided into *halves*, *quarters*, and on down to *forties*

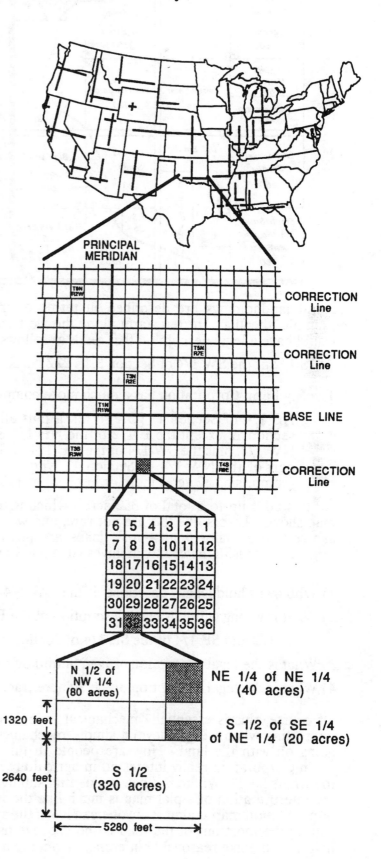

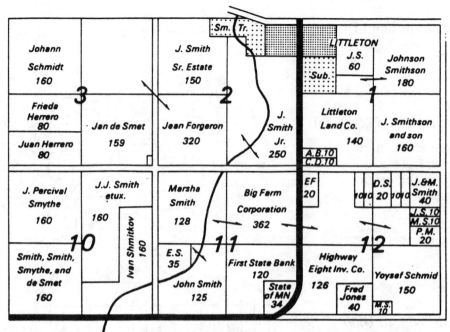

Rural landholdings are described in terms of fractions of sections. For example, the Juan Herrero farm along the west edge of the plat map above would have a legal description that reads as follows:

S 1/2 of the SW 1/4 of Section 3, T. 222 N., R. 44 W.

The Big Farm Corporation has a much more complex description:

NE 1/4 of Section 11 [OK so far?], plus all of the NW 1/4 of section 12 except the E 1/2 of the NE 1/4 & the W 1/2 of the NW 1/4, plus the SW 1/4 of the NE 1/4 of Section 12, plus that part of the NW 1/4 of Section 11 lying east of Smith's Creek (comprising 32 acres more or less), all in T. 222 N., R. 44 W.

All this adds up to a total of 352 acres, which is ten less than what the plat map shows. Errors like this are not rare, and we put one in here so that we can restate a major point -- plat maps are not legal documents; only the original records in the county archives have any standing in court.

1) Who owns land legally described as the NW 1/4 of the SE 1/4 of Sec. 1?

2) What is wrong with this legal description of the First State Bank Land?

N 1/2 and SE 1/4 of the SE 1/4 of Section 11

3) What is the legal description of Ivan Shmitkov's property?

4) What is the legal description of the 10-acre tract owned by AB?

Of course, this is essentially mechanical -- looking at a plat map becomes interesting when we get beyond simple mechanics and start to ask what is going on with the land. How are people in this area related? Is the Big Farm Corporation really interested in agriculture? How did the state come to own its land? Where is a new residential subdivision likely to form? Thus the interpretation of a plat map is much like the interpretation of a contour or population map -- almost anyone can learn the symbols, but the real key to getting the most out of the map is the creative use of other information to help you to make reasonable inferences from the map.

SAMPLE QUIZ QUESTIONS -- PUBLIC LAND SURVEY

You will be given part of a 1:24,000 topographic map.

_____ 1) Print the size (within 5 hectares) of the shaded area marked *A* on the map.

. . . 2) Print the legal description of the forty that point *C* is in.

_____

3) Print the legal description of the shaded field marked *F* on the map (assume it consists of simple fractions of sections).

_____

_____ 4) Print the number of acres in the landholding you just described.

5) Shade in the landholding legally described as follows:
   NW 1/4 of SW 1/4 of sec. 20 and E 1/2 of SE 1/4 of sec. 19

_____ 6) Print the number of acres in this landholding.

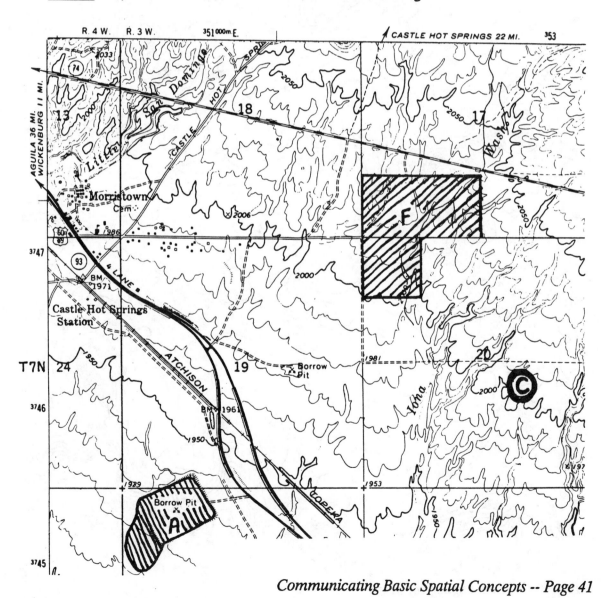

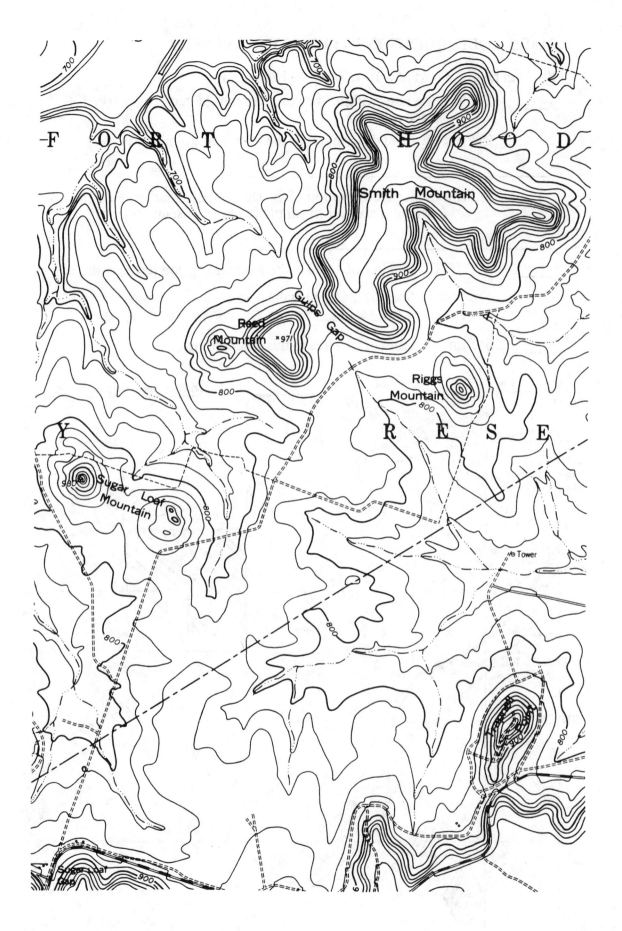

PART 2
DEPICTING THE SHAPE OF THE LAND

In this section, we will examine some of the symbols that people have devised to communicate ideas about the shape of the land -- the hills, valleys, and other features that rise above or dip below the *de facto* plane of a two-dimensional sheet of paper or computer screen. In general, these ways of showing three-dimensional surfaces tend to fall into four categories: models, pictorial clues, contour lines, and various optical "tricks" that convey a 3-D image to the reader. Of these, by far the most important are *contour lines*, which have been adopted as the conventional way of showing the shape of the land on the detailed maps published by the governments of most countries.

In the United States, the various kinds of *topographic maps* produced by the Geological Survey are the prime source of general-purpose spatial information for the nation. One series covers the country at a general scale of 1:250,000, with each map depicting an area that measures one degree of latitude by two degrees of longitude (about 70 by 100 miles). Another series shows areas at a much larger scale (1:24,000), with each sheet showing only 7-1/2 minutes of latitude and longitude (roughly 9 by 6 miles). An old partial series had a scale of either 1:62,500 or 1:63,360 and depicted 15 minutes of latitude and longitude on each map. A new series of metric maps has an intermediate scale (1:100,000), with each sheet covering one-fourth of the area shown on the "quarter-million" (1:250,000) topomaps. Finally, people with access to high-speed computers can also buy some topographic maps in digital form and display them at a variety of scales.

Older topographic maps relied mainly on time-consuming *field surveys*; modern topomaps are compiled primarily by *photogrammetry*. Sophisticated optical and electronic equipment allows the map maker to use aerial photographs and plot the locations of distinct objects (buildings, road intersections, survey markers, etc.) to within half a millimeter of their proper position on the map. Vertical position is also shown to a high degree of accuracy (within one-half of the *contour interval* shown in the legend at the bottom of the map). If more than 90% of the features on the map can satisfy those accuracy requirements, the map can claim to meet the *map accuracy standards* of the United States government.

A new series of printed maps has an aerial photograph as a base, to which the map maker adds lines, symbols, and letters to show the locations and names of selected features such as roads, cities, and political borders. These *orthophotomaps* give a clear visual image of the landscape, but they sacrifice some communicative precision in order to maintain the visual appearance of a photograph.

To obtain the detailed topographic map that covers a particular area, look in a library or camping store (or write to the USGS) for the *index map* for the state. This map has the major towns, roads, lakes, rivers, and an *overlay grid* that tells you the name of the map the covers each part of the state. Each individual map is named for a town, lake, or other prominent feature shown on it. The names of individual topographic maps are unique within a given state, but maps in several different states may have the same name, especially if it is a common one (e.g. Mud Lake, Pleasant Valley, or Lincoln). At the time of this printing, the DeLorme Company of Freeport, Maine, had published books of topographic maps for a dozen states, with more planned. If you are fortunate enough to live or travel in those states, check your bookstore for these books.

PRIMER -- MARGIN INFORMATION ON A USGS TOPOGRAPHIC MAP

    A standard *topographic quadrangle* actually has two parts: the mapped area itself, and the marginal clues that put the map into its spatial, temporal, and jurisdictional context.   Take the map provided by your instructor, or find a map that covers an area of interest. On the blanks by the letters A through Z, print the information requested.   Then, on the blanks to the right, indicate *where* on the quadrangle you found each kind of information.

A _____Name of the quadrangle _____

B _____Publishing Agency _____

C _____Representative fraction scale _____

D _____Date of publication _____

E _____Date of ground survey _____

F _____Date of aerial photography _____

G _____Date of field check _____

H _____Date of revision _____

I _____Minimum latitude _____

J _____Minimum longitude _____

K _____Maximum longitude _____

L _____E-W extent (answer K minus answer J) _____

M _____Map series _____

N _____Magnetic Declination _____

O _____Date of declination _____

P _____UTM grid declination _____

Q _____UTM grid zone _____

R _____UTM northing near center of map _____

S _____State coordinate zone _____

T _____State grid easting near center of map _____

U _____General location in state _____

V _____Name of quad just to the east _____

W _____Name of quad just to the northwest _____

X _____Contour interval _____

Y _____Contour datum _____

Z ___ Does this map comply with national map accuracy standards? _____

WARNING: map standards have changed through time, and therefore a given topographic map will not necessarily provide every kind of information listed here, nor will a given kind of information appear in the same place on every map.   The best way to learn how and where to find information on topomaps is to practice finding information on topomaps.   The sample on the next page shows where these kinds of information are printed on the Shakopee, Minnesota, quadrangle of 1972.

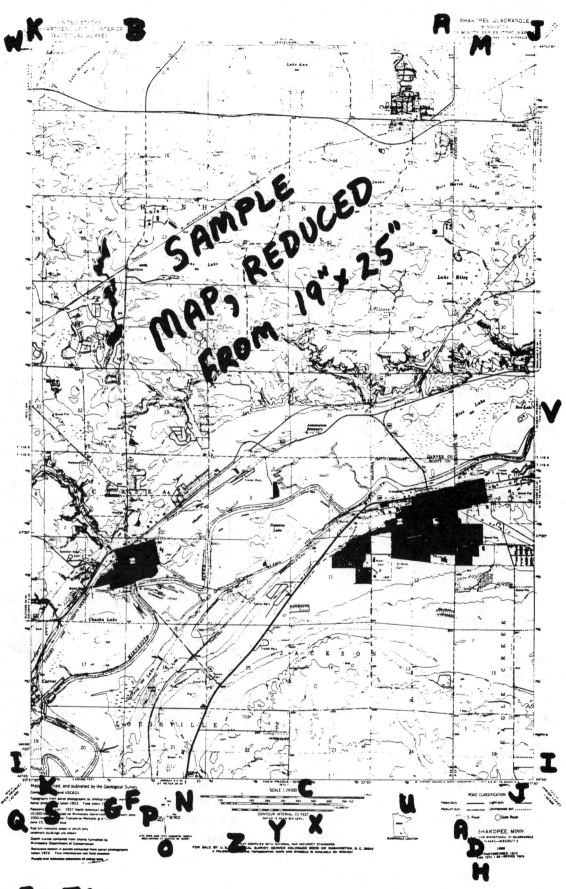

SAMPLE REDUCED MAP, FROM 19" x 25"

TOPOGRAPHIC MAP SYMBOLS

These are reproduced from a color booklet published by the United States Geological Survey. Symbols on older maps, the new metric series, and maps from other government agencies (and other countries) are somewhat different.

The "vocabulary" of a topomap also includes standard uses of color:

black - buildings, powerlines, pipe-lines, railroads, minor roads, and political boundaries

brown - contour lines, levees, and surface material: sand, gravel, tidal flats, mine dumps

blue - rivers, glaciers, reservoirs, lakes, and other water features

green - trees, orchards, vineyards, and other vegetation features

pink - residential and other built-up areas (gray on newer maps)

red - survey lines, fence lines, and major roads

purple - features added from aerial photographs during map revision; these are not field-checked

CONTROL DATA AND MONUMENTS

Horizontal control:

Third order or better, permanent mark ....

With third order or better elevation ....

Checked spot elevation ....

Vertical control:

Third order or better, with tablet ....

Third order or better, recoverable mark ....

Spot elevation ....

Boundary monument:

With tablet ....

BOUNDARIES

National ....

State or territorial ....

County or equivalent ....

Civil township or equivalent ....

Incorporated-city or equivalent ....

Park, reservation, or monument ....

Small park ....

LAND SURVEY SYSTEMS

U.S. Public Land Survey System:

Township or range line ....

Location doubtful ....

Section line ....

Location doubtful ....

Found section corner; found closing corner ....

Other land surveys:

Township or range line ....

Section line ....

Land grant or mining claim; monument ....

Fence line ....

ROADS AND RELATED FEATURES

Primary highway ....

Secondary highway ....

Light duty road ....

Unimproved road ....

Trail ....

Dual highway ....

Dual highway with median strip ....

Road under construction ....

Underpass; overpass ....

Bridge ....

Drawbridge ....

Tunnel ....

BUILDINGS AND RELATED FEATURES

Dwelling or place of employment: small; large ...

School; church ....

Barn, warehouse, etc.: small; large ....

House omission tint ....

Racetrack ....

Airport ....

Landing strip ....

Well (other than water); windmill ....

Water tank: small; large ....

Other tank: small; large ....

Covered reservoir ....

Gaging station ....

Landmark object ....

Campground; picnic area ....

Cemetery: small; large ....

RAILROADS AND RELATED FEATURES

Standard gauge single track; station ....

Standard gauge multiple track ....

Abandoned ....

Under construction ....

Narrow gauge single track ....

Narrow gauge multiple track ....

Railroad in street ....

Juxtaposition ....

Roundhouse and turntable ....

TRANSMISSION LINES AND PIPELINES

Power transmission line: pole; tower ....

Telephone or telegraph line ....

Aboveground oil or gas pipeline ....

Underground oil or gas pipeline ....

CONTOURS

Topographic:

Intermediate ....

Index ....

Supplementary ....

Depression ....

Cut; fill ....

Bathymetric:

Intermediate ....

Index ....

Primary ....

Index Primary ....

Supplementary ....

MINES AND CAVES

Quarry or open pit mine ....

Gravel, sand, clay, or borrow pit ....

Mine tunnel or cave entrance ....

Prospect; mine shaft ....

Mine dump ....

Tailings ....

SURFACE FEATURES

Levee ....

Sand or mud area, dunes, or shifting sand ......

Intricate surface area ....

Gravel beach or glacial moraine ....

Tailings pond ....

VEGETATION

Woods ....

Scrub ....

Orchard ....

Vineyard ....

Mangrove ....

MARINE SHORELINE

Topographic maps:

Approximate mean high water ....

Indefinite or unsurveyed ....

Topographic-bathymetric maps:

Mean high water ....

Apparent (edge of vegetation) ....

COASTAL FEATURES

Foreshore flat ....

Rock or coral reef ....

Rock bare or awash ....

Group of rocks bare or awash ....

Exposed wreck ....

Depth curve; sounding ....

Breakwater, pier, jetty, or wharf ....

Seawall ....

BATHYMETRIC FEATURES

Area exposed at mean low tide; sounding datum ..

Channel ....

Offshore oil or gas: well; platform ....

Sunken rock ....

RIVERS, LAKES, AND CANALS

Intermittent stream ....

Intermittent river ....

Disappearing stream ....

Perennial stream ....

Perennial river ....

Small falls; small rapids ....

Large falls; large rapids ....

Masonry dam ....

Dam with lock ....

Intermittent lake or pond ....

Dry lake ....

Narrow wash ....

Wide wash ....

Canal, flume, or aqueduct with lock ....

Elevated aqueduct, flume, or conduit ....

Aqueduct tunnel ....

Water well; spring or seep ....

GLACIERS AND PERMANENT SNOWFIELDS

Contours and limits ....

Form lines ....

SUBMERGED AREAS AND BOGS

Marsh or swamp ....

ELEVATION

The primary purpose of a topographic map is to display the *elevation* of the land, in both absolute and relative terms. As with most of the spatial ideas described in Part 1, people have developed many different ways of showing the vertical extent of landscape features. These include:

1) **Pictorial images.** The most primitive way to show a mountain is to draw a picture of it on the map. In a more abstract way, one might use big triangles or lumps to represent big mountains and little ones to depict small hills. The use of pictorial images can be documented on maps that date back many centuries in different parts of the world. The apparently separate invention of the technique in different places is an indication of how effective it can be in communicating the shape of the land to a map reader. In the hands of an artistically talented map maker, the pictorial representation of topography can still be extremely effective; the series of black-and-white landform maps drawn by Erwin Raisz are still in wide use after many decades.

2) **Hachures.** Short vertical lines can show the direction and steepness of slopes, and thus can provide an indication of the heights of mountains. This technique was especially common in Europe about the time the printing press was invented; short discrete lines are a reasonably easy way of producing images for use with early copper-plate and lithographic printing technology.

3) **Shaded relief.** With the development of photography and halftone printing, it became possible to display a range of grays as well as the simple black-and-white of a hachure or pictorial line. This, in turn, allowed people to depict elevations by showing one of the most obvious effects of elevation: the shadows cast by tall objects when illuminated from one side. The use of *relief shading* to portray landforms is especially effective on a map that also has other messages to communicate, because a subtle gray shading does not conflict much with the messages being carried by bolder lines, dots, circles, or printed letters and numbers.

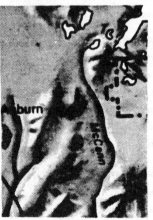

4) **Colors.** Another indirect method of showing elevation is to paint part of the map a color that indicates the kind of vegetation that is likely to grow there. This technique is quite effective in communicating the idea of elevation to someone who knows that a typical high mountain is like a layer cake of different vegetation zones, with a white snowy top, then a pale green tundra zone, a dark green coniferous forest, a greenish brown (or red or yellow, in autumn) hardwood zone, and, near the bottom, a zone of desert shrubs that might be a variety of colors, depending on season, but often are a dry yellow or tan.

5) **Absolute elevations.** At certain selected locations, surveyors have tried to measure the absolute height of the land. This deceptively simple sentence hides a number of problems. For example, there is the question of the base level (or *datum*) for the elevation measurements; the concept of elevation has no meaning until someone specifies the level above which the land height is measured. The datum for most topographic maps is *mean sea level*, but the average elevation of the sea surface is a rather abstract notion when you really look at the ocean. The level of the ocean changes in many different ways as it responds to different forces, each with its own unique "signature" in time and space:

a) *Ripples,* that change sea level every fraction of a second
b) *Waves,* that change sea level every few seconds
c) *Wave groups,* that change sea level every few minutes
d) *Tides,* that change sea level several times a day
e) *Moon phases,* that change sea level from week to week
f) *Seasonal cycles,* that change sea level from month to month
g) *Oscillations* ("El Nino"), that change sea level from year to year
h) *Weather cycles,* that change sea level from decade to decade
i) and a host of longer geologic changes in erosional processes, the sizes of polar ice-caps, and continental position that can change sea level over hundreds, thousands, or millions of years.

One result of the interaction of all of these factors is that the level of the ocean surface on one side of a narrow neck of land (such as where the Panama Canal crosses Central America) may be many meters higher than on the opposite side. Map makers have agreed to ignore this variability by arbitrarily designating a particular elevation as *mean sea level* for the purposes of a given survey. However, the designation may change through time, and therefore the map reader must pay attention to the fine print in order to get the correct message from a map.

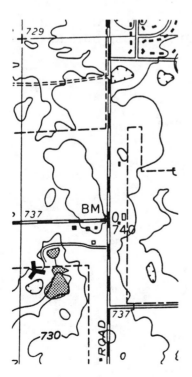

A typical topographic map has a number of *spot elevations* indicated by blue or black numbers printed near road intersections, on lake or river surfaces, or close to brown or black crosses printed on the map. In theory, each spot elevation has been accurately surveyed, but in practice it can be wrong because of inaccuracy in locating the spot horizontally on the map. Small triangles show places where horizontal accuracy is checked, usually by a resurvey. The letters "BM" next to a printed cross or triangle show the location of a *benchmark,* a brass plate that has been "permanently" put in the ground at a place where the elevation and horizontal position was surveyed as accurately as feasible. A given benchmark may actually be in the "wrong" place or at the "wrong" elevation, but the error is simply ignored -- benchmarks have been legally defined as accurate, and that is that (at least until the problems get serious enough to warrant a resurvey).

6) **Relative elevations.** Brown *contour lines* trace curving paths among the benchmarks and other spot elevations on a topographic map. Each contour represents a particular elevation, though usually only the major lines actually have their elevation printed on them. The job of a contour line is to *separate* areas with higher elevation from areas where the elevation is lower than the value of the line. Because all points on a given contour line are theoretically at the same elevation, and because each contour line has its own elevation, contour lines can never cross one another, divide, or meet. (Every rule has an exception -- in very steep terrain, where contour lines must be drawn close to each other, the simple mechanics of printing may cause the lines to merge together.) Although it may not be visible on a given map, a contour line eventually curves around to meet itself again -- the zero-elevation contour encloses the entire continent of North America, while the 20,320-foot contour is a tiny circle that goes around the very top of Mount McKinley in Alaska.

The approximate elevation of any specified place on the map can be estimated by noting the elevations of the contour lines on either side of the place. All by itself, this information is not really all that useful, but a good topomap reader can keep track of the relative elevations of many different points. This skill, in turn, allows the map reader to decide whether a given point is on a hilltop or in a valley, on a slope that faces south or north, higher than its neighbors or surrounded by higher places, etc. And that information, in turn, can be useful in deciding on where to put a hiking path, cabin, gun emplacement, ski slope, or place to store toxic wastes.

PRACTICE: A few contour lines have been drawn, at least partly, around the spot elevations printed below. Finish the map by adding lines at ten-meter intervals.

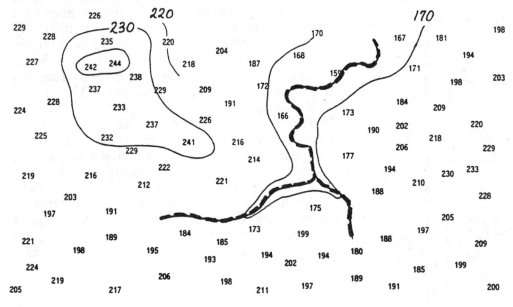

SLOPE

The steepness and ruggedness of the land in a place has a profound effect on erosion hazard, ski resort suitability, avalanche risk, transportation efficiency, land use, and many other traits of the place. Because of this importance, people have created a number of ways to describe and analyze slopes:

1) **Local relief** is the difference between the highest and the lowest elevation in a designated area. The local relief on the author's Wisconsin farm is about 120 feet; in the southern Appalachian Mountains, it is about 5500 feet; and in the first 50 miles west of Denver, the local relief is a bit more than 9000 feet. This measure provides basic information about the landscape but does not tell much about the smoothness or ruggedness of the terrain; some of the slopes on my farm are steeper than in the Rockies.

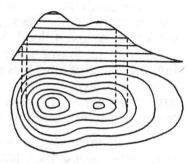

2) **Contour spacing** gives a good quick impression of the slope in part of a landscape, because the contours on a steep slope will be closer together than on a gentle slope (assuming the map maker used the same contour interval, of course). This measure is not adequate all by itself, however, because a set of closely-spaced contours may indicate a long mountainside or a bunch of steep up-and-down hills.

3) Some more precise **mathematical expressions** of slope include:

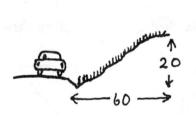

a) *Slope ratio*, which is the vertical distance (difference in elevation) divided by the horizontal distance. For example, suppose the top of a roadcut is sixty feet from the road edge and twenty feet higher than the road surface. This cut has a 1:3 slope (20 feet up and 60 feet out). Slopes in nature are rarely that steep, and it is often easier to describe them in terms of feet per mile. For example, a canoe stream with a slope ratio of 70 feet per mile (70/5280, or about 1:75) would be a challenge for an expert.

b) *Slope percentage*, a form of ratio, in which the vertical and horizontal measurements are made in the same units and the result multiplied by 100. An island with a 1500-foot summit that is three miles from shore would have a slope of about ten percent (1,500 feet divided by about 15,000 feet and then multiplied by 100). Railroad and highway slopes are usually described in percentage terms; few highways have slopes that exceed ten percent.

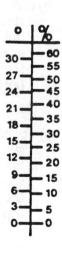

c) *Slope angle*, which is a measurement of a slope in terms of degrees of inclination from horizontal. The 10 percent slope in the example above has an angle of about six degrees (see the table in the margin to convert from slope percent to angle and vice versa). Geologists and avalanche forecasters usually express slopes in terms of degrees; many kinds of loose earth material are unstable when the slope exceeds an angle of thirty degrees.

4) The **aspect** of a slope is its horizontal orientation -- the direction that one would head in order to go downhill as steeply as possible. On the map segment to the right, the aspect of the slope at point X is southeast. We could also describe this as a southeast slope or say that it "faces to the southeast." Aspect is an important concept for ecologists who try to analyze the stresses that plants and animals are likely to encounter on a site. Aspect is also significant for an architect who wants to design buildings that take advantage of solar light and heat.

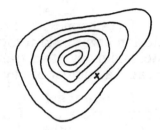

5) **Grade** is the term for the "slope" along a road, path, or other line that does not necessarily go directly down or up the topographic slope of a hill. A railroad engine cannot pull a loaded train up a grade that exceeds a few degrees (the *limiting grade* for a given load and engine) and therefore railroad tracks usually go diagonally uphill whenever they ascend a slope that exceeds the limiting grade. The limiting grade of a hiker is much more variable, because it depends on the nature of the trail surface, the length of the slope, the hiker's skill, pack weight, time of day, aspect, air temperature, wind direction, and all the other things that conspire to make long steep south-facing hills so miserable on hot afternoons.

6) The **geometry** of a slope is a vocabulary for communicating more about the shape of a slope than just its aspect and average angle. Slope geometry is an important consideration in trying to decide where to put things like houses, fences, or roads. People who are trying to predict landslides or soil erosion are also concerned with the geometry of the slope; they often classify slopes into six categories:

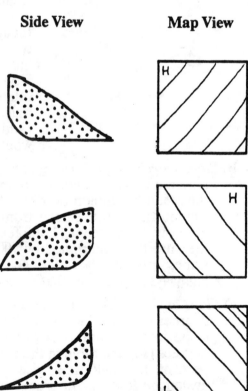

Side View   **Map View**

a) *uniform* -- the slope at any point is about the same as the average slope from valley bottom to hilltop. Contour lines are evenly spaced on a uniform slope.

b) *convex* -- the slope gets less steep as you go up the hill. Contour lines are spaced farther apart near the top than at the bottom of a convex slope.

c) *concave* -- the slope gets steeper as you go up the hill. Contour lines are spaced farther apart near the bottom than at the top of a concave slope.

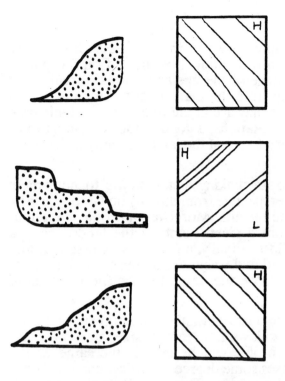

d) *sigmoidal (s-shaped)* -- this very common slope shape has a convex *shoulder* high on the hill, a uniform *face*, and a concave *foot* (or *toe*) at the bottom of the hill.

e) *terraced* -- reasonably level areas alternate with steeper slopes. Closely spaced contours mark the steep *scarps* between the level *benches* of a terraced slope.

f) *complex* -- the angle of the slope varies in an irregular manner from top to bottom. The spacing of contour lines is also uneven.

The geometry of the slope has been noted for seven lettered lines on this fragment of a 1:24,000 topographic map. The labels for two of the last four lines are incorrect; identify which two and write the correct answer below.

A. concave

B. uniform

C. sigmoidal

D. convex

E. convex

F. uniform

G. concave

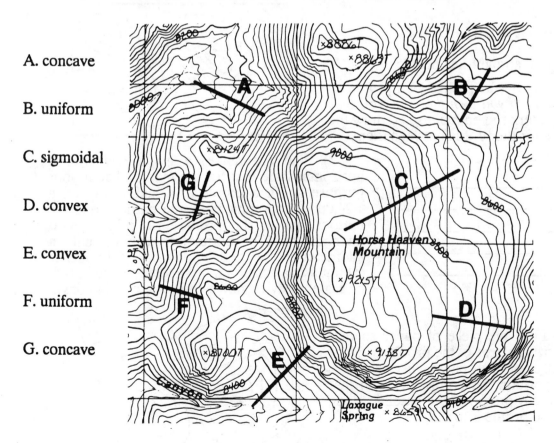

SIDE PROFILES

A topographic map gives a "straight-down" view of the terrain, as if you were directly above each place on the map. Unfortunately, it is printed on flat paper, which does not allow it to give a literal image of the ups and downs of real-world topography. Hills do not physically rise up from the plane of the map, and valleys are not lower than the surrounding area (as they are in the real world and might be on a good plastic model). Despite these limitations, a good reader of topographic maps is able to "see" the three-dimensional surface of the land with only the contour lines as clues.

Most people, however, can benefit from making a *side profile* to help them interpret a contour map. The change in perspective from directly down to side view can help form a better mental image of the terrain. Moreover, a profile can tell us whether a particular feature is visible from a given point on the landscape -- a desirable bit of information if a person is lost. Finally, a profile is an essential tool for someone designing a highway or railroad and trying to minimize the amount of dirt that needs to be moved in order to achieve the desired grade (no puns about required courses, please).

Profiles are generally constructed along a straight line between two points, but it is possible to construct a profile that follows a stream course, trail, or other irregular line. The vertical scale of the profile can be exactly the same as the horizontal scale of the map, but in most cases some degree of *vertical exaggeration* is useful in order to highlight the details of the terrain. This need for exaggeration is partly a result of a quirk of the human mind -- most people remember slopes as being much steeper than they actually are.

MAKING A SIDE PROFILE

To make a straight-line profile:

1) Locate the path of your profile on the map. *If you own the map*, you may wish to mark the endpoints and draw the *baseline* for the profile between them.

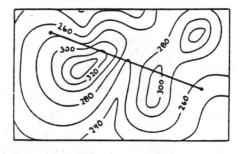

2) Find (or make) a *graph grid* with a horizontal scale that fits the map and suits your purpose. For a profile of a hiking trail on a 1:24,000 topographic map, the marks along the bottom line of the profile grid might be at intervals of 2.1 centimeters (about half a kilometer in the real world) or 1-5/16 inches (about a quarter of a mile -- reread pages 21-24 on scale to review how to do scale conversions).

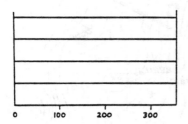

3) Fold the piece of paper so that the horizontal axis of the profile grid is at the edge of the paper, like a ruler. Then, position the profile grid with that axis directly on top of the baseline along which the profile is to run.

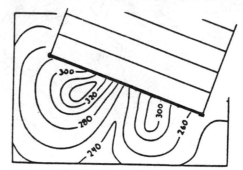

About 250,
320 plus

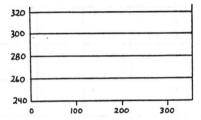

4) Examine the contour lines, spot elevations, and benchmarks, and note the highest and lowest elevations along the line of the profile.

5) Select appropriate values for the horizontal lines (the ones that represent elevation on the vertical axis of the graph). These values should be round numbers (or other easy-to-remember values) that extend from *near or below the lowest elevation* to *near or above the highest elevation* along the line of the profile.

6) At every place where a major contour line intersects or touches the horizontal axis of the profile grid, go "up" from the bottom of your graph and place a dot at the appropriate elevation.

7) Note the positions of hill tops, valley bottoms, and other major changes in the slope of the land along the profile line. Place dots at the appropriate elevations and horizontal positions for these key features. (After you get reasonably proficient at profile drawing, you may be able to omit step 6 and concentrate on these "information-rich" locations along the profile).

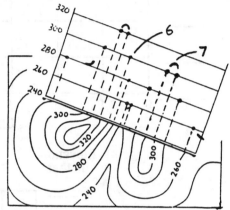

8) Draw a smooth line connecting the dots on your graph. Let the other contour lines on the map help you shape the details of the profile line -- it should slope steeply where contours are close together and more gently where they are farther apart. This line shows the shape of the land as seen from one side.

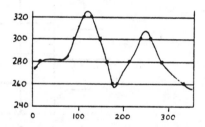

9) Label key features of your profile with placenames from the map. Add other information (e.g. forest cover, house density, underlying geology, etc.) with appropriate symbols if you wish to illustrate the relationship between the surface topography and the other kinds of landscape features.

10) Practice -- the forms on the next page fit standard 1:24,000, 1:62,500, and 1:100,000 topographic maps. After you get fairly good at making profiles along a straight line, try making some along a hiking path, canoe stream, or other curved path.

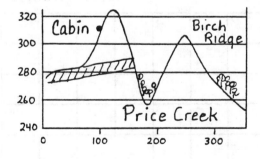

TOPOGRAPHIC MAP PROFILE FORMS

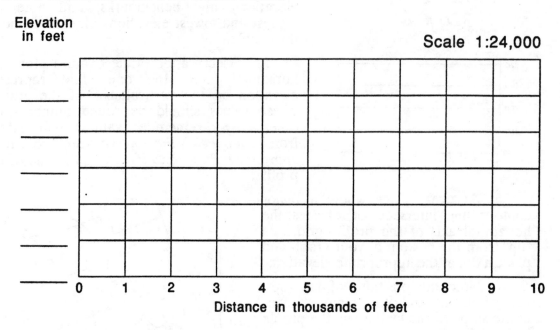

Elevation in feet

Scale 1:24,000

Distance in thousands of feet

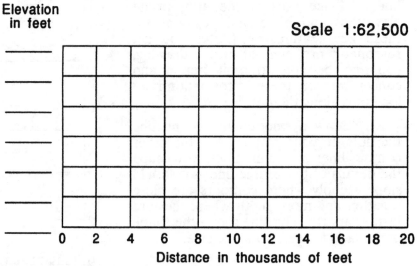

Elevation in feet

Scale 1:62,500

Distance in thousands of feet

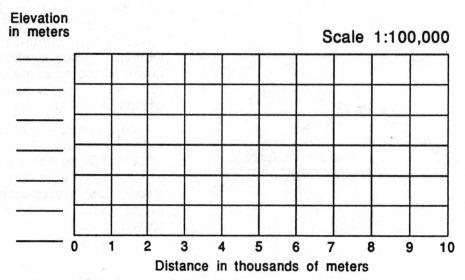

Elevation in meters

Scale 1:100,000

Distance in thousands of meters

ROUTES

A profile on a topographic map does not necessarily have to go in a straight line from one point to another. Indeed, one of the most common uses of topomaps is to select travel routes that avoid hazards such as cliffs, rivers, swamps, or stretches that exceed a tolerable gradient. The ability to construct a profile along a proposed route is essential in order to decide whether the gradient is acceptable for a particular purpose.

One easy way to do this is to take a small card or piece of paper and put a few marks along the edge; these marks should be spaced just as far apart as the contour lines on the steepest slope you can manage to overcome. For example, suppose you have a 7-1/2' quadrangle (scale 1:24,000) with a contour interval of 40 feet, and the steepest acceptable slope is eight percent. In this case, the contour lines on a barely acceptable slope would be about 500 feet apart (40 / 500 = .08). On a 1:24,000 map, 500 feet is about 6 millimeters (or 1/4 inch). In practice, you do not need to figure the distance in inches or millimeters, because it is easy to use the bar scale on the map to put your marks the right distance apart. These marks then act as a kind of judge: any slope that has contour lines spaced closer than the marks on your card is too steep.

The next step is to turn the card so that its edge does not go directly up and down slope. At some critical angle, the marks on the card will fit right on top of the contour lines on the map. At that angle, a path would be an acceptably gentle slope. Whether it is the best route depends on other things, such as the nature of the terrain elsewhere along the route and the relative ease of walking or driving up different degrees of slope.

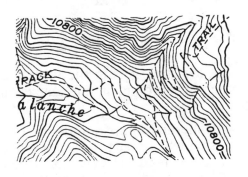

In extremely hilly terrain, a travel route may take several miles to go only one mile "as the crow flies." The route on a steep slope may be a series of *switchbacks*, which trace a zig-zag path up the slope in order to keep the grade of the path below the limiting angle. This is easier for hikers than for railroads or automobiles, which have trouble with sharp turns as well as steep slopes.

Heavy earthmoving equipment has allowed highway engineers to substitute construction energy for transportation energy, but that has not decreased the importance of topographic map analysis. Indeed, detailed contour maps are the primary source of information to guide engineers in deciding where to fill in low areas and where to cut through hills. A good cut-and-fill design allows a road to be built with a minimum amount of expensive hauling of rocks and earth into or out of the project area.

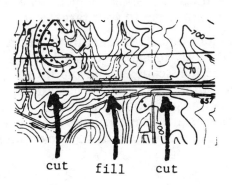

cut   fill   cut

PRACTICAL ROUTEFINDING

Finding a good hiking path through roadless terrain is the essence of map reading for some people (notably those steeped in the Scout tradition). While we would argue that there is more to map interpretation than simple routefinding, that fact remains that wilderness routefinding is uncommonly rewarding fun. Many interesting books have been written on the subject, but out in the real world the skill boils down to a few commonsense rules:

- practice walking along paths with known distances until you have a good idea how far you go during some some easy-to-remember interval of time (e.g. 5 minutes) or number of steps (e.g. 100 steps)

- measure the distance to your destination and convert it into your personal distance-measurement terms (e.g. 2.3 miles is about 50 minutes of walking with a thirty-pound pack; see pages 10-11)

- determine the straight-line direction to your destination, and express it in terms of degrees from magnetic north (see page 16)

- use a good compass to find magnetic north and turn yourself so that you are sighting in the direction you want to go

- pick out some object on the horizon (or as far as you can see) and head toward that object, counting minutes or steps as you go (and adjusting for slope and obstructions if they really alter your speed or pace length)

- if a well-defined barrier (such as a lake) gets in the way, you can "box" it as shown on this sketch; note that side B of the box is the only distance that counts toward the target, but sides A and C must be the same length if you are to stay on the intended path

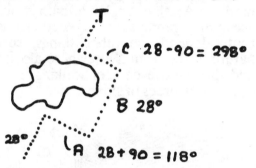

- never lose elevation unnecessarily -- if a low area gets in the way, it is often easier to follow a rough contour line around it and make an adjustment for distance on the map

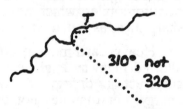

- deliberately aim a little to one side when going toward a place on a road, stream, or other linear feature; then, when you hit the feature, there will be no question about which way to turn to get to your target

- *backsight* from peaks and other prominent objects frequently to verify your position on the map (see page 36). The best way to avoid getting lost is to stay found (which is easier said than done in some landscapes -- the blunt fact is that finding your way above timberline in the Colorado Rockies is like kindergarten compared with hiking through a nearly level forested swamp in eastern Canada, where roads are nonexistent, magnetic compasses are several points off, local iron-ore deposits make them unreliable, and the mosquitoes seem to be thick enough to interfere with backsighting).

ROUTEFINDING -- PRACTICE

Figure out a good hiking path between any two of the four places shown on this 1:24,000 topographic map. Try to avoid swampy areas and excessive up-and-down movement. The grade of your path should not exceed about 15 percent for any significant distance. Use a colored marker to show your path, and note the magnetic compass direction and distance of each major segment of the route. If you choose to use a road or contour line rather than a straight line for part of your route, describe that segment carefully so that another person could follow your directions.

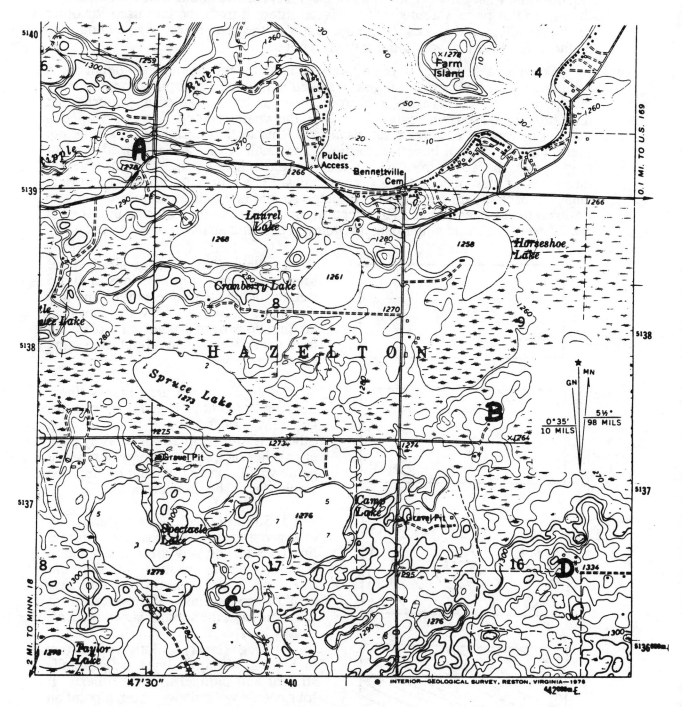

TOPOGRAPHIC POSITIONS

Someone learning to read a language that has an unfamiliar alphabet (e.g. a child with any written language, or an adult American learning Russian) has to look carefully at each individual letter at first. In time, however, the *unit of perception* becomes the syllable, then the whole word, and perhaps even a group of words. The speed of reading increases dramatically as the mind learns what information is essential and what can be ignored. For example, did you notice that the heading at the top of this page is a *sans serif* typeface, different from the one used for other section headings in this book ? Compare it with the heading on page 59 and note all the differences that your mind casually ignored.

Likewise, a beginner is often overwhelmed by the amount of detail on a standard topographic map, whereas a skilled map reader seldom bothers to trace individual contours. Taken as a group, contour lines often form patterns that indicate familiar terrain features. Over the years, people have developed a number of ways to classify *terrain elements*. This section introduces a simple but useful classification of basic landforms. The small X on each idealized contour map shows the point from which four people might try to walk in different directions, as described in the text paragraphs. The four paths are always at right angles to each other, but the set is oriented so that one individual goes directly up or down the steepest slope. (In effect, we have adjusted the paths so that they fit the *aspect* of the slope rather than just going in the *cardinal directions*; see page 52).

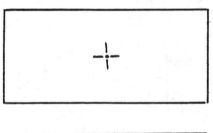

1) **Plain (flat)** -- a generally level area, with few contour lines and no significant change in elevation in any direction. If four people walked away in all directions from a point on a plain, all four would remain at about the same elevation.

2) **Slope** -- a flat area that is tilted, not level. Contour lines on a slope are generally straight and parallel to each other. If four people walked away from each other on a slope, one person would go downhill, one would climb, and two would stay at the same elevation.

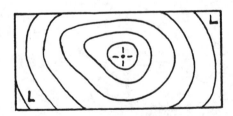

3) **Summit (peak)** - the highest point in a given area. At least one contour line goes all the way around a summit. If four people walked in different directions from a point on a summit, they would all go downhill. If they descend at the same rate, the summit is *symmetrical*.

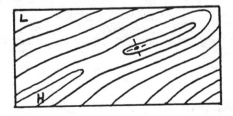

4) **Ridge (crest)** - a long and narrow high area. Contour lines are generally straight and parallel to each other. If four people walked away from a point on a ridge, two would go downhill and two would stay at the same elevation.

5) **Spur (nose)** -- a tilted ridge, where the contours form a roughly parallel set of rounded "V" shapes. If four people walked away from a point on a spur, one would climb, one go gently downhill, and two would have to descend more steeply.

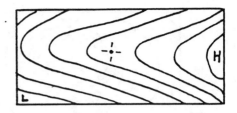

6) **Cliff** -- an abrupt and very steep slope, with crowded parallel contours. If four people walked away from a point near the top of a cliff, two would stay about the same level, one could stay level or climb, and one may not survive the fall!

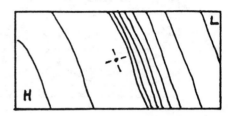

7) **Bench (terrace)** - a level area on a slope, with parallel straight contours. If four people walked away from a point on a bench, all would start out level, but one would soon climb and another would go downhill, while the other two stayed generally at the same level.

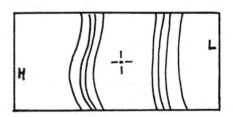

8) **Valley** -- a long and narrow low area, like an upside-down ridge. The contour lines are often straight and parallel to each other, although a valley, like a ridge, can curve. If four people walked away from a point in a valley, two would stay at about the same elevation and two would go uphill.

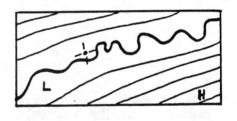

9) **Draw** -- a tilted low area, like an inverted spur. Contour lines form a parallel set of rounded "V" shapes. If four people walked away from a point in a draw, two would climb steeply, one would go more gently uphill, and one would descend.

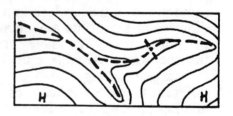

10) **Depression (hole or pit)** -- the lowest point in a local area (an upside-down summit). At least one contour line completely encircles a depression; tiny *hachures* indicate the downhill direction. Four people walking away from a point at the bottom of a depression would all have to go uphill.

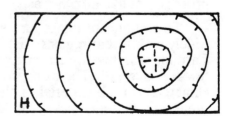

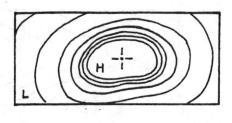

11) **Butte** -- hill with a flat top and steep sides, marked by closely spaced concentric contours that encircle a level area with few lines. If four people tried to walk away from each other on a butte, no one could walk too far! (A big butte is called a *mesa*).

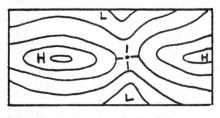

12) **Pass (saddle)** -- a low point in a high area, with contours that look like a combination of two spurs and two draws. If four people walked away from a point in a pass, two would go downhill and two would have to climb.

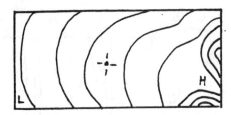

13) **Fan** -- a wide spur, where the contour lines form a set of nested arcs or concentric half-circles. If four people walked away from each other on a fan, one would climb gently uphill and the other three would descend slowly.

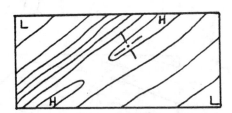

14) **Scarp** (**cuesta** or **hogback**) -- an asymmetrical ridge, with one slope significantly steeper than the other. If four people walked in opposite directions from a point on a scarp, two would stay nearly level, one would go gently downhill, and one would go steeply downhill.

These *topographic positions* (*terrain elements*, or *topographic features*) do not exist in isolation. On the contrary, they tend to occur in more-or-less predictable groups (*associations*) of related landforms. Two summits, for example, usually are separated by a pass, which in turn serves as the top of two draws. Similarly, a long draw leading out onto a plain in a dry region will usually have a fan where it leaves the hillier area. In many cases, these associations of topographic features can provide some valuable clues about the geologic structure that underlies the landscape (see pages 68-70). At the same time, however, the close association of different topographic features can make it difficult to separate one feature from another (or even to decide whether a particular feature actually exists in an area). In short, the identification of topographic features is at least partly an arbitrary process, just like all other aspects of the language of maps.

To complicate things further, the *scale* of individual terrain elements can vary widely in different regions. For example, a pile of dirt exposed to the rain in North Carolina will develop an intricate set of draws and tiny fans, often no more than a few feet across. The same process working a long time in the radically different climate and rock material of Nevada can build fans that are many miles wide and thousands of feet thick. With practice, a map reader learns what shapes and spacings of contour lines are normal within a given region. Perhaps even more important, a skilled reader can "read between the contour lines" and see what the slope actually is like. For example, a wiggly contour line may indicate a rough and rocky slope with many irregularities too small to show with individual contour lines.

TERRAIN INTERPRETATION -- PRACTICE

Find a topomap for an area that interests you and take a mental "hike" through the map. Try to choose a route that is not too steep, stays out of swamps, goes by interesting features, etc. As you "walk" along, describe the terrain you might see. For example, suppose you started in a cabin in the middle of Camp Woodstock on the map below. "I go a few hundred feet northward along the edge of the lake and then northwest along a creek to the road. Here, I turn left, pass by a gentle summit, and, just before the road heads downhill to the junction, I turn north on a lane that leads to a house. From there, I go a few hundred feet to the northwest and climb a summit that might have a spectacular view to the north. Heading west from the north end of this summit, I go by two mines next to the road. From here, I head generally west across a small plain."

As you become more skillful, put features together into a three-dimensional landscape: "When I reach the western edge of the bench, I walk diagonally southwest down a slope until I get to where a swamp empties into a draw; maybe there's a beaver dam here? After crossing the stream, I curve southward onto a bench and then climb a spur to the highest point on my trip, a small summit with a long steep slope to the west. A big swamp lies between my hill and one just slightly higher to the east. From here, it's a simple matter of following the spur to the northeast to the dirt road and letting it take me back to the camp entrance, though I might save some breath by following a contour line southeast from the road junction."

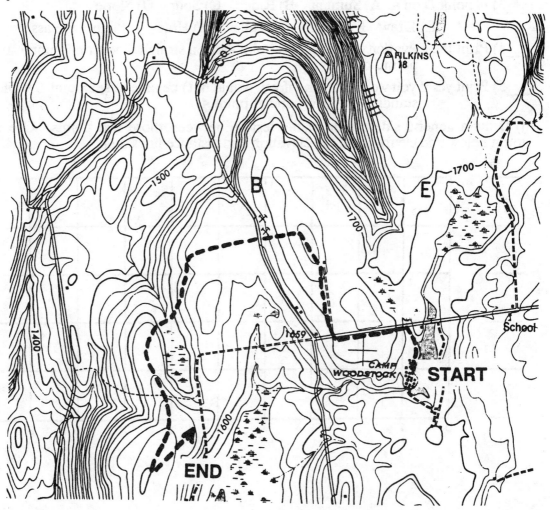

SAMPLE QUIZ QUESTIONS -- ELEVATION AND SLOPE

You will be given part of a 1:24,000 topographic map.

___1) Print the contour interval on this map.

___2) Print the maximum elevation (nearest meter or foot) that point *F* on this topographic map could possibly have.

___3) Print a reasonable interpolated elevation for point *G*.

___4) Print the elevation difference between point *C* and *I*.

___5) Print the slope angle (nearest 5 degrees) that corresponds to a slope gradient of *35* percent.

___6) Print the average gradient (nearest 5 percent) of a direct path from point *A* to point *B* on the map.

SAMPLE QUIZ QUESTIONS -- TERRAIN AND PROFILES

You will be given part of a 1:24,000 topographic map.

___1) Print the direction (nearest 10 degrees) that you would head to go down the steepest slope from point *C* on the map.

___2) Print the grade (nearest ten percent) of that slope.

___3) Is point *D* on a A) Summit B) Ridge C) Spur D) Slope
     E) Draw F) Bench G) Valley H) Hole I) Plain J) Pass

___4) Print the elevation of the highest point along a straight line from point *F* to point *J* on the map.

___5) Print **yes** if you would (and **no** if you would not) be able to see point *C* while standing on the ground at point *A*.

6) Draw a general side profile of the terrain between those two points. Use the graph below and clearly label the elevation and distance lines on it.

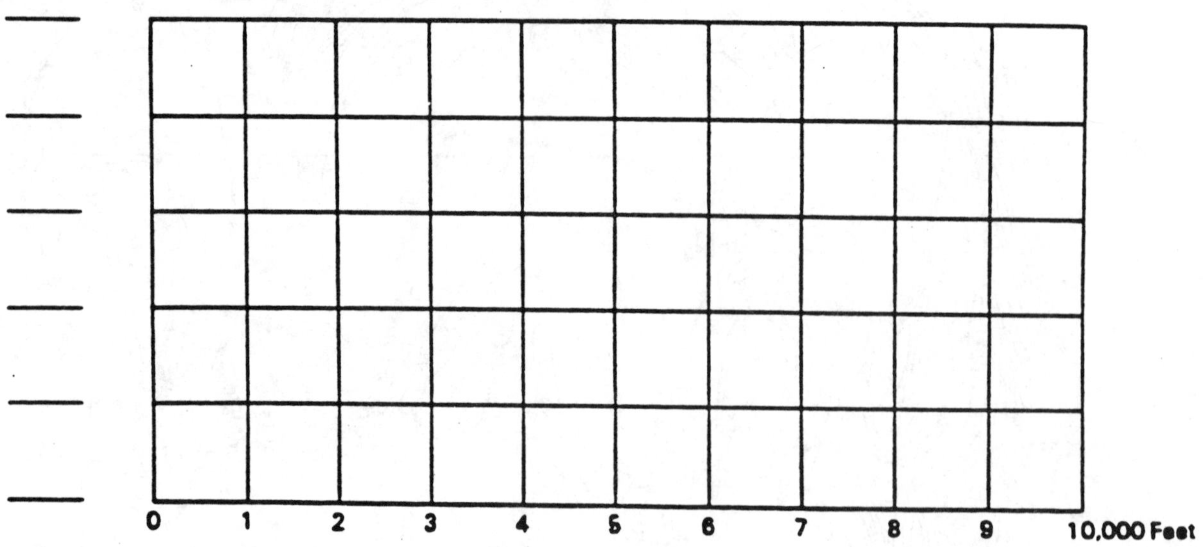

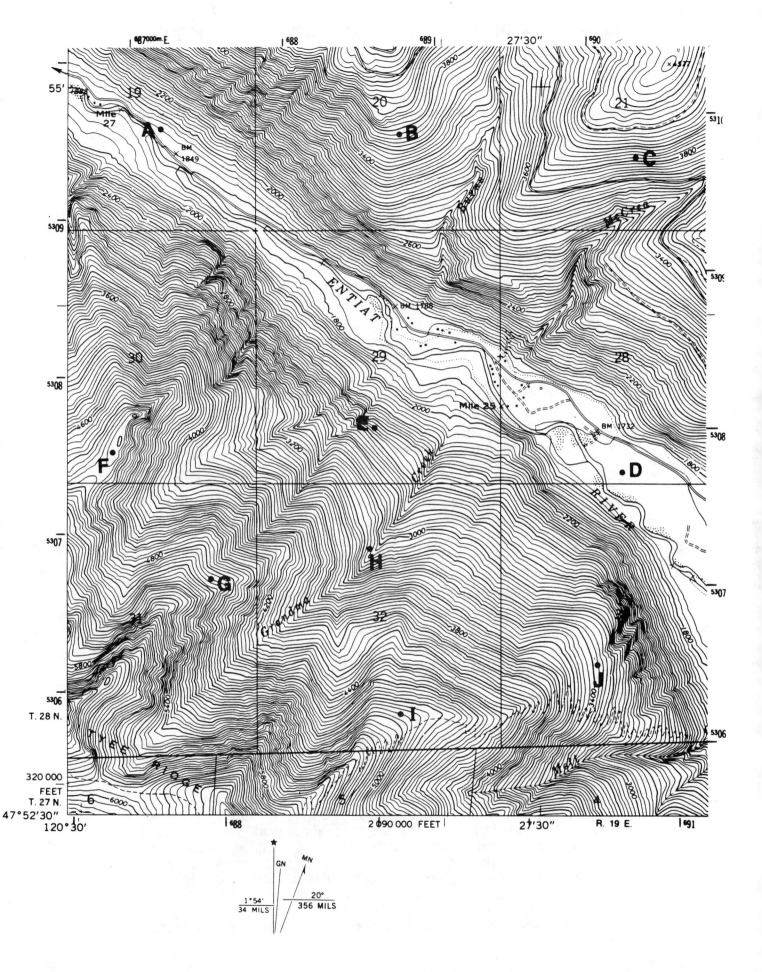

TRANSITION -- THE GREAT TERRAIN ROBBERY (sorry about that!)

The safest place for a mountain to hide is on the ocean bottom. Land above sea level is exposed to relentless assault by a number of *geomorphic* (landforming) *agents* -- wind, glaciers, streams, waves, and its own weight. These "sculptors of the land" all get their energy from gravity, but they apply that energy in different ways and therefore make different landforms. To understand the shape of the land, one must try to figure out:

- *what* processes are at work on the landscape, and
- *where* those processes tend to focus the force of gravity.

These profile diagrams show the effects of various landforming agents. The dashed line represents a simple V-shaped valley. A solid line shows a profile of the same valley after a particular landforming process has been at work for awhile. For example, profile F is the result of landslides, which start on steep slopes and run out of energy on flat land. The result of this pattern of energy is a concave scar on the slope and an irregular pile of earth in the valley. Match the appropriate profile with each landforming agent:

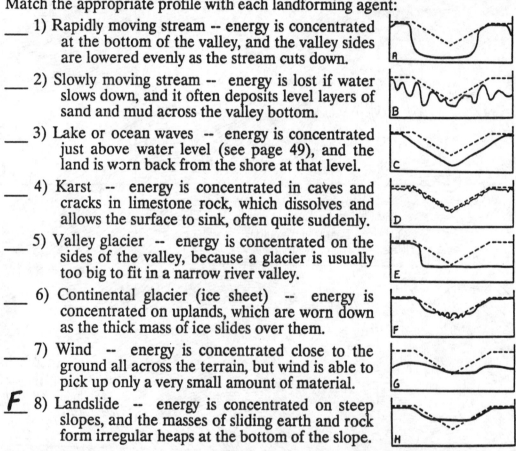

___ 1) Rapidly moving stream -- energy is concentrated at the bottom of the valley, and the valley sides are lowered evenly as the stream cuts down.

___ 2) Slowly moving stream -- energy is lost if water slows down, and it often deposits level layers of sand and mud across the valley bottom.

___ 3) Lake or ocean waves -- energy is concentrated just above water level (see page 49), and the land is worn back from the shore at that level.

___ 4) Karst -- energy is concentrated in caves and cracks in limestone rock, which dissolves and allows the surface to sink, often quite suddenly.

___ 5) Valley glacier -- energy is concentrated on the sides of the valley, because a glacier is usually too big to fit in a narrow river valley.

___ 6) Continental glacier (ice sheet) -- energy is concentrated on uplands, which are worn down as the thick mass of ice slides over them.

___ 7) Wind -- energy is concentrated close to the ground all across the terrain, but wind is able to pick up only a very small amount of material.

F 8) Landslide -- energy is concentrated on steep slopes, and the masses of sliding earth and rock form irregular heaps at the bottom of the slope.

These idealized cross-sections are rare in the real world, because nature can add at least five complications to any of the processes described above:

- differing degrees of rock resistance -- weak rocks wear down faster
- different climates in the past -- landforms in an area may still show the effects of processes that are no longer at work there
- changing sea levels -- the energy in waves and rivers depends on the elevation of the ocean (or any temporary barriers to river flow)
- isostasy -- landmasses, like boats, respond to a removal of weight by rising to "float" higher above the molten interior of the earth
- tectonic movements -- earthquakes, volcanoes, and other effects of large-scale crustal motion can dramatically alter local landforms

PART 3
INTERPRETING TOPOGRAPHIC MAPS

The shape of the land has a pervasive influence on many things, from the kinds of native plants that can grow in a place to the problems encountered by someone trying to build a house there. A good map reader sees much more than elevation and slope on a topographic map; like a well-educated reader of poetry, a good map reader can make *inferences* that go far beyond the *literal meaning* of a map symbol. The messages one can draw from a map depend on the background of the map reader and the purpose for looking at the map. Here are a few generalizations:

- Map inferences can be *obvious* or *subtle*. The spacing of contour lines provides an obvious indication of those parts of a trail that are likely to involve strenuous climbing. Walking directly toward a bright sun can also be annoying, but one must have a rather sophisticated understanding of slopes, directions, and hourly sun angles in order to look at a map and judge whether the sun will be a nuisance on a specified path at a given time of day.

- Map inferences can be *direct* or *indirect*. Water in a Kansas stream has a direct logical link with the pattern of green color on a topographic map: the extra moisture in the soil near the stream allows trees to grow in a region that is otherwise too dry. Climatic conditions in a valley in eastern Kentucky would also be favorable for trees, but flat land is so valuable that the farmers probably cleared the forest from the valleys in order to plant crops there. The pattern of green on a topomap of this area is thus the result of an indirect series of links among terrain, human perception, agriculture, and forest cover.

- Map inferences can be *forward* or *backward*. Running water will shape the terrain in a distinctive way, with V-shaped valleys and level floodplains. At the same time, the rate of erosion by water depends on the length and angle of the slope, and therefore present topography has an influence on the ability of running water to shape the land. Scientists call this kind of action-reaction system a *feedback loop*. In time, a feedback system tends to reach an equilibrium between process (erosion) and form (slope). A person who understands feedback can therefore visualize landforming history and predict future erosion, as well as interpret present landforms.

- Map inferences can be *straightforward* or *complex*. A hydro-electric generator gets its energy from falling water and therefore must be located right at the lower end of a pipe or tunnel that extends down from a stream or reservoir. A simple link between turbine efficiency and relative elevation imposes some strict limits on the location of the power plant. By contrast, the site for a used-car lot depends on a host of factors, such as road access, landholding size and shape, property taxes, competition, previous land use, and the personality quirks of the owner. Complex tradeoffs among seemingly unrelated factors like these are part of trying to explain some patterns on a topographic map.

Topographic map readers are aided by the fact that the symbolic language of a given series of topographic maps has been standardized. Skill in reading one kind of maps can be deceiving if you encounter a topographic map from another agency or country, which may use a different set of conventional symbols. In this section, we have deliberately chosen a restricted map language for our illustrations, so that the general ideas can be used in interpreting a variety of topographic maps from different sources.

LANDFORMS ON TOPOGRAPHIC MAPS

The form of the land surface in a particular place is the result of the interplay of rock structure, destructive (erosional) and constructive (depositional) processes, and time (complicated by the fact that different landforming processes may have operated at various times in the past). Many different landforming processes can help shape the terrain, and the work of each one usually leaves recognizable clues on contour maps:

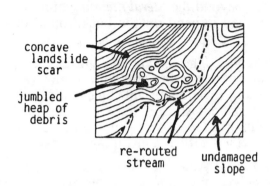

concave landslide scar

jumbled heap of debris

re-routed stream

undamaged slope

1) **Mass movements** -- Rock or soil can move downhill under the influence of gravity; mass movements often are triggered by an earthquake or big storm, but the shaping of the terrain is done without assistance from any other "earth-moving agents" such as rivers, glaciers, or wind. Mass movements vary widely in speed and size, and the shape of the resulting landform depends on the kind of earth material and the environmental conditions in which the movement occurs.

2) **Pedimentation** -- Flash floods can carry earth material downhill in many normally dry areas. Storm runoff is usually energetic enough to pick up material from the steep slopes of a mountain, but the water loses speed and has to drop some of its load when it flows out onto a more gentle slope. The details of flash flooding are still open to debate, but the result in most places is a distinctive "apron" or "fan" of earth and rock that extends in a gentle slope away from the foot of the mountain.

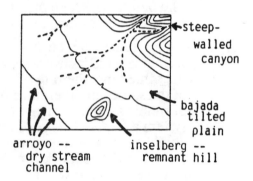

steep-walled canyon

bajada tilted plain

arroyo -- dry stream channel

inselberg -- remnant hill

3) **Streams** -- Water in confined channels also can carry earth material downhill. An actively eroding stream usually carves a deep V-shaped valley for itself. The angle of the slopes on each side of a stream depends on the interplay of mass movement and stream action. In general, streams tend to undercut the bank on the *outside* of a curve -- a stream that is curving to the left as it flows downslope will remove material from the base of the right-hand bank and thus make that slope steeper. Material deposited by a stream on the inside bank or in other places where the water slows down is usually nearly level.

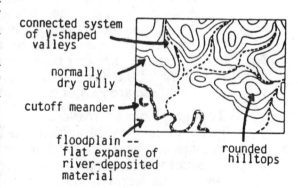

connected system of V-shaped valleys

normally dry gully

cutoff meander

floodplain -- flat expanse of river-deposited material

rounded hilltops

4) Valley glaciers -- These "rivers" of ice carry earth material down steep-sided valleys in high mountain areas. Most glaciers move only a few meters per day, whereas rivers flow hundreds of times faster. A glacier must therefore be hundreds of times as big as a river in order to carry away the same volume of water. This extra size is why a glacier makes a big U-shaped valley, much wider and more steep-sided than the narrow V-shaped valley carved by a typical stream (exception: a U-shaped valley can also occur around a river that is depositing material on the floor of its valley).

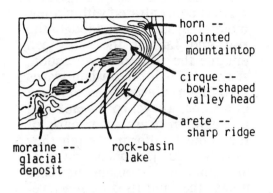

horn -- pointed mountaintop

cirque -- bowl-shaped valley head

arete -- sharp ridge

moraine -- glacial deposit

rock-basin lake

5) Ice sheets -- Continental glaciers are now rare except in Antarctica and Greenland, but they covered a large part of North America 20,000 years ago. These glaciers form when snow accumulates to the point that it recrystallizes and then begins to flow outward, like thick syrup on a pancake. The outward spread of a mile-thick mass of ice can move vast amounts of rock and soil; the result is a maze of scoured basins and rock outcrops near the origin of its journey and lumpy deposits of boulders, sand, and gravel where the ice melted.

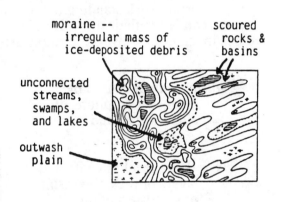

moraine -- irregular mass of ice-deposited debris

scoured rocks & basins

unconnected streams, swamps, and lakes

outwash plain

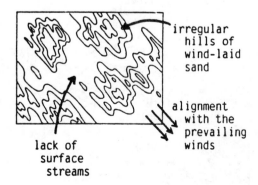

irregular hills of wind-laid sand

alignment with the prevailing winds

lack of surface streams

6) Winds -- Moving air can carry sand and dust away from exposed surfaces. Actual "sandblasting" of fresh rock is rare, because wind is very weak compared to moving ice or water. However, the steady removal of fine particles will eventually produce one of the characteristic features of arid places: a surface layer of rocks and gravel (*desert pavement*). Deposition of wind-carried material in the form of sand *dunes* or silty *loess* layers is quite common at the edges of regions with seasonally or permanently dry climates.

7) **Waves** -- Surf pounding on a shore can carve steep cliffs and make *beaches* and *bars* out of sand and rock. The energy of a wave is concentrated within a few meters of sea level, though the rise and fall of the tides can enlarge the zone of wave action. A *sea cliff* is formed when waves take material away from the base of a slope; a level rock *bench* and a fringing *reef* are other parts of the same landform, though they usually occur just below sea level and therefore remain invisible unless the land rises or sea level goes down.

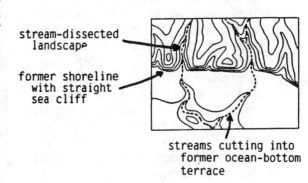

stream-dissected landscape

former shoreline with straight sea cliff

streams cutting into former ocean-bottom terrace

8) All terrain-forming processes operate at rates that are controlled partly by the resistance of the rocks in an area. Where rocks of different kinds occur together, erosion may remove the weaker rock and leave the more resistant rock standing out as a hill or cliff. In this way, many geologic events can leave their own distinctive "signatures" on the landscape. These clues include such diverse features as:

- *volcanic cones* caused by explosive eruptions of cinders, gas, and ash

- *lava flows*, level or contorted layers of rock, the result of steady eruptions of molten material

- *sinkholes* and vanishing creeks, where limestone rock dissolves and caves form (and, occasionally, collapse)

- *fault traces*, linear cracks where rocks slide past each other during earthquakes

- *hogbacks* ("tombstone topography") caused by unequal erosion of tilted rock layers of greatly differing resistance

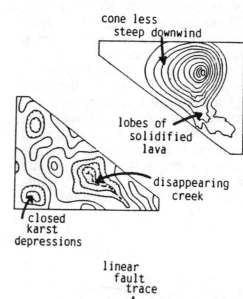

cone less steep downwind

lobes of solidified lava

disappearing creek

closed karst depressions

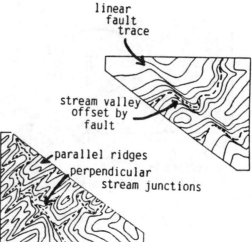

linear fault trace

stream valley offset by fault

parallel ridges

perpendicular stream junctions

DRAINAGE PATTERNS ON TOPOGRAPHIC MAPS

Natural rivers and artificial drainage features exist for only one purpose -- to take surplus water from high ground and carry it to a lower place, often all the way to an ocean. The streams in an area usually follow the lines of least resistance. For that reason, a study of drainage patterns can tell a map interpreter much about the underlying geology, landform history, climatic seasonality, land value, and economy of a region.

NATURAL DRAINAGE PATTERNS

1) **Dendritic** -- a tree-like arrangement of small streams ("branches") that join to form a large river (the "trunk"). A dendritic drainage pattern is the "null hypothesis" in landform analysis: it is the pattern of streams one expects to find in a region that has reliable rainfall and no unusual geologic structures, extraordinary economic pressures, or other influences. Tiny creeks usually form a dendritic pattern; the modifying effects of geologic structure or other outside influences often are not apparent until the stream system gets quite large.

2) **Parallel** -- an elongated variant of the dendritic pattern, in which the tributary streams flow in the same general direction and usually join at small angles. A parallel drainage pattern occurs in places with a regional slope, prevailing wind, or some other factor that causes most streams to flow unusually far in one direction before merging with other streams to make bigger rivers.

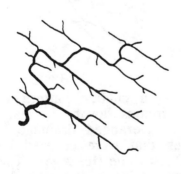

3) **Trellis** -- a squared-off drainage pattern in which streams often flow directly toward each other from opposite directions and then make right-angle bends when they meet. Trellis patterns are common in places where layered sedimentary rocks are tilted up from horizontal; the rivers usually follow the layers of less-resistant rock until they get big enough to break through the resistant layers. Those gaps, in turn, often have enormous strategic value for transportation.

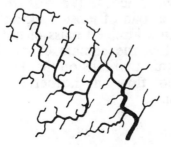

4) **Rectangular** -- another pattern of straight channels and sharp curves, but these rivers turn abruptly at right angles almost at random all along their courses. Rectangular drainage patterns occur in regions with granite or other kinds of jointed bedrock, especially if the area is subject to earthquakes that may extend and open the joints.

5) **Radial** -- a circular arrangement of streams that flow outward in all directions, away from a central high area. Radial drainage patterns are common in the vicinity of volcanic cones, salt domes, granite intrusions, and other localized geologic uplifts.

5) **Centripetal** -- another circular pattern of streams, but this time the water flows inward from all directions toward the center of the pattern. Centripetal drainage is likely to appear in two very different environments: deserts, where intermittent streams flow toward a temporary salt lake (a *playa*), and *karst* areas, where long streams are rare because surface water flows into depressions (sinkholes) caused by cave collapse or dissolving limestone rock.

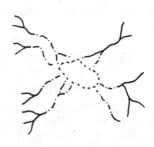

7) **Meandering** -- a pattern of sweeping curves and loops. Meanders are common where terrain is flat enough to allow a river to move sideways, undercutting its bank on the outside and depositing material on the inside of the curve. This lateral movement is responsible for a distinctive cycle of loop formation and enlargement, followed by abandonment of old channels (now called *oxbow lakes*) when the river takes a shortcut across the neck between two enlarged meanders.

8) **Braided** -- a rope-like pattern of twisting channels that separate and then join again all along the stream. Stream braiding is common in semiarid regions, where floods bring more sediment into the channel than the normal flow of the stream is capable of carrying away. A maze of *sandbars* and low islands may form during periods of low water and then be destroyed when floodwaters carry the material farther downstream to form a new arrangement of islands.

9) **Deranged** -- a chaotic pattern of lakes, swamps, and streams flowing in many unrelated directions. Deranged drainage is typical of landscapes that were covered by glaciers during the Pleistocene (Ice Age). The thick masses of moving ice slid across the landscape, picked up a load of loose rock and soil, and then left it in a jumbled mass of hills and closed valleys when the climate changed and the ice melted. Rain that falls on that kind of terrain often cannot flow any farther than the nearest depression.

ARTIFICIAL DRAINAGE PATTERNS

1) **Channelized streams** -- straightened and shortened segments of streams, in places where natural curves are judged undesirable because their hydraulic efficiency is too low or the adjacent property is too valuable to "waste." As you might expect, channelization is common in urban areas and in productive farm districts. Unfortunately, an artificially straightened channel usually starts to meander unless maintained regularly.

2) **Levees and diversions** -- earth banks designed to keep waterfrom flowing where it otherwise would, especially in time of flood. Diversions are common on river *floodplains* in humid regions, especially where the protected land can be used for housing, industry, or high-value crops.

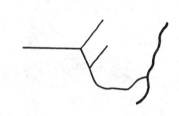

3) **Drainage ditches** -- channels cut across level or undulating terrain in order to remove excess water that would otherwise interfere with the intended use of the land. Surface drainage is necessary on many river floodplains, coastal plains, and the glacial *till plains* and abandoned *lake plains* of the Upper Midwest.

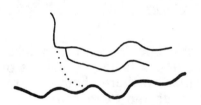

4) **Contour ditches** -- level channels designed to transport water around a hillside rather than straight downhill. Contour ditches are most common in dry regions, where they bring irrigation water to fields. A parallel system of ditches is often present to carry salty drainage water away from the fields.

5) **Barge canals** -- straight or broadly curved channels designed to allow barges to move products from one place to another. Barge channels are usually quite wide and deep and often end in large dock areas in mining or industrial districts. *Locks* are needed where the channel must change elevation to stay even with the surrounding terrain.

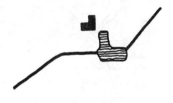

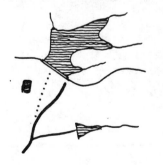

6) **Reservoirs** -- artificial lakes created by digging a pit or damming a gully or natural stream channel. *Dug* reservoirs are often square or rectangular in shape; *dam* reservoirs usually have one straight or gently curved border where the dam is located.

INTERPRETING FOREST COVER ON TOPOGRAPHIC MAPS

Forests occur where tree seeds fall on adequate soil, seedlings can get enough heat and moisture to grow, and trees are not forcibly removed. The interaction of topography, climate, soil, hazards, and human land-use can produce a variety of distinctive forest patterns:

1) **Riparian habitats** appear as strips of green along stream channels, both *perennial* and *intermittent*. These trees are kept alive by moisture from a river in dry seasons or dry regions. When all other things are equal, riparian strips will be wider in wetter climates, along bigger rivers, in flatter valleys, and in coarse sandy soils, where water from the river can seep sideways through the soil and "subirrigate" the trees.

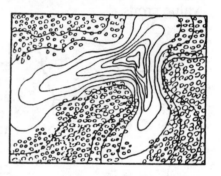

2) **Timberline groves** are patches of green extending upward to the edge of the *tundra* zone on a mountainside. Forests always encroach upslope, a generation at a time, until they are stopped by the combined effects of low temperature, snow, wind, fire, sun, and thin soil. Timberlines usually are quite irregular, due to differences in seed dispersal, slope, soil depth, exposure to the wind, and frequency of catastrophes such as fire, windthrow, or insect attack.

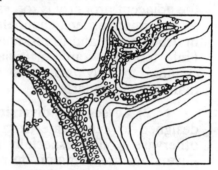

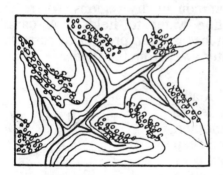

3) **Sun-slope forests** are patches of green on slopes facing southwest or south (in the northern hemisphere!) These trees need the extra heat on the sunnier side of a hill in a cool climate. All other things being equal, the patches will be larger in warmer regions, coarser soils, and sites with some shelter from cold northwest winds. Sun-slope forests rarely extend all the way down to the bottom of the hill, because cold air tends to drain down into low places.

4) **Moist-slope forests** are green areas that look like inverted timberlines above desert valleys. As you go up a mountainside, rainfall tends to increase while temperature goes down. At a critical elevation, the balance between rainfall and evaporation tips and there is enough moisture for trees to survive. In general, moist-slope forests appear at lower elevations on the shadier and cooler north and northeast slopes.

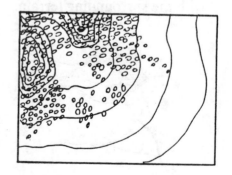

5) **Favorable-soil forests** are patches of green that just seem to stop, mysteriously, partway across a map. Sometimes, a change in stream pattern, house spacing, or average slope will serve as a clue that underlying geology and soil quality have changed, making part of the landscape unfavorable for trees (or preferable for crops, a different idea with similar map consequences).

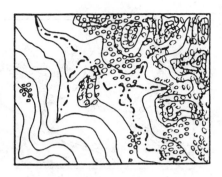

6) **Landslide scars** occur on very steep slopes in a mostly wooded area. Forest trees are easily destroyed by landslides or avalanches moving down clearly defined *chutes* in mountainous terrain. The trees are not likely to reappear until the soil has been rebuilt to an adequate thickness by the slow processes of rock weathering and the accumulation of nutrients and organic matter. Meanwhile, the treeless chutes tend to favor repeated avalanching that keeps the chutes clear.

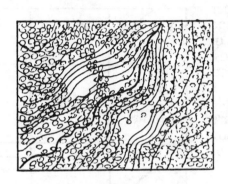

7) **Fire survivors** are patches of green on the downwind side (usually to the east, northeast, or southeast in the United States) of rivers, swamps, lakes, steep cliffs, or other fire breaks. Prairies or shrublands are often kept treeless by fires that sweep across the landscape; some patches of trees usually survive just downwind of any obstruction that does not allow the fire to burn through.

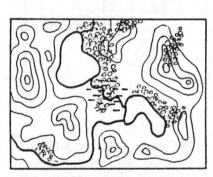

8) **Tree islands** are patches of green on hillier places in swamps or wet prairies. These forests often occur on *salt domes*, former islands, or beach ridges, where soils are coarser and better drained than in the surrounding swamp; the drier soil allows tree roots to grow better (especially in coastal swamps, where the groundwater may be salty and tides can be a problem).

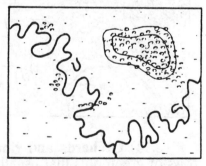

9) **Swamp forests** are patches of green on low or level spots in a typical humid agricultural landscape. These forests remain on land that cannot or has not been artificially drained for crops. Swamp forests are common in glaciated landscapes, outwash plains, river floodplains, and some filled-in beds of former lakes.

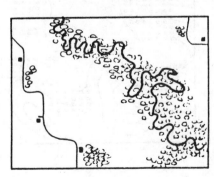

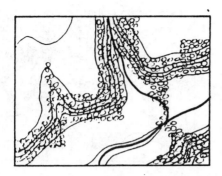

10) **Slope forests** are patches of green on steep slopes facing in all directions. These forests remain on rough and rocky slopes after the more level areas have been cleared for agriculture. One typical trait is some unpredictability in the pattern, caused by the fact that different farmers have different ideas about how steep a slope can be safely farmed.

11) **Woodlots** are isolated patches of green, commonly rectangular in shape and often located toward the middles of the survey *sections*, away from roads. Woodlots are remnants of former forests that covered most of the area. Pasture and crops now occupy the more accessible land, but patches of woods still are perceived as useful for some reason (lumber, firewood, recreation, or aesthetics).

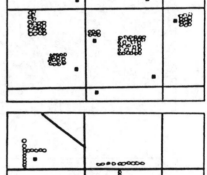

12) **Shelterbelts** are distinct patches and strips of green around buildings and along fences and roads. These trees usually were planted in an otherwise treeless region in order to protect structures or fields from sun or wind. Unlike farm woodlots, shelterbelts often are not self-maintaining; they must be tended like any other crop.

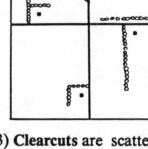

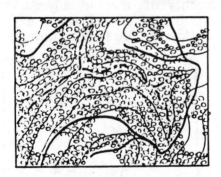

13) **Clearcuts** are scattered white patches in otherwise green parts of a map. Cutting all of the trees from large tracts of land is now illegal in most states, because that kind of logging can cause erosion, floods, and other kinds of environmental damage. Small clearcuts usually have a distinctive combination of three traits: straight sides, access roads or trails, and no apparent natural reason to be treeless.

14) **Orchards** and **vineyards** are rows of green dots that usually occur on gentle slopes. Hilltops can be poor sites for orchards in some marginal climates, because wind can damage trees. Valleys are also risky in some places because cold air settles down into them at night. A site partway up the side of a hill may be as much as ten degrees warmer than either the summit or valley bottom.

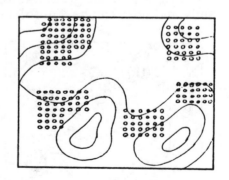

SURVEY SYSTEMS ON TOPOGRAPHIC MAPS

It is difficult to interpret the present landscape of a region unless you understand the way in which the land was divided and distributed to its owners or managers. The original land survey took place in a particular environmental, economic, and political setting. Conditions may be very different now, but old survey boundaries are very persistent and therefore can have a profound impact on modern land use decisions. We offer three brief examples:

1) Many modern farm problems can be blamed on the square or rectangular 160-acre *homestead*, which was a bargain a century ago but may be too small for efficient use of modern farm machinery. Moreover, a square field is often very poorly shaped for erosion control, and field access can be a problem when a creek crosses between a farmer's house and field.

2) Many public buildings, transportation corridors, and urban renewal projects are located at junctions between different surveys, where legal uncertainty about ownership made private investment in building construction or maintenance risky. Slums or squatter settlements often form in these areas.

3) Some big oil or mineral deposits are untapped because the land surface, mineral rights, and water rights are separately owned (often by different people) in many parts of the country, and the resulting legal tangle can inhibit exploration and mineral development.

In effect, whenever a land-use decision depends in part on the size and shape of the land, the original survey will come back to haunt the present-day manager. This effect has a definite geographic pattern, because different parts of the United States and Canada were surveyed and divided according to at least eight major "land alienation" systems:

Irregular sizes
and shapes

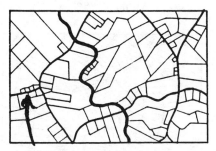

Small house-lots
along road

1) **Metes-and-bounds** surveys are common in the original thirteen colonies and parts of Appalachia. Property lines in this system are defined in terms of features on the landscape (e.g. "from the oak tree to where the creek goes past the Elliott barn"). Landholdings were often surveyed independently of each other and claimed in priority order. As a result, individual parcels of land may vary widely in size and shape. Road and fence patterns on a topomap are often chaotic, because different people may have had different reasons for choosing the kind of land they wanted to own. Disputes about ownership are common, because the original survey often had many gaps and overlaps and the survey markers are not permanent (trees die, rivers move, etc.)

2) **Town Charters** are the basis for land ownership in much of New England and eastern Canada. Blocks of land were granted to corporations or individuals, who could then subdivide the land and distribute it as they saw fit. Local details may vary, but chartered towns usually have a few distinctive map clues: straight boundary lines coming together at odd angles, placenames like Cooper's Grant or Lot 14 Church, and clusters of villages with a common name (e.g. Troy, East Troy, Troy Center, Troy Hill, Old Troy, etc.). In some remote parts of the region, towns were defined but never settled. These *unorganized towns* are known only by numbers.

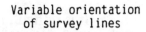

Variable orientation
of survey lines

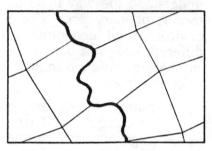

Use of river
as boundary

Spanish Grant
Boundary

3) **Spanish Grants** are common in California, New Mexico, Texas, and adjacent states. Tracts of land, often quite large, were granted by the Spanish rulers to church missionaries or military officers. The new owners usually were careful to claim deep valley soils and reliable sources of water in this rocky and arid part of the country. Unlike New England towns, which occur side by side and fill all of the available land, Spanish grants often are surrounded by unsurveyed land or land that was later divided into the checkerboard pattern of the Public Land Survey described below.

4) **Longlots** are common where French-speaking people settled in Quebec, Louisiana, Texas, and scattered strips along many lakes and rivers in eastern North America. Property in a longlot system is defined in terms of its frontage on a transportation artery (a river at first, a road later). Ownership usually extends back an unspecified distance from the river or road. When the head of a family dies, the land often is divided among the heirs by splitting the river frontage and thus making a long and thin landholding even thinner. Map clues to a longlot system include unusually close spacing of rural houses and fences that run at right angles to a road or river.

Narrow ends of lots
along river

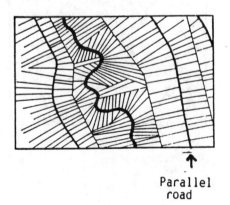

Parallel
road

5) Round Towns occur in several southeastern states. These distinctive circular boundaries are the result of a rule that a town may claim jurisdiction over all land lying within a specified distance of a marker in the middle of town. In the dense forests and rolling hills of the Southeast, this simple rule enabled towns to get started without the cost of a time-consuming land survey. The low cost was a big advantage, but it does have a penalty: plantations and farms that were surveyed according to some other system may lie partly inside and partly outside the town boundary. Uncertainty about jurisdiction over these border properties could affect the way the town expands.

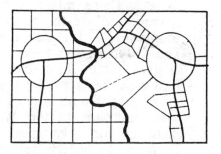

Round town within metes-and-bounds area

Round town within area surveyed by Public Land Survey

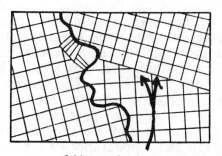

Remnant long-lot area within state surveys

Odd sections at survey junctions

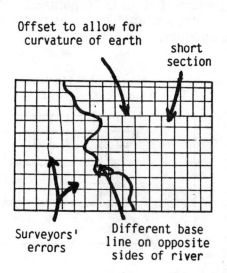

Offset to allow for curvature of earth

short section

Surveyors' errors

Different base line on opposite sides of river

6) State Surveys were conducted in parts of Georgia, western Kentucky and Tennessee, eastern Ohio, southern Indiana, and Texas. These surveys subdivided the land before settlers were allowed into an area, and the rules were designed to avoid the haphazard nature of a metes-and-bounds or town-charter system. The state surveyors usually tried to divide the land into uniform square or rectangular tracts. However, different state surveys had different road spacings and landholding sizes, and some of the road grids were oriented at angles that were not exactly true north-south. One distinctive feature is thus a host of triangular tracts of land at the junctions of different surveys.

7) The United States Public Land Survey is the major system of land subdivision in Alabama, Mississippi, the states around the Great Lakes, and most of the area west of the Mississippi River. The survey has its legal basis in the Land Ordinance of 1785; this was an attempt to ease conflict by establishing strict rules for surveying Western lands before settlers would be allowed to claim or purchase property. As described on pages 38-40, the survey divided the land into square "Townships" that contain 36 square-mile "Sections". The Townships are numbered on the basis of their position with respect to arbitrary Base Lines and Principal Meridians.

8) **Checkerboard Grants** occupy several wide strips of land across the plains and mountains to the Pacific Coast. These mixtures of public and private land are the result of a special adaptation of the Public Land Survey. The national government was interested in linking the old settled areas of the East with the "new" West, and therefore it encouraged a number of companies to build railroads to the West Coast in exchange for government land grants. To promote orderly settlement and to prevent local land monopolies, the government usually granted the railroad companies every *other* section of land (arranged like the dark squares on a checkerboard) for ten or twenty miles away from the proposed rail line.

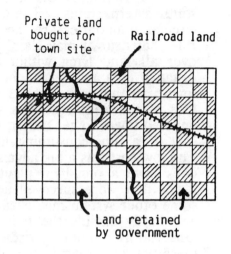

Private land bought for town site — Railroad land

Land retained by government

9) **Plats** are private surveys that developers conduct on their own land in order to sell lots to individuals. The boundaries of the developer's land are fixed by the survey system that prevails in the region. However, the description of an individual lot in a development may be something like "Lot 171, Turkey Subdivision Number 2." The process of fixing boundaries for lots can follow virtually any rule the developer makes up. For that reason, no generalization about the map appearance of a platted subdivision is valid in every case. Some patterns, however, appear in many plats: fairly uniform sizes of landholdings, a road pattern that looks "organized," and a name that sounds like it was made up by a developer.

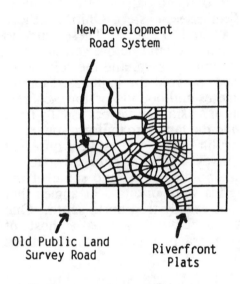

New Development Road System

Old Public Land Survey Road

Riverfront Plats

10) **Reservation** is a general word to describe an unsurveyed tract of land. These are most common in the Western states, where the land is dry, rocky, and/or mountainous. Much of this land did not seem desirable for settlement. Other tracts were reserved for Native Americans, set aside in the form of parks and national monuments, or held back for military reasons. Reservations usually are clearly labelled as such on topographic maps, though a few military reservations appear simply as blank areas on the map -- even contour lines are considered "classified information."

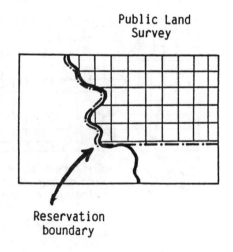

Public Land Survey

Reservation boundary

TRANSPORTATION PATTERNS ON TOPOGRAPHIC MAPS

The movement of goods and people from place to place usually leaves a recognizable imprint on the landscape. As the volume of traffic increases, it often becomes feasible to alter the terrain in order to make travel easier. In time, each mode of transportation usually produces some unique features on topographic maps, and the interactions between terrain, transport mode, origin, destination, and amount of traffic can create distinctive arrangements of transport routes in a region:

1) **Contour patterns** -- It takes energy to overcome distance or increase elevation. The actual route chosen by someone trying to get from one place to another is often a compromise between the desire to move along as straight a line as possible and the conflicting desire to avoid unnecessary change in elevation. The result is often a form of contour-line travel, in which the route stays at about the same elevation (or changes elevation very gradually) as it goes around a topographic obstruction.

Different modes of travel have different tradeoffs between distance and elevation change. For example, a railroad is more efficient than a truck in carrying bulky goods over level land, because the steel wheel has much less friction with a steel rail than a rubber tire does with a concrete highway. This reduction in friction, however, makes it impossible for an ordinary railroad to climb as steep a hill as a truck can. A canal is even more limited in its ability to cross irregular terrain, since it can change elevation only by means of costly and time-consuming locks.

2) **Interfluve patterns** -- Many regions are "built" on level layers or masses of rock in which a stream system has carved a system of deep connected valleys (see page 71). The *interfluves* (areas between the stream valleys) are often fairly flat, and therefore may be favorable for farming, industry, or house building. The river valleys, on the other hand, can be narrow, winding, swampy, flood-prone, inundated by a reservoir, or plagued by a combination of several of these traits. The best way to serve a population in this environment is to build the transportation arteries on the ridges that serve as divides between the river valleys, and to go down into the valleys only when absolutely necessary to cross the rivers.

3) **Valley patterns** -- In steep mountainous terrain, by contrast, the interfluves are often narrow and rugged. People tend to live in the lowlands, and the roads follow the major streams. Valley transportation networks usually are more costly to build than interfluve systems, because the routes are rarely straight and many bridges are needed. Valley transport systems also tend to be costly to maintain, because floods and landslides are more likely in the bottom of a valley than on a flat upland divide.

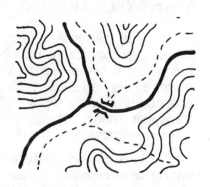

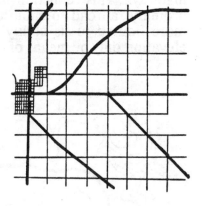

4) **Grid patterns** -- In nearly flat terrain (river floodplains, glacial till plains, former lakebeds, outwash plains, etc.) the original survey of the land and the planning of a road system may have taken place at the same time. The result is a rectangular *grid* of straight roads, usually spaced at intervals of a mile or two and running due east-west or north-south. Grid patterns tend to merge into interfluve or valley patterns where the topography gets more rugged and the cost of straight roads becomes too high.

5) **Radial patterns** -- Large cities often are linked to the surrounding area by a system of highways and railroads that radiate outward in all directions, like spokes on a bicycle wheel. A radial pattern will be distorted if hills and valleys are aligned, or if there is more need to travel in certain directions (e.g. to reach a port or ore deposit). Radial routes often cross an underlying grid at odd angles, which in turn leads to odd-shaped tracts of land near intersections.

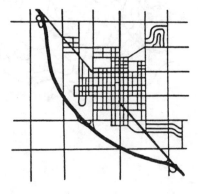

6) **Bypass patterns** -- Expansion of a city usually increases congestion near the center. In time, most urban planners have tried to reduce congestion by building two types of high-speed roads: *radial links* for those going to the city center, and *bypasses* around the city for those heading to another destination. Land near the intersections of *radial* and *circumurban* freeways is often extremely valuable as a site for a shopping center or office complex, because it can be reached by more people in a short time than almost any other place in the city.

EVOLUTION OF A TRANSPORT NETWORK

As time passes and traffic on a transport link increases, the road tends to go through a predictable series of changes in shape and alignment:

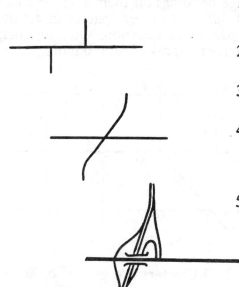

1) The right-of-way gets wider to accommodate the traffic

2) Flows of traffic in opposite directions are separated

3) Curves become more gradual to handle higher speeds

4) Intersections are first controlled (e.g. by a traffic light) and then separated (e.g. by a bridge or cloverleaf interchange)

5) The road becomes isolated from the surrounding terrain, as bulldozers smooth the ground and noise barriers block visual contact with the landscape.

Additions

Later additions to a transportation network must overcome not only the barriers of terrain and distance but also the problems posed by other development that is linked to the existing transportation pattern. One consequence of this situation has been a tendency for later additions to go between existing transportation arteries. For example, a powerline often runs directly through the middles of the square-mile sections that were created by the Public Land Survey and reinforced by the road network. Land in the middle of a survey section is often cheaper because houses are built near roads and it is easier to condemn a strip along the back of a farm than it is to compensate a farmer for a swath through the middle of it. The same principle applies in cities, where major roads often attract stores and offices that are more expensive than the houses or small apartments on minor streets. Indeed, you can often spot the locations of the slums of half a century ago by the alignments of modern urban freeways -- planners often put roads right through the slums, where buildings were less costly, and then traced around high-class neighborhoods, where the economic advantage of a straight line was offset by the political clout of a local aristocracy.

Conflicts

Hints about the economic and political significance of transportation have been scattered throughout the paragraphs above. Easy access to good transportation can increase the value of land, because things that must be brought to the site or sold from it are easier to ship and therefore will be less expensive. At the same time, being next to a busy transportation route is often a nuisance and occasionally a danger. This situation is complicated by the inherent difference in the preferred alignments of different modes of transportation. A single topographic map thus may contain evidence for many conflicts among transport modes and other land uses.

RURAL SETTLEMENT PATTERNS ON TOPOGRAPHIC MAPS

The pattern of human settlement of rural areas has two separate but related components: the way in which the land is divided among its owners, and the way in which the owners arrange buildings on their land. We have already examined the map imprints of different survey systems in another chapter; this section is about the other part of the question. On a topomap, one can find examples of several distinctive patterns of rural buildings:

1) **Dispersed houses** are the dominant rural pattern for much of the United States. Each house sits amid some barns and other buildings on the parcel of land from which the occupants derive their livelihood. Building densities range from less than one per square mile in the dry plains of North Dakota to more than ten in the tobacco districts of North Carolina.

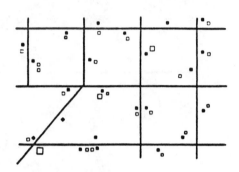

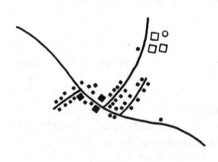

2) **Clusters** are groups of houses that occur near a restricted resource such as a mine or a logging site. Retail stores often occupy some large buildings within the clusters. In many cases, the houses and/or commercial buildings are owned by the industrial, logging, or mining, or company that developed the resource. These company towns may be named for the resource ("Tin City") or a relative of the owner ("Edith").

3) **Strings** are groups of houses arranged in a linear pattern along a transportation artery that leads to a place of work. Unlike clusters, rural strings may have no commercial buildings other than gas stations, because a person who is willing to commute to work is also likely to travel in order to shop or be entertained.

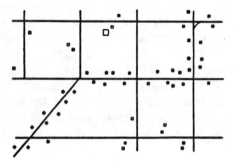

4) **Waystations** are groups of houses and other buildings that serve a transportation artery. Concentration of truck terminals, gas stations, repair shops, and restaurants commonly occur on freeway interchanges or other sites that just happen to be the right distance away from a major traffic center.

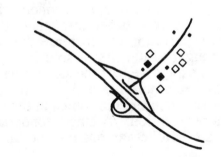

5) Sprawl is common at the fringes of an expanding urban area. In its classic form, sprawl consists of some densely populated residential areas interspersed with open fields, isolated houses, older clusters, commuter strings, and/or other rural settlement forms. The spacing of the buildings is often a good indicator of the price of the houses in a sprawl.

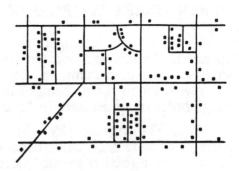

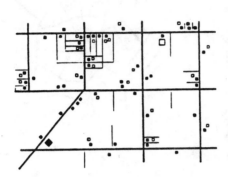

6) Rips are small (2 to 10 acres) landholdings taken out of ("ripped from") larger farms, usually within commuting distance of a city but beyond the sprawl zone. Garages and small sheds usually surround the houses on a typical rip lot. Rips occur when farmers sell small tracts in order to meet rising taxes or unusual expenses. Once an area is dominated by rips, it becomes difficult for a developer to put together enough land for efficient subdivision-style building.

7) Resorts are strings or small clusters of residential and specialized commercial structures that occur near lakes, ski slopes, golf courses, or other scenic or recreational areas. The houses in a resort may be occupied only during favorable seasons. The residential areas are interspersed with parking lots and other facilities that serve visitors who come for only a day.

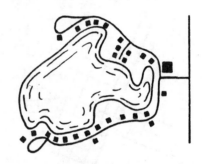

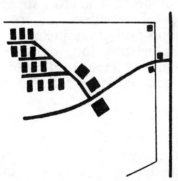

8) Military bases are usually labeled as such on a map. Neat rows of elongated *barracks* are the most striking feature; large open spaces are common; entrances and exits have guardhouses; fences are prominent; and small clusters of retail stores and entertainment buildings often cluster near the entrances to the base.

CAUTION: The form of a rural settlement usually reflects its first use, but the use of a particular structure can change through time. For example, a string of cottages along a rural lake can become the permanent homes of commuters if a new employer locates nearby or a new highway provides easier access to an urban area. In this manner, nearly every rural settlement form on this list can change its function; look at the rest of the map for clues about those factors that can influence the use of buildings.

URBAN STREET PATTERNS ON TOPOGRAPHIC MAPS

Cities have changed through history, as needs and technology changed. Distinctive associations of street patterns, residential densities, lot shapes, house placement, and commercial buildings on a topographic map can reveal much about the age and economic status of a neighborhood. In rough order of appearance in American cities, here is a list of major types:

1) **The organic city**. Streets in early cities were built when needed and in whatever direction seemed necessary at the time. The map pattern is usually chaotic, because streets are rarely large enough or direct enough to serve more than a local purpose. House lots have irregular shapes and sizes, a result of gradual subdivision of formerly large rural landholdings. There is little separation of land uses: residences, shops, and small factories may occur together in the buildings. Roads are named for their destinations or the early owners of adjacent property.

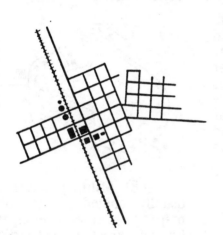

2) **Speculative grids**. Street layouts in these "planned towns" were designed for efficient surveying and sale of lots to immigrants, who may not be able to examine the site before buying. The street grid usually has a main road that runs parallel to and was named for a river, lakeshore, canal, or (later) a railroad. A commercial district often occurs at the junction of this road with a principal crossroad. Side streets often are numbered, and cross streets bear the names of presidents or trees. Other common grid traits include rectangular blocks, narrow lots, dense settlement, and, unfortunately, traffic and ownership problems wherever different grids meet.

3) **Railroad suburbs**. Railroads appeared about the time of the Civil War, and they changed the shape of cities. The speed of the railroad allowed people (if they could afford the fare) to live in "ideal" small towns built beyond the limits of the crowded organic city in which people worked. Features of these *dormitory towns* include larger lots than in the city, stores near the railroad station, and curving streets with names that have rural/romantic connotations: Greenfield, Briarcliff, Idyllwylde, etc.

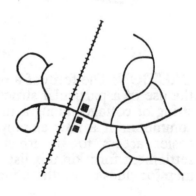

4) Streetcar grids. Streetcars, at first pulled by horses and later driven by electric motors, helped to shape cities in the late 1800's. They allowed access to residential areas along major routes, which were often spaced a mile or half-mile apart in a square grid. Stores and apartment buildings line the main roads, while blocks of narrow houselots fill the less valuable land far from the streetcar lines. Numbered or lettered streets and avenues are typical, especially in those parts of the cities that were being urbanized at a very rapid rate.

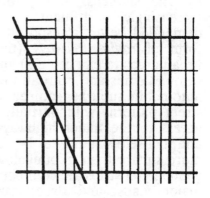

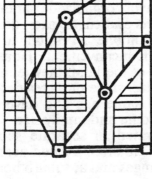

5) The city beautiful. Wide *boulevards* going diagonally through a rectangular grid are the hallmarks of this design, which was a deliberate attempt to overcome the dullness of the streetcar city. The avenues focus on public buildings and pedestrian squares, with statues or monuments at strategic locations. Unfortunately, plans for the city beautiful were expensive as well as imaginative, and therefore most of them were never finished, though nearly every major American city has a few districts.

6) Tangletowns. Complex mazes of curving streets often occur in small hilly areas within grid cities. These enclaves attracted people with above-average incomes and a willingness to trade convenience for privacy. Dead-end streets and confusing mixtures of names (e.g. Buena Vista Avenue, Vista Road, Sunny Knoll Avenue, Sunny Knoll Place, Sunny Knoll Vista, you get the idea) are some of the strategies used to "keep outsiders out."

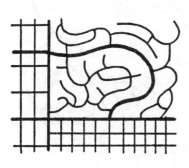

7) Bungalow grids. Automobile ownership became widespread in the 1920s, but the automobile was just part of a radical change that included farm mechanization, rural-to-urban migration, and mass production of consumer goods. Cities grew even more rapidly than in the streetcar era. Compared with the earlier grids, the bungalow districts have lower population densities, larger lots, and elongated blocks, often with alleys behind the closely spaced single-family houses and duplexes.

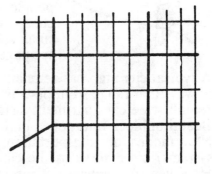

8) **Tract suburbs.** After World War II, increasingly affluent commuters demanded better transportation, in the form of *radial freeways* (through old urban areas to city centers) and *bypasses* (around cities and railroad towns). The automobile suburbs featured rectangular street patterns with partially restricted access to the major highways. Blocks and houselots tend to be larger and more square than in bungalow districts; commercial strips are common along the major roads; and street names often change at suburb boundaries.

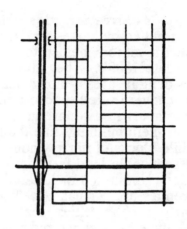

9) **Suburban hills.** After the postwar building boom, suburb planning began to favor organized patterns of curving streets and cul-de-sacs, designed to allow automobile access but to make through traffic inconvenient. House lots occupy most of the land; they tend to be uniform in size, since most residents are of about the same age and have about the same income and family size. Stores are concentrated in separate shopping malls, which are often located near freeway interchanges and at suburb borders.

10) **Planned unit developments.** These communities of the 1970's feature curved streets, concentrated clusters of houses or condominiums, open spaces, bicycle paths, local recreational and shopping areas, and other conscious efforts to reduce the use of energy for transportation and heating. Strict laws required most developments to provide housing for a wide range of income groups, although the builders often put them in separate places.

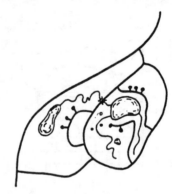

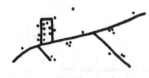

11) **Rurbia.** At each time in history, some people were willing to trade commuting time for cheap land, and they lived in a haphazard zone of small subdivisions, strings, and individual lots (*rips*; see page 85) just beyond the margins of the city.

A typical city map has remnants of many of these patterns, often modified in ways that range from obvious (closing streets to prevent traffic through a rebuilt streetcar apartment district) to rather subtle (subdividing a big City Beautiful block in order to build bungalows on the old gardens and alleys). New modes of transportation (especially freeways and light-rail transit systems) often serve as the catalyst for major changes in the urban map. However, the changes are rarely so thorough that a skillful map interpreter is unable to reconstruct at least part of the former landscape.

INDUSTRIAL PATTERNS ON TOPOGRAPHIC MAPS

An industry, to be successful, must be located where it can bring its raw materials in, process them, and ship the finished product out at a cost that is less than the general selling price of the finished goods. That truism is the basic idea of industrial location theory, but it is complicated by the fact that different industries have different requirements for raw materials, labor, power, capital, waste disposal, or transportation of their finished products. These differences can be used to help interpret the patterns of industrial and commercial structures on thematic or standard topographic maps. The key idea is the notion of *industrial orientation*, which says that different industries have different economic needs that guide their choice of location:

1) **Raw-materials-oriented industries** are those that take a large volume of raw material and process it down into a small quantity of finished product. That kind of factory will be more profitable if it can locate near the source of raw materials, because the cost of transporting the inputs is greater than that of the outputs. Examples include concentration and freezing of orange juice or processing of taconite (the crushing and reduction of several tons of low-grade iron ore to make one ton of high-grade pellets). Maps may show mines or other raw-material sources nearby, often connected by railroad track or pipeline to the factory.

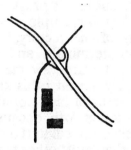

2) **Market-oriented industries** are those that take a small volume of raw material and produce a product that is bulkier, more perishable, or otherwise more costly to transport than the original materials. This kind of industry tends to locate as close as possible to the final market. Examples include soft-drink bottling, cement mixing, boat building, and, to a lesser extent, auto assembly (which was concentrated in Detroit until the cost of shipping cars to growing markets like Atlanta and Los Angeles became too great). Market-oriented factories often occur near freeway junctions in urban areas.

3) **Power-oriented industries** are those that consume vast amounts of energy. Examples include aluminum refineries, metal foundries, and some kinds of chemical processing. These factories tend to be located near a source of energy, but the prime sources of energy have changed several times through history. For example, textile (cloth) mills used to be located near waterfalls, but now their most obvious clue is a nearby concentration of electric power lines. This change in power source has allowed owners of textile factories more freedom of location, and many have moved from New England to the South. Other map clues to power-oriented industries include pipelines and oil storage tanks (unless the industry is an oil refinery or petrochemical plant!), railroad sidings with bulk coal unloaders, or hydroelectric dams.

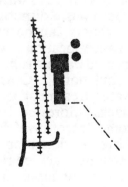

3) **Labor oriented industries** are those that require a lot of human labor in order to produce their product. The need for "human power" is the reason these industries are often located in a large city, where an adequate supply of labor with the necessary skills is likely to be present. Other common sites for this kind of industry are small towns in resort areas, rural areas that have lost farm or timber jobs, and areas of rapid immigration (such as the Los Angeles Basin or the Rio Grande border with Mexico). Examples of labor-oriented industries include clothing sewing and some electronics assembly and testing. These industries can often use buildings with several stories, since they have little bulky or heavy materials to move around. Map clues include large parking lots near the factory; small blocks, apartments, and other evidence of crowding in nearby residential areas; good access to highways or mass transit systems; and, often, a scarcity of competing industries nearby.

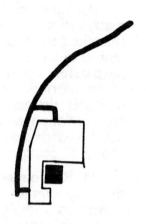

5) **Space oriented industries** are those that need a lot of room for their process. Examples include mobile-home building, cattle or hog slaughtering, paint testing, some chemical processing, and aircraft assembly. Most space-oriented industries are found near the edges of urban areas or small towns. Other map clues include large buildings, outdoor storage areas, and multiple parking lots for employees who work in different parts of the factory. Rail sidings, oil tanks, truck terminals, and other evidence for orientation toward raw materials or market may be notably absent; this kind of industry is also rare in areas of high population density or rapid population growth, because the high cost of land in these areas will hurt a space-oriented industry more than most other types..

6) **Waste orientation** -- Industries in this group produce a lot of waste and therefore need to be located where waste disposal is cheap and where conflicts with neighbors can be minimized. The key map clue is relative location: waste-oriented factories tend to be located *downstream* and *downwind* from big clusters of population. Other topomap clues include private water treatment facilities, tall or numerous smoke-stacks, forested "buffer zones" around the factory, some "decorative" fountains and lagoons that actually serve as detention areas for industrial waste, and separate truck or rail sidings on different sides of the factory for input raw materials, output products, and waste by-products. In extreme cases, some of the houses and other buildings in the neighborhood may be abandoned or converted to other uses.

7) **Commensal industries** are those that are aided by face-to-face contact among people in different factories. Examples include machinery (New England in the mid 1800's), auto designing (Detroit in the early 1900's), petrochemicals (Delaware in the mid 1900's), and electronics ("Silicon Valley" in 1970s California). Commensal factories usually occur in distinctive strips or clusters of small buildings, often in enclaves on the "clean" side of town, because the people who get involved in innovative "high-tech" kinds of industries are usually better educated and wealthier, less willing than the rest of the population to tolerate crowding or pollution.

8) **Footloose** is the generally accepted term for industries that do not show any of the major orientations listed above. Examples of footloose industries include the printing of business forms or wedding invitations and the manufacture of lawnmowers, toys, missile heat shields, or mousetraps. Since the key idea is that these industries are not drawn toward any particular location by some characteristic of their process, it is almost impossible to make any generalization about them except the obvious one: none of the above rules about industrial orientation apply to footloose industries.

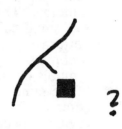

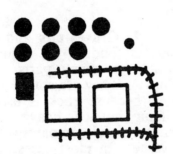

9) **Industrial storage** is a specialized land use that occurs in areas that have a lot of other kinds of industry. A single factory may choose to store its raw materials and products on-site; owners of a group of factories may find it more convenient to bulk-order some things and store them in a common area. Clusters of buildings and/or tanks are the most obvious map features, along with good highway, rail, or canal links to the outside world.

10) **Recycled plants** -- All of these rules about industrial orientation are subject to one big caveat -- some kinds of industry are willing to locate in a less-than-ideal location if it already has a building that can satisfy their needs. Examples include the canoe builders and computer programmers that occupy an old textile mill by a waterfall in a New England town. They are typical of the whole host of small manufacturing firms that move into existing structures when other industries move out. As if that weren't confusing enough for a map reader, some towns reconstruct old schoolhouses or auditoriums, purchase old factories, or even build new general-purpose buildings in order to attract industries to the area. Such tactics can be very costly in the long run, because industries that are not located favorably with respect to their basic orientations are also not likely to be as competitive in a tightening world economy.

MINING FEATURES ON TOPOGRAPHIC MAPS

Mines are located where useful minerals occur, but the reverse is not necessarily true -- mineral deposits may remain untapped for a variety of reasons: geological inferiority, inaccessibility, political instability, corporate strategy, or simply because the resource has not yet been discovered. An operating or abandoned mine has some unique features that can be seen on a topographic map. Those clues, in turn, can provide information about the nature of the mine, the underlying geology, and the surrounding economy:

1) The simplest and most numerous kind of mine is a small **exploration pit** (often called a "glory hole"), dug by a prospector searching for potentially valuable minerals. These holes are usually too small to make a noticeable pattern of contour lines on a topomap. Tiny pick-and-shovel symbols often show the locations of the mines. They are especially common in rugged mountainous regions, because the processes that act to concentrate metallic ores in nature are the same forces that make mountains.

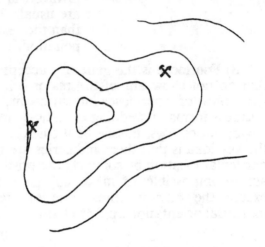

2) **Gravel pits** and **stone quarries** tend to be ubiquitous (located in many parts of the country). They are common near cities, because rock is used for building, but it is heavy, hard to transport, and comparatively low in value. In most cases, a map will have the words "gravel pit," "sand pit," or "quarry" next to the terrain depression that is the actual site. Large quarries and pits often have some buildings and maybe a rock crusher nearby.

3) **Placer mines** were common in some of the famous "Gold Rush" areas of California, Nevada, Montana, and Alaska. These mines used jets of water to wash rock and earth into a trough, where the heavy metal would settle to the bottom (and the lighter rock and sand would be washed out and dumped on the land). The most noticeable symptom of a large placer mine is the irregular jumble of hills ("spoil heaps") made out of the worthless material that was left after the mining operation.

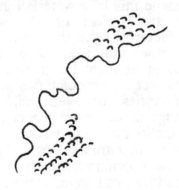

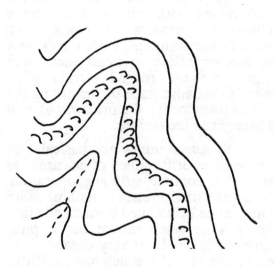

4) Strip mines, like placer mines, leave vast quantities of *spoil* in heaps on the landscape (unless restored to the original contour, which is now the law in most places). Strip mines remove the surface material (*overburden*) in order to get at a horizontal layer of rock that is not buried too deeply. Coal is by far the most important substance that is mined by stripping; a railroad or a conveyor to a power plant are often associated with the mine.

5) Contour strip mines occur where level or gently tilted rock layers (including coal seams or other valuable deposits) have been eroded by rivers or glaciers (see pages 68-70). With a level rock structure, the layers of coal will outcrop at about the same elevation on every hillside; mining consists of scraping the surface soil away from the seam and then removing the coal. Prior to passage of reclamation laws, miners would simply shove the "overburden" into the valleys, leaving a distinctive cliff and nearly level bench after removing the coal; now, they usually must replace overburden and reshape the land to the original slope.

6) Open-pit mines are the normal way to get at iron, copper, nickel, and other metals that occur in comparatively small deposits of rich ore at modest depth. The distinguishing feature of a big open-pit mine is a spiral arrangement of cliffs and benches with railroad tracks or roads on them. If there is a source of inexpensive electricity or other energy nearby, a *smelter* to refine the ore may appear on the same topomap. Otherwise, a railroad, canal dock, or other means of transporting the heavy ore will be present, often prominent.

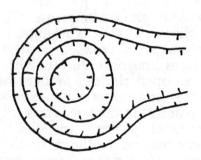

7) **Shaft mines** consist of vertical tunnels leading down to ore deposits that are too far underground to be recovered by open pit or strip mining technology. The *mine head*, other buildings, railroads or roads, ventilator shafts, and heaps of discarded spoil are common features on aerial photographs or topomaps. This kind of mine is almost always much more costly than a surface mine, and therefore the mineral must be intrinsically valuable (gold or diamonds), highly concentrated (high-grade iron ore), or strategically important (chromium or vanadium).

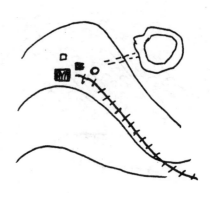

8) **Drift mines** are horizontal shaft mines, with tunnels that enter a hillside and penetrate sideways, deep beneath the summit. Drift mines may be less expensive to build than shaft mines, but the rugged terrain often cancels that advantage by increasing the cost of transporting the ore away after it is brought to the surface.

9) **Auger mines** are basically an inexpensive drift mine, often used as part of a contour stripping operation. An auger mine consists of nothing more than a huge drill aimed horizontally into the hillside; when turned on, it pulls some of the coal out very cheaply (and leaves the rest of it much more difficult to mine than it was before -- profitable for a company but terribly shortsighted as far as the whole nation is concerned).

10) A drilled **well** is the normal way to recover petroleum, helium, natural gas, and other liquid or gaseous minerals. Old or shallow oil wells may appear on topomaps as crowded clusters of dozens, maybe even hundreds, of small open circles. Modern wells are arranged more strategically to maximize production, especially if the pool is deep, and therefore there may be a uniform spacing of symbols (e.g. one well in the center of each survey section). Pipelines and one or more solid black circles (the standard symbol for a tank) are often associated with the wells.

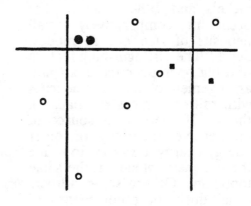

PLACENAMES AND CULTURAL FEATURES ON TOPOGRAPHIC MAPS

The human act of naming a landscape feature has several implications in the context of a course on the Language of Maps. First, a collection of widely used placenames is a cultural structure, like a house, fence, or road, which were all built in order to make life more convenient. As described in Part 1 of this book, a *landmark vocabulary* is easier and faster than most other ways of communicating the basic spatial concepts of location and direction, and a set of unambiguous placenames is an essential part of landmark communication.

The process of naming places is much like the evolution of language in general. In most cases, an individual just starts to use a particular word for a particular feature, and it "catches on." In other situations, someone makes a deliberate decision to invent placenames. The motives for this decision span a range of human emotions, including an urge to "make your mark" in the world, a desire to memorialize a friend, a compulsion to fill in gaps on the map, or a pragmatic need for an easy way to describe a place that just became important for some reason (a gold strike, for example). In time, the clutter of placenames can get so confusing that someone decides to take responsibility for imposing order, and a *gazetteer* of placenames (like a dictionary of words) is born. Early versions of these books inevitably go through a period of testing and revision, and, in time, the vocabulary of the language becomes more or less standard.

In the United States, the *Board for Geographic Names* publishes the "official" spelling of the "official" names of places all over the world. A quick look at a topographic map, however, will reveal a horde of places -- small hills, clusters of houses, side valleys, spurs, gaps, branches of streams, ponds, etc. -- that have no names. Any person can suggest names for these features (Geographic Names Information Management, U. S. G. S. Topographic Division, National Center Stop #523, 12201 Sunrise Valley Drive, Reston, VA 22092). The Board will evaluate the suggested name in terms of several criteria. The first criterion is importance: the feature must be prominent enough to deserve a name. The second criterion is taste: pornographic or profane words are discouraged. The third criterion is uniqueness: our maps already have quite a few "Pleasant Valleys" and "Round Lakes," and the Board tries to avoid duplication of existing placenames. Names that reflect unique local conditions or historical events are preferred, because they continue a rich tradition of allowing placenames to mirror the landscape and its inhabitants.

The placenames used in an area can be a great source of information about the people living there, both at present and in the past. A name like "Lynch Nigger Creek," for example, is a source of embarrassment or anger for most Americans today, because it evokes a strong image of an unsavory part of our culture in the not-too-distant past. In a similar way, placenames can tell us about hopes (Richland, Liberty Center), shattered dreams (Poverty Ridge, Nowater Valley), ethnic identity (Niew Amsterdam, Blackfoot Ridge), environmental conditions (Sawtooth Mountain, Hungry Leech Lake, Alkali Spring), humor (Mountain, North Dakota), or perhaps ecological ignorance (Ponderosa Canyon on the Atlantic coastal plain, thousands of miles from the nearest stand of Ponderosa pines and nowhere near where Spanish people gave the name "canyon" to steep-walled valleys). Obviously, the more one knows about regional environments, cultural history, and group psychology, the more information can be extracted from the names on a topographic map.

Interpreting placenames might begin with a review of some of the general traits of the languages spoken by the people who may have occupied a particular region. The Native Americans of the Southeast, for example, had languages that were rich in vowels and repetitive syllables, which have become prominent features of Dixie vocabulary -- Altamaha, Chattahoochee, Mississippi, Tallahassee. The languages of the Pacific Northwest, by contrast, tended toward clusters of consonants and sharper vowels -- Kitsap, Klikitat, Puyallup, Skagit. Someone trying to interpret native American words on a map must remember that these people had no written language, *as we know it*. Europeans of different nationalities heard native Americans speak and tried to write their placenames with European letters. In the process, words like "Tsalagi" (used in the western North Carolina mountains) was apparently recorded several times by different people, and in time became our modern name for a group of Indian tribes (Tsalagi, Tsarakee, and then Cherokee) and the mountain region they used to occupy ("Appalachian," shown on early maps as Tsalagi, Atalatsy, and Apalathean). In a similar way, variants of the name of a widely known Indian "spirit being" occur all around the Great Lakes -- Manitou, Manitoulin, Manitoba, Manitowoc, Manitowadge, Manitowish, etc.

To a lesser extent, many other placenames reflect this process of borrowing words and recasting them into the language conventions of a different group of people (as anyone who has heard the local pronunciations of Berlin, New Hampshire; Detroit, Michigan; Des Plaines, Illinois; Stuttgart, Arkansas; the Arkansas River, Kansas; San Jacinto, California; or Moscow, Idaho can testify). Even so, it is still possible to learn something about the former occupants of many regions by trying to "see through" the placenames that are now used there. To do this, it is useful to learn some of the terms for landscape features in different languages. The major languages for "generic" terms on United States topographic maps are native American, English, French, Spanish, and, to a lesser extent, German, Italian, Russian, and various Scandinavian languages (see page 97).

Foreign words are common in placenames on American topographic maps, and the use of foreign words goes far beyond borrowing generic terms from the languages of immigrant groups. A knowledgeable individual can trace the probable national origin of people who named places after major European cities (New Orleans, Birmingham, Stuttgart, Venice), patron saints (San Francisco, Saint Louis, Saint Olaf), military or cultural figures and events (King William, Napoleon, Wellington, Waterloo, Marengo, Bismarck, De Soto, Pulaski, Martin Luther King), and friends or relatives with distinctively national names. A quick scan through the telephone book for a given town can help support or refute a theory about the nationality of the people in a place with an intriguing name. As with most aspects of map interpretation, a map reader should always consider evidence from surrounding features in forming a generalization -- for example, there is a town called El Paso, near Panther Creek and the Woodford-McLean County Line, half an hour east of Peoria, Illinois. Despite its Spanish name, this town is much less likely to be of Spanish origin than the El Paso that has Our Lady of Guadalupe Church and is across the Rio Grande from Ciudad Juarez, near the border between Texas and New Mexico. The Illinois El Paso, as it turns out, was named for a railroad intersection, where the Toledo, Peoria, and Western railroad "passes over" the tracks of the Illinois Central -- hardly compelling proof of Spanish origin.

	English	French	German	Spanish
Directions				
	east	est	osten	este
	north	nord	norden	norte
	south	sud	süden	sur
	west	ouest	westen	oeste
Colors				
	white	blanc	weiss	blanco
	black	noir	schwarz	negro
	red	rouge	rot	rojo
	green	vert	grün	verde
Features				
	land	terre	boden	tierra
	sea, lake	mer, lac	meer	mara, lago
	island	ile	insel	isla
	water	eau	wasser	agua
	snow	neige	schnee	nieve
	fire	feu	feuer	fuego
High/low places				
	high	alta	hoch	alto
	mountain	mont, montagne	berg	montana, sierra
	plateau	plateau	hoch bene	mesa
	plain	plaine	ebene	llano
	valley	vallee	tal, thal	valle
	cave	caverne	höhle	cueva
	river, creek	riviere	fluss, bach	rio, arroyo
	mouth, bay	boche, baie	mündung, bucht	boca, bahia
Plants/ animals				
	forest	foret	wald	bosque
	oak, pine	chene, pin	eiche, kiefer	roble, pino
	desert	desert	wüste	desierto
	meadow	prairie	wiese	pradera, cienega
	bear	ours	bär	oso
	horse, cow	cheval, vache	pferd, kuh	caballo, vaca
Minerals				
	iron	fer	eisen	ferro
	gold	or	gold	oro
	silver	argent	silber	plata
	stone, rock	pierre	stein	piedra, pena
Buildings				
	castle	chateau	schloss	castillo
	church	aglise	kirche	iglesia
	house	maison	haus	casa
	road	route, rue	strasse	camino, calle
	town, city	ville	dorf, stadt	pueblo, ciudad
Miscellanies				
	beautiful	beau, belle	schön	bello
	dead	mort	tot	muerto
	spirit	esprit	geist	espiritu

TOPOGRAPHIC MAP INTERPRETATION -- PRACTICE

There is a good reason for the lack of practice exercises in this section on topographic maps. It makes more sense to get topomaps for an area you already know fairly well and to practice with them first, because you can go look at the landscape to check your interpretations (and perhaps find out what has changed since an old map was made!). If you are taking a formal course about maps, your instructor has probably prepared some local exercises for your class. If not, you can get the index for your state (sources on page 183) and order some maps that cover areas near where you live. After that introduction, let your interests guide your selection of maps to study. Once you have learned some basic vocabulary and grammar, the way to master a language is to use it often. And a good way to do that is to use topographic maps to plan a vacation or learn more about areas that already are of interest to you.

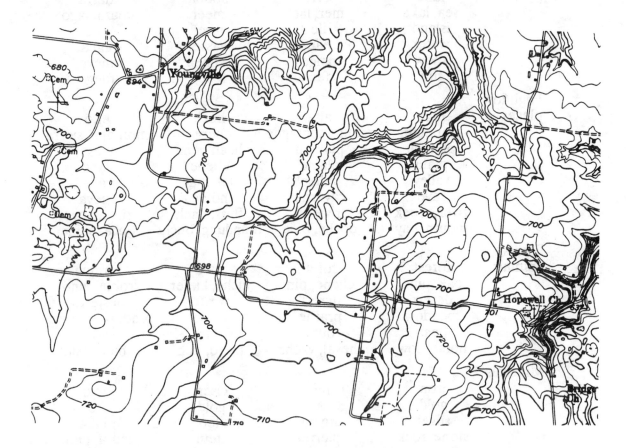

SAMPLE QUIZ QUESTIONS -- TOPOGRAPHIC MAP INTERPRETATION

You will be given part of a 1:24,000 topographic map.

1) Briefly interpret the *physical features* of the mapped landscape -- its underlying geologic structure, landforming process, surface or underground drainage, vegetation cover, and soil fertility (as inferred from the land use pattern). Cite specific map locations as examples where appropriate.

2) Briefly describe the *cultural features* on this landscape -- the survey system, rural and/or urban settlement pattern, transportation infrastructure, placenames, and land use patterns. Cite specific features as examples where appropriate.

EXTRACTING THEMES FROM TOPOGRAPHIC MAPS

On this 99th page about maps, let's stop and reflect for a moment. We have said that basic spatial ideas -- position, distance, direction, enclosure -- can be expressed in many ways, and that topographic maps contain an extraordinary wealth of detailed information about the world. As people get better at reading maps, they often shift from one "dialect" to another and use one kind of information (e.g. road patterns or drainage) to help interpret other features (e.g. settlement patterns or geologic structure). Thus, the different map vocabularies and the mass of available information are not necessarily confusing; indeed, they can actually help a person interpret a map (if given enough time). This is yet one more parallel with a spoken or written language; familiarity with different map vocabularies can help a map reader, just like knowledge of Latin or French can help a person use some English words more precisely to express a particular idea.

If, however, you want to tell someone else about a pattern that you have painstakingly dug out of a topographic map, it usually helps to simplify the map. In other words, the mass of detail that helped you *discover* a pattern can actually interfere with *communicating* it to another person. Look back over this part of the book -- most of the diagrams are simplified sketches rather than fragments of actual topomaps. In effect, we were trying to *extract a theme* from the mass of detail and to show the theme as clearly as possible.

Extracting a theme from a topomap illustrates the process a map maker must follow in making a map of <u>any</u> specific real-world feature -- e.g. roads, burglaries, music festivals, or cases of lutefisk poisoning. The first step is to describe the characteristics of the thing the map is supposed to show. This usually involves making a clear list of traits an object must have before it is put on the map. For example, to make a map showing polluted rivers, a cartographer must first define "river" and "polluted" in unambiguous terms.

In the real world, the process of feature definition is usually complicated. How much water must flow in a channel (and on how many days of the year) before we call it a "river"? How many people must be present to make an area "urban"? In defining "auto accidents," what should a map maker do with piles of glass left by people who are too scared to report the collision? What about "police junkies" who report all kinds of events as accidents?

In short, the process of feature definition almost always involves some arbitrary lines drawn through "logical space." That, in turn, usually puts some dissimilar things or events together in a single logical category. The resulting simplification of the real world is not necessarily bad; as stated above, theme extraction can help us communicate a clear message about some aspect of the world to another person.

THEME EXTRACTION -- PRACTICE

Find a 1:24,000 topographic map that covers an area of interest. Use the form on the next page and plot the locations of a few important towns, roads, or rivers. These provide a *frame of reference* for the theme. Then, pick some feature that is well represented on the map (e.g. buildings, longlots, sinkholes, bungalow neighborhoods, riparian forests, shopping centers, irrigation canals, good building sites, avalanche chutes, playgrounds, or any one of a thousand other features that may be common in the area). Formulate a clear definition of the feature you have chosen as a theme. Put a mark on your small map at each place where that feature occurs. Revise your definition, if necessary, to keep things clear.

QUADRANGLE

THEME

_____
_____
_____
_____
_____

PART 4
READING THEMATIC MAPS

Mapmakers have traditionally classified their products into two broad categories, each with its own rules about grammar and symbol selection:

- *Reference maps* focus on an area and try to depict it accurately. What are the prominent features in the area? Where are they with respect to each other? How many features of a particular kind are within a designated area? A reference map is usually read by finding a place and looking at what the map says is around it. Obviously, a map cannot show everything in an area; a map is by definition a simplification of the real world. *Prominence* is the key rule in choosing what to put on a reference map -- important things should be included, while minor things can be left off. Unfortunately, the definition of "important" often depends on the intended use of the map. For example, a motorist thinks that roads are more important than fences, but a map that has a focus on roads is no longer a pure reference map; it has some of the traits of the other category of maps. Without further ado, then, the other category of maps:

- *Thematic maps* focus on a feature and try to show its spatial pattern accurately. Where is this feature prominent, present, absent? How is its spatial pattern changing through time? A thematic map is usually read by comparing it with another map (whether printed or in the mind of the map reader). Comparing one map pattern with another can suggest causal relationships that may be worth investigating. This comparison is easier if both maps are drawn on the same basemap, with the same scale and projection. It is even easier if the maps also show some major towns, roads, rivers, or borders. However, a map that is cluttered up with a lot of background material is no longer a pure thematic map; it has some of the traits of reference maps.

The distinction between *reference* and *thematic* is thus more than a little blurry, a fact worth underlining before we start to look at the symbolic languages of different kinds of thematic maps. Beneath the straightforward descriptive prose in this part of the book is a pervasive idea -- the language of maps, like most written languages, is not a simple one-to-one code, with a single word used to express each separate idea. Such a language might be efficient in conveying simple ideas, but it would lack flexibility in dealing with complex shades of meaning. In effect, the language of maps, like all other languages, must seek a balance between ease of learning and flexibility of use.

Mistakes often occur when a language has several alternative ways to express one idea. Some mistakes are difficult to unlearn, and therefore people may make the same error throughout an entire lifetime. Of course, when enough people make the same "mistake," it becomes an acceptable part of the language and thus ceases to be a mistake in a practical sense. The most dangerous kinds of mistakes, therefore, are those that occur often enough for some people to think they are correct while others are mislead by them. You should begin, as soon as possible, to *evaluate* as well as *read* the symbols on the maps you see. The purpose of this section is to describe a variety of symbolic "vocabularies" and the kinds of spatial ideas they can be used to express. The key word to keep in the back of your mind is "appropriate" -- some kinds of symbols are more appropriate than others for communicating particular spatial ideas. With that in mind, let us look at how different spatial ideas can be described, classified, and communicated.

CLASSIFYING INFORMATION

A map is a group of symbols whose job is to tell a reader something about the arrangement of things in space. A map maker, in choosing symbols to convey a particular idea, must consider both the nature of the message and the traits of the map reader. The first of these considerations is called the "conceptual" part of symbol selection -- how do we choose an appropriate symbol to represent our concept of what we are mapping? The second is the "perceptual" aspect of the symbol-selection process -- how will the map reader perceive and interpret the symbols on the map? In effect, an individual bit of information is a qualitatively different thing within each oval of the communication model shown on page 4:

- out in the world, it is a *phenomenon*, an observable entity;

- in the map maker's mind, it is a *datum*, a recorded observation;

- on the map, it is a *symbol*, a graphic object; and

- in the map reader's mind, it is a *perception*, a mental image.

In order to choose appropriate symbols, a map maker must look at part of the world and try to figure out what *kind* of phenomenon is really there. A map reader, in turn, must be able to "look through" the symbol in order to reconstruct what the map maker saw. These tasks are not always easy, because the world has many different kinds of information, which can be described in many different ways. Some of the most useful classifications are based on:

A) **Tangibility** -- the physical reality of the data

1) *Tangible* - actually existing, capable of direct measurement (snowfall, depth to water table, wheat yield from a field)

2) *Abstract* - computed or derived from other sources (percent in white-collar jobs, median school years completed)

B) **Temporality** -- the situation of the data in time

1) *Status* - showing things as they are at a particular time (land value in 1986, December unemployment, continent position in the Triassic)

2) *Trend* - showing how things change through time (urban expansion since 1900, decline in lake level, change in the ozone layer)

C) **Continuity** -- the presence of data between observation places

1) *Discrete* - occurring in some parts of the map but not in others (city parks, locations of deaths due to emphysema)

2) *Discontinuous* - occurring throughout the mapped area, but with abrupt changes (political jurisdiction, land ownership, rock type)

3) *Continuous* - occurring throughout the mapped area, with smooth changes from place to place (temperature, distance from a road)

D) **Dimension** -- the spatial extent of the data within the map plane

1) *Point* - having position but no length on the surface being mapped (camp site, bus stop, elevation of a survey benchmark)

2) *Line* - having length but no width on the mapped surface (hiking path, telephone line, boundary between Canada and Alaska)

3) *Area* - having both length and width on the mapped surface (Lake Erie, low-income neighborhood, regional shopping center)

E) **Presence** -- the location of the data with respect to the map plane

    1) *Restricted* - existing only on the surface being mapped, not above or below it (pasture land, road intersection, visitors' parking lot)

    2) *Compressed* - extending up or down from the map plane, but also present in it (building height, depth of a water well)

    3) *Projected* - occurring above or below the map plane, but not present in it (jet stream, mean sea level, mineral deposit)

    4) *Computed* - not physically present in or around the map plane (average income, probability of severe storm)

F) **Logical scaling** -- the comparability of data values for different places

    1) *Nominal data* (NAME) are qualitatively dissimilar from each other: this is not like that, but we have no idea if it is more or less (Spain is not the same as France; pine forest is different from aspen grove)

    2) *Ordinal data* (RANK) are arranged in order: this is greater than that, but we have no idea how much difference there is between them (city is bigger than village; prime is better than marginal land)

    3) *Interval data* (SERIAL) are measured on an arbitrary scale; we can add or subtract the numbers, but it is not valid to multiply or divide them (1800 A.D. is 190 years before 1990, but it is not nine tenths as big; 80 degrees Fahrenheit is not twice as hot as 40)

    4) *Ratio data* (NUMBER) are measured on an absolute scale; we can do all mathematical operations and comparisons with real numbers (14 is 10 more than 4; $2,000 is exactly half as much as $4,000)

    5) *Percentage data* are really a kind of ratio data, but they must add up to 100, and therefore we can use partial information to make some speculations about unmeasured values (if a census tract is 86% Norwegian, there can't be more than 14% Hispanics)

Map makers can describe a given bit of information with many of these criteria. For example, a census table of average family income in counties should be classified as abstract, status, discontinuous, area, computed, ratio data. Although it sounds rather academic, that classification is useful because it eliminates at least half of the different kinds of symbols from the list of appropriate options a map maker might use to show average family income by county. (We chose the words in that last phrase very carefully: "$4.37 in my pocket" is tangible, status, discrete, point, restricted, and ratio data, and a quite different kind of symbol would be appropriate to communicate this information accurately.)

CLASSIFYING INFORMATION -- PRACTICE

A map maker must classify information in order to make an intelligent selection of map symbols. If all map makers did that, map reading would be much easier. In this imperfect world, however, a good map reader must stay alert; in effect, you must make your own classification of the data and then see if the symbols on a map are really an appropriate way of displaying the kind of data you think the map maker had. If the symbols are not appropriate, you have a clue about what kinds of perceptual error they might be causing in an unwary reader. In the following practice exercise, put the letter of each data type in the appropriate cell of the classification (the first two are done as examples).

CLASSIFYING DATA BY TWO IMPORTANT CRITERIA

	NOMINAL	ORDINAL	INTERVAL	RATIO
POINT		*A*		
LINE				
AREA	*B*			

A) Major and minor auto accidents in Vilas County
B) Land used for a pecan orchard in the San Saba Valley
C) Passengers landing at California airports in July

D) Routes of mainline and branch railroads in South Dakota
E) Wheat yields in bushels per acre in Kansas counties
F) Locations of regional and local shopping centers in Miami

G) Dates and positions of Cherokee Indian treaty boundaries
H) Average SAT scores of students in Cincinnati high schools
I) Traffic flow in vehicles per hour on Illinois freeways

J) Course of the North Platte River through Wyoming
K) High- and low-income suburbs of Denver
L) Minimum overnight temperature in central Florida

M) Location of the Homestake Mine office
N) Individual and supporting members of Ohio Public Radio
O) Park Service jurisdiction in the Rocky Mountains

CAUTIONS -- stay alert when you classify phenomena or data, because it is possible to *change* these classifications in a number of ways:

1) Generalizing a map (changing its scale; see pages 21-24) -- a city is an *area* on a road map but only a *point* on a world map.

2) Measuring things in a particular way -- rainfall is best classified as a tangible, continuous, volume phenomenon, but a rain gauge measurement is sampled, discrete-point data (which, in turn, can become an ordinal-area symbol if a mapmaker colors all of the regions where gauges recorded "above normal," "normal," and "below normal" amounts of rain).

3) Combining data with other data -- describing murder in terms of reported cases per 100,000 people has made abstract-ratio-area data out of a nominal, point, and horribly tangible phenomenon.

4) Transforming data mathematically -- grouping city blocks into high, medium, and low average income per capita has changed tangible and countable dollars into abstract ratio data and then into discontinuous ordinal symbols (see pages 142-144).

5) Choosing conventional symbols -- the contour lines on a topographic map are restricted-line symbols that try to show projected-point data (surveyed elevations). Actually, some people prefer to call it compressed-volume data; the apparent confusion serves as yet another reminder that the classification of data, like all other aspects of a language, is also partly arbitrary).

SYMBOLIZATION

Map symbols are the "words" in a graphic language, the vehicles that carry messages about a place or the relationships between places. A map symbol can resemble the thing it represents or be an abstraction of it. Some map symbols have been used in roughly similar ways by many people for a long time; these symbols have become parts of a standard language of maps. Other symbols must be defined when they are used, which is one purpose of a map legend. Graphic symbols are able to represent many different kinds of data because symbols can vary in many ways:

A) **Spatial extent** (the dimensionality of a symbol)

1) *Point symbols* (dots, graduated circles, letters, icons, pie graphs) are used to mark the locations of things, to depict quantities that were measured at particular places or within certain areas, or to summarize the characteristics of a surrounding area.

2) *Line symbols* (lines, dot strings, flowlines, contours, color bands) are used to mark the locations of rivers, highways, or other linear features, to enclose or separate areas, to show the shape of a landform or other surface, to point out the connections between places, or to clarify a map layout.

3) *Area symbols* (shading, coloring, crosshatching, or dot patterns) are used to indicate regions that are uniform, to identify areas that have common traits, and to separate parts of a map layout (especially to identify the surrounding country or other non-important part of an area).

B) **Abstractness** (the representative nature of a symbol)

1) *Iconic symbols* are pictorial, with shapes and/or colors that map readers are likely to associate with the things being mapped.

2) *Linguistic symbols* are letters that are usually associated with the mapped phenomena in the language of the map reader.

3) *Abstract symbols* are geometric shapes that have been arbitrarily selected to represent the phenomena being mapped.

C) **Traits** (other characteristics of map symbols)

1) *Shape* -- distinctiveness of form or outline

2) *Size* -- dimensional extent of the inked area

3) *Complexity* -- amount of detail in the boundary

4) *Value* -- light reflected from the surface

5) *Color Hue* -- red, orange, green, purple, etc.

6) *Color Chroma* -- gray, weak, or intense color

7) *Pattern* -- arrangement of marks in an area

8) *Orientation* -- arrangement with respect to border

9) *Association* -- connection with other symbols

APPROPRIATENESS

Combining these variables can give us thousands of ways to alter the visual appearance of a map symbol. Some combinations are clearly better than others for expressing a given map idea. The choice of symbols is not always a simple task, because the appearance of a symbol is affected by everything around it. For example, a red circle half an inch in diameter will stand out clearly on a map that consists of thin black lines and gray-shaded areas. Put the same circle in a swirling mass of intense colors on a wall map, and it promptly gets lost. (You'll have to use your imagination for that, or else pay an extra ten dollars for color plates in this book. That little dilemma is a good illustration of the tradeoffs involved in deciding what symbol is appropriate for a particular map idea -- a map maker has to balance the clarity and force of a symbol against the importance of surrounding ideas, the cost of map production, and the skill and patience of the map reader.)

Amid all this potential confusion, we should keep sight of one fact -- people have used particular symbols to express particular kinds of ideas for a long time, and, as a result of this long use, we can safely conclude that some symbols are more appropriate than others for expressing a given idea. The purpose of this part of the book is to describe a variety of common "symbolic vocabularies" that have evolved among map users over the years. For each kind of map, we offer examples, comments about the kind of data that it can communicate most clearly, and cautions about interpretation. The sequence of examples goes roughly from concrete to abstract, and from point through line to area within those broad groups, but it will soon become obvious that few real-world maps deal with only a single kind of data, and even fewer real-world phenomena are customarily shown with symbols that have the same scaling, continuity, presence, etc.

Next on the list of general cautions is this simple plea: look at each map as a whole, as well as studying its parts. Like a spoken phrase, a map can communicate a message by its overall tone as well as individual symbols. For example, the English words "I love it" can mean a wide variety of things, depending on the object, the setting, and the speaker's facial expression and tone of voice. At one extreme, this short sentence might express gratitude for a caress or delight with the taste of a hamburger; at the other, irritation about cleaning the basement or disgust with the promotion of an undeserving and obnoxious co-worker.

We are not trying to imply that a printed map has all of the nuances of a sentence spoken by a live human being. But it most surely can have some of them, and the presence of all-too-human personality quirks and private jokes can affect the message carried by the map. A confession to illustrate the point: once upon a time, I was making a map of organic soils (a muddy subject, indeed). In mountain regions, these soils occur in tiny patches, a few hectares in size, in passes and draws (see pages 61-2). They are scattered from Montana to New Mexico, and the entire region may have a total of a thousand square kilometers of organic soils. The map legend said that one dot should represent one thousand square kilometers of each kind of soil, and therefore the map maker had a lot of freedom in deciding where to put the single dot for mountain organic soils. I chose, without too much thought, to put it halfway between Mt. Harvard and Mt. Yale in Chaffee County, Colorado. That was roughly in the middle of the Rockies, and at the time it seemed clever to endow the Ivy League Mountains with their own dot. To make a long story short, someone decided to translate that dot map (page 122) into a bounded-area map (page 124), and the official United States Department of Energy map of Energy Resources has a small blob that shows a major peat deposit, halfway between Mt. Harvard and Mt. Yale, in Chaffee County, Colorado.

Is that appropriate?

HISTOSOLS

One dot represents
1000 square kilometers

The map above shows the general distribution of *histosols*, the taxonomic category that includes all organic soils: peats, mucks, saltwater swamps, and all kinds of transitional forms. The map was printed in a professional geographic journal (the *Annals of the Association of American Geographers*). The map below, copied from a United States Department of Energy report entitled *Peat Prospectus,* is the fourth in a chain of six maps that were apparently "borrowed" from one another; the fifth version is a straightforward copy of this map with an even more optimistical title: *Energy from Peatlands: Options and Impacts*. Changes in the legends and symbolic vocabularies of the maps have "transformed" some scattered mountain bogs and salty desert playas into "major energy resources" for the nation.

PHOTOMAP -- FIELD BOUNDARIES

This is an example of a *photomap*, a map made by aiming a camera to record a map-like view of the landscape. A photomap is, in many ways, the least abstract of all map types. The camera simply cannot ignore some features and emphasize others to the extent that a human map-maker can.

This ability to show an entire scene with all of its details can be both an advantage and a disadvantage in communication. The amount of image distortion (whether accidental or deliberate) is usually very low. The apparent honesty of the image, however, can blind some readers to the fact that the "maker" of a photomap does have a great deal of control over what part of the landscape will be shown. Moreover, the main message can often get lost in the mass of detail on a typical photomap. Misinterpretation is even more likely if the reader forgets that the same object can look quite different on different photomaps -- its image can be affected by a host of conditions, including airplane speed and height, season, weather, and time of day, as well as by actual changes in the object. Despite these limitations, photomaps are some of the most useful sources of information for people studying patterns and changes in the landscape. A series of aerial (or satellite) photographs can illustrate changes in land use that can, in turn, have a profound effect on related systems such as traffic flow, stream discharge, air quality, school enrollment, or the local economy.

An interpreter of a photomap is like a detective who tries to decide what is really there by piecing together a mass of clues of different kinds:

1) *Size* -- areal or linear extent (gas station or shopping mall?)
2) *Shape* -- geometric or irregular (tree, shed, or oil tank?)
3) *Shadow* -- long, short, or wide (roof or swimming pool?)
4) *Brightness* -- amount of light reflected (snow or water?)
5) *Texture* -- roughness of the surface (field or parking lot?)
6) *Pattern* -- spacing and regularity (forest or orchard?)
7) *Association* -- surrounding objects (factory or school?)
8) *Topographic location* -- position on the landscape (golf clubhouse or ski chalet?)

In addition to its obvious use as a record of the actual appearance of objects, a photomap has another use that is even more important for a modern map-maker. This role depends on an adaptation of a principle from plane geometry. When a camera takes a picture from a particular point, only objects that are directly beneath the camera are recorded in their "exact" positions. All other objects are *displaced* in a way that follows a basic geometric rule, as shown in the diagram. A computer or optical plotter can take two aerial photographs of the same area, use the idea of displacement to calculate the elevation of the surface at any point in the area, and in that way make a contour map directly from a series of photomaps.

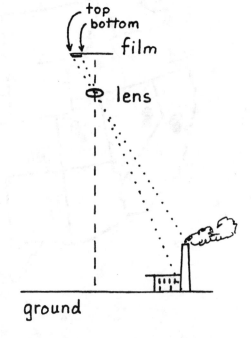

The Agricultural Stabilization and Conservation Service (part of the United States Department of Agriculture) used this aerial photograph to determine the amount of land used for specific crops on this farm. A technician marked the print with numbers to identify various fields and show their sizes in acres

PLANIMETRIC MAP -- HIGHWAYS

The major purpose of this kind of map is to show the locations of a selected number of features very precisely. Unless it is drawn at a very large scale (e.g. a blueprint for a small building), a planimetric map has to exaggerate the sizes of things that are of interest (so they can be seen easily), and therefore the map maker must be rather ruthless in eliminating other landscape features from the map. Even so, a planimetric map rarely tries to cover a large area -- a folded map of part of the United States is close to the limits of usefulness of this kind of map. Attempts to show more of the earth usually result in problems with scale or direction in parts of the map, because it is impossible to put much of the spherical earth on flat paper without causing some distortion (see pages 30-32). This, in turn, defeats the purpose of a planimetric map, which is to allow someone with a compass and ruler to determine directions and distances directly from the map.

Symbols on a good planimetric map are simple and almost intuitively obvious: big lines for big roads, small lines for minor roads, blue lines for rivers, small dots for towns, colored areas for cities, etc. Unlike most other kinds of maps, on which the general spatial arrangement of the phenomenon being mapped is of primary importance, the major message of a planimetric map is the individual spatial relationships of a host of minor details -- e.g., is the junction with highway 21 in the middle of Friendship or on the other side of town?

There are two common ways to translate the message of a planimetric map into terms that you can use in telling a driver which way to turn in Friendship. The first way is to keep the map oriented in a conventional north-is-up way and to picture your vehicle as a dot moving along the lines on the map. Translation of "go northeast" into "turn right" then takes place in your mind after you have located the vehicle on the map and decided on the route to take. The alternative to this "geocentric" strategy is a "vehicle-centric" one, which requires the map reader to turn the map so that the map line for the road is roughly parallel to the vehicle and the map symbol for the destination is toward the top of the map (i.e., ahead of you). The correct way to turn the vehicle (right or left) is easy to figure with this system, but translating road signs (e.g. I-90 WEST) from an upside-down or sideways position may take some thought. To use this approach, you may need to practice reading numbers and names at all kinds of angles. The designer of a planimetric map should use a typeface that makes that kind of reading as easy as possible, because many people do choose to use the map in that way.

A planimetric map, contrary to popular opinion, is not a good tool to use in trying to find out where you are after you get lost. The maker of this kind of map has tried to keep it readable by omitting many features of the real world, and the resulting scarcity of clues can make it hard to find your position on the map. For this reason, you should treat a planimetric map as a *preventive* medicine -- use it to keep track of your location, and check your progress frequently by noting whether side roads and towns actually appear to be where the map says they should be. In short, the best way to avoid getting lost is to make sure you know where you are at all times.

Other uses for the planimetric technique include location maps in newspapers and magazine articles ("Where is El Salvador?"), site designs for landscape architects, and other kinds of survey or reference maps. Many of these make use of the *inset* technique, in which a small map is printed along with the main map in order to show how the main map fits into a larger area or to provide a detailed look at part of the main map. This is particularly important if the main map is of an odd-shaped or small area, which may not be familiar to the readers.

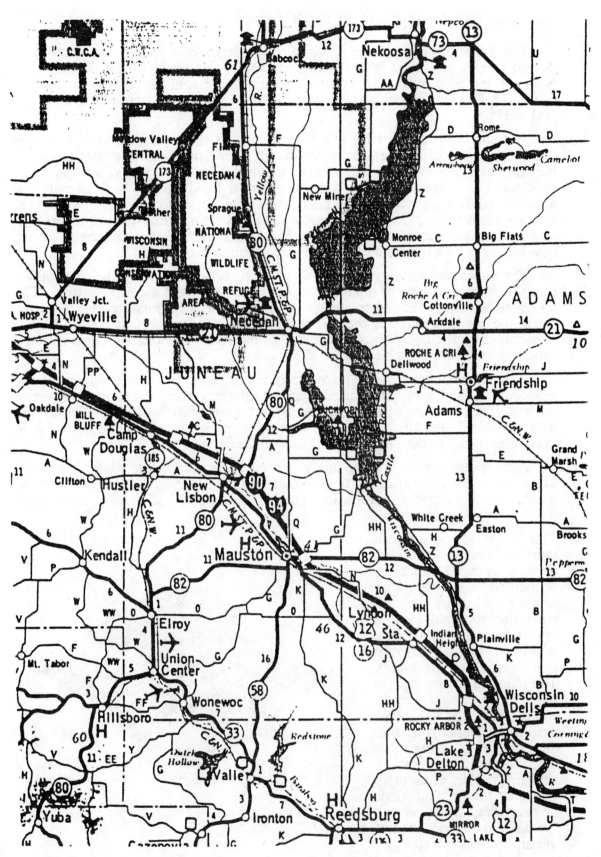

Source: Wisconsin Department of Transportation

PERSPECTIVE MAP -- CAMPUS BUILDINGS

This kind of map language is basically a variation of a planimetric vocabulary, in that its primary intent is to communicate the *locations* of things. In this case, however, the map maker has chosen to compromise some positional accuracy in order to help the map reader recognize a feature when it is approached out in the real world.

A recurring problem with this kind of map is the choice of view to use in displaying a particular feature. A *consistent perspective* (e.g. one that shows all buildings as if they were viewed from the southeast) has the virtues of simplicity and predictability -- the map user can see what a building will look like if it is approached from a particular direction. In the real world, however, the locations of walkways and roads usually force people to take certain routes through an area. If that is the case, then a map maker can make life easier for the reader by showing how buildings look when viewed from those common paths.

The alternative strategy, *continually changing perspective*, might be exemplified by a tourist map of historic buildings in Venice as seen from the canal system. The maker of this map decided to show only the side of each building that faces the canal; the size and shape of the rest of the building is a mystery as far as the map reader is concerned. Obviously, that kind of map is more valuable if you are on a canal-boat, rather than a bicycle.

Pictorial-perspective maps were very popular in the late 1800s, when mayors, city councils, and speculators used them to advertise their towns to prospective settlers. The recent construction boom in the business districts of big cities has led to a revival of this kind of map. Perspective maps are also quite common in museums, theme parks, and other recreational areas.

A computer can draw some kinds of perspective maps quite easily. The map maker must first determine the three-dimensional mathematical coordinates of key points (building corners, hilltops, streambanks, road junctions, etc.) and enter them into the computer memory.

This "numerical image" can then be enlarged, moved, rotated, reduced, updated, or painted bright green with a few easy keystrokes on a computer terminal (and a few thousand person-hours of work writing the program that does all of the math). The diagram to the right is part of a *digital terrain model*, much like those now used for airplane navigation and missile guidance. A map maker can use a similar graphic vocabulary to depict many other kinds of "surfaces," such as the "peaks" and "valleys" of unemployment in a city.

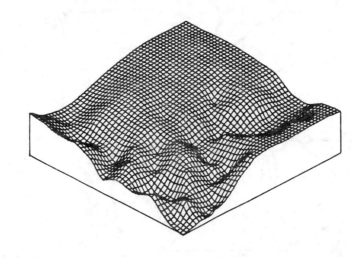

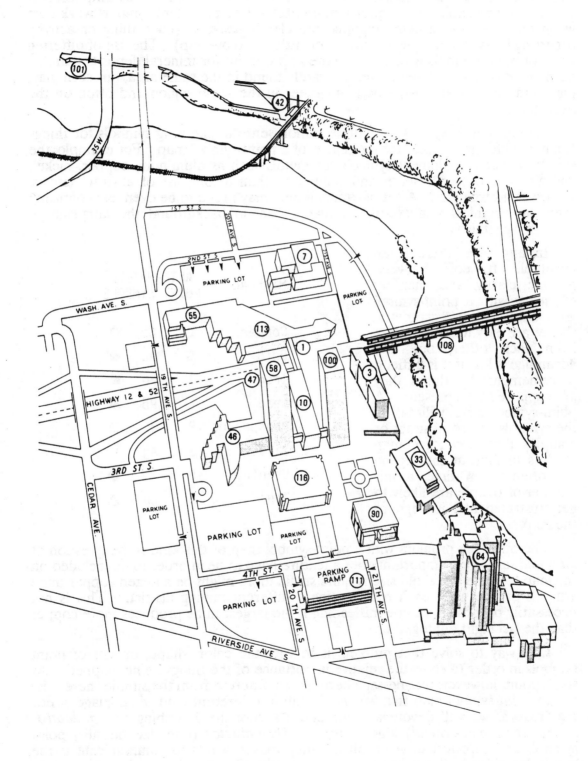

Source: Greg Chu

POINT-SYMBOL MAP -- MINERAL DEPOSITS

This kind of map is very popular with authors of elementary-school textbooks, which use point-symbols maps mainly as a result of the (erroneous) assumption that children are not able to interpret a more abstract map.   Point symbols work best when the phenomena being mapped are clearly *discrete* (each thing or activity occurring in its own unique location, with little or no overlap).   The use of differing kinds of point symbols is therefore more appropriate for mineral deposits than for farm crops -- coal and metal ores are rarely found in the same area, but corn, hay, pigs, and dairy cows usually occur together in the same region and often on the same farm.

A map maker who uses a little common sense in choosing symbols for things can make life much easier for the reader of a point-symbol map.   For example, the standard chemical-element symbols for metals such as aluminum, copper, nickel, and zinc are easier to learn and remember than a long list of abstract circles, squares, and triangles.   A set of capital letters may prove to be even less confusing than the chemical symbols, if the reader has no background the language of academic chemistry.

In any case, there is an inevitable tradeoff between graphic clarity and memory efficiency with a point-symbol vocabulary. Simple geometric shapes are easy to differentiate from each other, but that advantage is lost if it is difficult to remember the things they are supposed to represent. A point-symbol map will fail if the symbols are so abstract or complex that they force map readers to look at the legend too often.   In time, a fair number of people are likely to get frustrated and just ignore the map.

MINERAL	ALTERNATIVE POINT SYMBOLS		
Copper	C	Cu	○
Gold	G	Au	●
Iron	I	Fe	▪
Lead	L	Pb	▲
Phosphorus	P	P	▢
Silver	S	Ag	▽
Uranium	U	U	◆
Zinc	Z	Zn	△

The other big problem with a point-symbol map of this kind is the question of *threshold size* -- how important does a feature have to be in order to be included on the map? If the threshold size is quite small, there might be a dozen copper mine symbols on the map, each representing a different mining district.   This is not necessarily bad, but it can be misleading if the largest mine produces more copper than the last eight put together.

One way to solve that problem is to vary the color, shape, or size of point symbols in order to show the relative importance of the things being mapped.   At some point, however, the message becomes so different from the simple "here it is" of the point-symbol map that we should call it a different kind of language.   For that reason, we will devote another entire section to describing the *graduated-symbol* (or *scaled-symbol*) kind of map.   *Ungraduated* (one size fits all!) point symbols are appropriate when all the map maker wants to communicate is the simple locations of things like bathrooms, missile silos, burglarized houses, meteor craters, and other nominal point information.

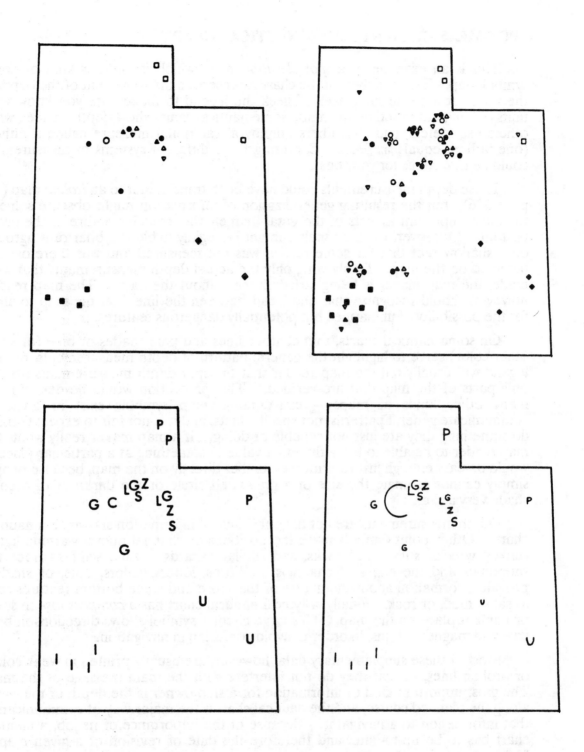

These maps of mines in Utah show how the communication efficiency of a point-symbol map depends on the choice of symbols and the threshold size of the phenomena being mapped. The top left map depicts only the largest mines; the top right one shows all major mines; the map on the lower left uses mnemonic symbols to show the largest mines; and the one on the lower right tries to indicate differences in importance by scaling the sizes of the symbols. Data source: adapted from <u>Atlas of Utah</u>, W. Wahlquist, editor.

SPOT-MEASUREMENT MAP -- NAUTICAL CHART

This is an example of a *spot elevation* map, which is another kind of point-symbol map. Each number on the chart represents a measurement of the depth of the water at a particular place. Check the legend to make sure you know what units of length are used on the map; some nautical charts show depths in feet, while others use meters, and still others employ a traditional measure called a fathom (one fathom equals six feet). Confusing these different systems of measurement could be hazardous for your boat.

These depth measurements could have been translated into an *isoline* map (see page 136), but the resulting generalization of information might obscure some of the most important aspects of the data, namely the irregular nature of the ocean bottom. Moreover, the map maker might be legally liable if a boat runs aground on a shallow reef that for some reason was not measured and was therefore not depicted on the map. By showing only the actual depth measurements that were made, the map maker is being strictly honest about the data. The map reader, however, should recognize that and "read between the lines" on the map to allow for the possibility of unmapped but potentially dangerous features.

On some nautical charts, thin contour lines and pale shades of blue (or some other color) serve to highlight the general pattern of depth measurements, but the legend will usually tell the map reader that the spot depth measurements are the only parts of the map that are verified. This precaution would be desirable on many other kinds of maps -- conventional map symbols exist in order to communicate general patterns, not specific facts, and it is not fair to expect them to do something they are just not capable of doing. If a map maker really wants the map reader to be able to learn the exact value of something at a particular place, it would be easy enough just to print the number directly on the map, because people simply cannot estimate the size of a graduated circle or the darkness of a color shade very accurately.

Depth measurements are not the only kinds of information shown on a nautical chart. Other point symbols mark the positions of channel buoys, warning lights, sunken wrecks, submerged rocks, and similar hazards. Line symbols trace the shorelines and the edges of channels. Words, letters, colors, dots, or shading provide information about the nature of the shore and some bottom features such as sand, mud, or rock. Finally, a typical nautical chart has a *compass rose* in some prominent place on the map. This large circular symbol shows directions in both true and magnetic terms, in order to avoid confusion in navigation.

Most of these supplementary data, however, are usually printed in weak colors or broken lines, so that they do not interfere with the main message of the map. The most important kind of information for a ship owner is the depth of the water along the planned course, and the nautical chart is the major way of communicating that information to a navigator. Because of the importance of its job, a nautical chart has to be up-to-date, and therefore the date of revision of a given map is featured prominently on the map.

For sailors in many coastal areas, the time of day is even more significant than the date of map revision, because the daily rise and fall of the tides can make all of the printed numbers wildly inaccurate at any given time. A pilot must therefore use a tide chart to adjust the figures on a nautical chart in order to get an accurate impression of the sea bottom in a particular place. This need to consider both time and space is one reason why the reading of a nautical chart is not as easy as it may seem at first glance.

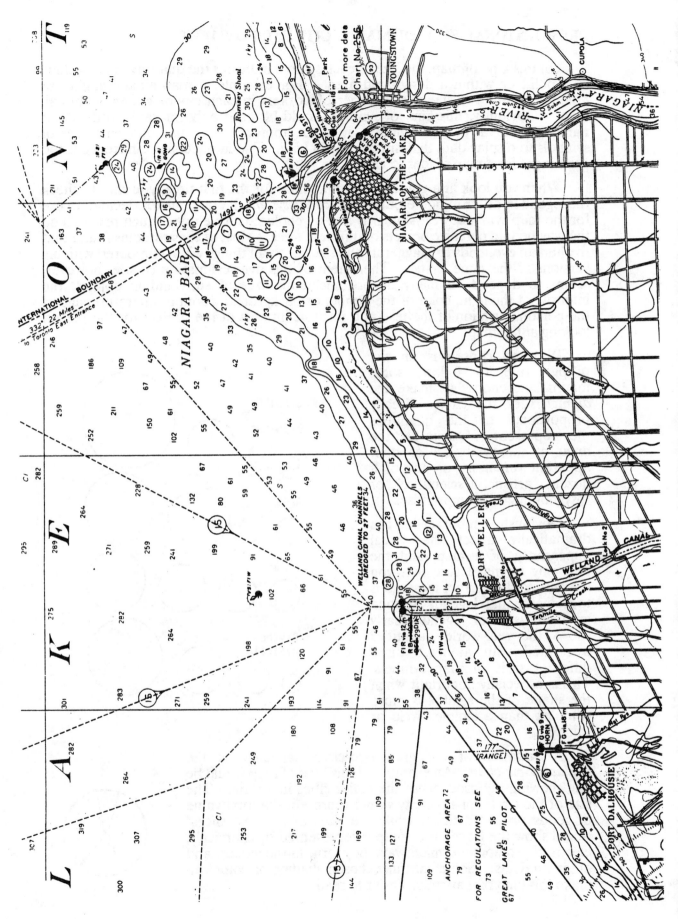

PROPORTIONAL-SYMBOL MAP -- CITY EMPLOYMENT

On this kind of map, the size of each symbol indicates the quantity of something at a point or within a designated area. For example, a map-maker might use graduated circles to show the number of workers in each city or county within an area. Obviously, this kind of symbol should be used only for rank (ordinal) or number (interval or ratio) data -- it is not appropriate to use different *sizes* of symbols to display data that differs only in *kind*. The implied size difference is too prominent for a map reader to ignore.

When you look at a graduated-symbol map for the first time, you should check the legend in order to figure out which *scaling system* the map maker decided to use for the map symbols. Physiologists and psychologists have done much research on the way people perceive objects of different sizes. Most of these studies found that the human eye tends to exaggerate the sizes of small things when compared with big versions of the same shape. The extent of this over-estimation of size, however, seems to depend on many factors, including sizes of surrounding objects, the intensity of the light, color of the symbol or background, room temperature, age of the person, duration of the test, and intrinsic interest of the subject for the person looking at the map.

With no consensus on the proper rule to follow, some mapmakers choose to make the *diameters* of the circles directly proportional to the quantities they represent. Others use the *areas* of the symbols, or their apparent *volumes*, or any of a dozen "artistic, "scientific," or "psychophysical" compromises.

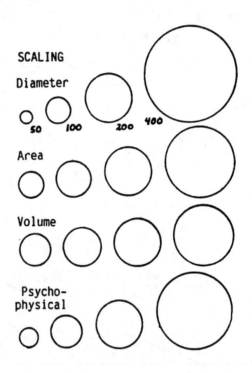

Obviously, symbol scaling can dramatically affect the visual appearance of a map, and the only way to make sure that you are getting the correct message is to study the map legend. A good graduated-symbol legend clearly shows the real-world quantities associated with at least three different sizes of map symbols. This is especially important when the shape of the symbol is more complex than a simple circle or square.

A variation of the graduated-circle language is the *graduated-pie-chart*. An example of this kind of map would be one showing the products of the major cities in a state. The size of the circle for each city would represent the total value of goods produced there, while the sizes of the "pie slices" would show the fractions of output represented by chemicals, electronic equipment, microwave popcorn, music videos, and other products. Some carefully chosen shading or color can make this kind of map much easier to read.

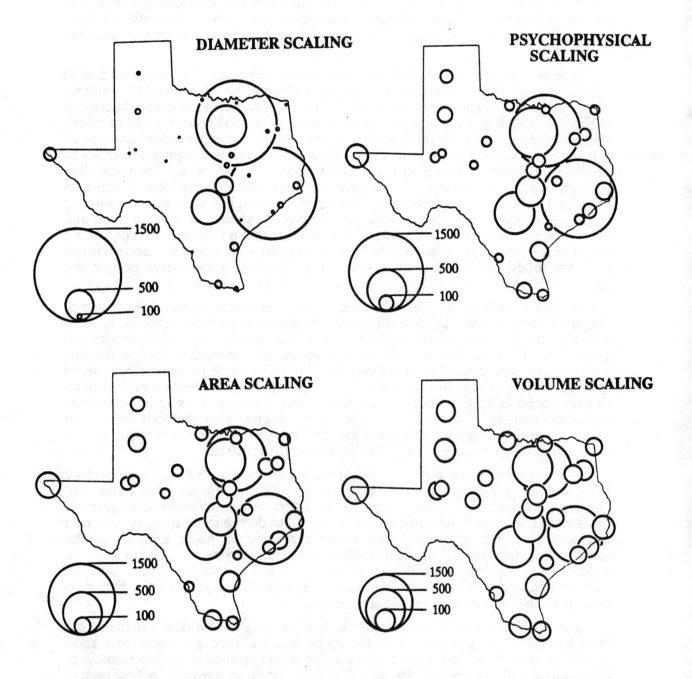

DIAMETER SCALING

PSYCHOPHYSICAL SCALING

AREA SCALING

VOLUME SCALING

These maps use graduated circles scaled in four different ways to show employment in Texas urban areas (in thousands of employees). The resulting visual impression is strikingly different. The visual appearance of the circles would also differ if they were black, gray, or some other color. A map maker should provide a legend showing the values associated with at least three different sizes of circles; a map reader should check the legend carefully before trying to compare symbols in different areas. Source: Texas Bureau of Business Research, 1988

FLOWLINE MAPS -- RIVERS, MIGRANTS, AND URBAN TRAFFIC

The symbolic vocabulary on these maps is the line equivalent of a graduated circle -- both kinds of symbols try to show the *quantities* of something by varying the *sizes* of the symbols. In these examples, the width of each line represents a quantity of something: traffic on a road network, people moving to new homes, or water in a river system.

A map of streamflow is generally easy to make, because river channels stay in about the same places, water flows only one direction (downhill), and the number of major streams is small enough to justify a set of permanent recording devices on them. Most of these *gauging stations* produce a printed record of streamflow; some modern ones report the data to a master station through a telephone line or satellite radio link. The mapmaker still must make some assumptions in order to produce line symbols based on the gauging station records, which are point data (see page 102). In general, it is reasonable to assume that the flow of water in ungauged streams is probably about the same as in similar streams with gauging stations (as long as the areas around the streams are similar in size, features, and amount of rainfall). It is also reasonable to assume that a river will continue to get larger as it flows along, unless it goes over geologic structures that can absorb water (e.g. dry sandy areas or limestone caverns) or through areas where people are removing water (e.g. cities, large industrial areas, irrigation districts).

A map of traffic flow poses a somewhat more complex problem. Like a stream gauging station, a mechanical traffic counter (usually a pressure-sensitive hose or wire that counts each tire passing over it) is willing to work day and night with few complaints about the weather. However, a typical road network is large, and traffic counters are expensive. Few cities can afford to record data on more than a small fraction of their roads at any one time. As a result, the record may contain measurements of traffic along one stretch of road during a week in June and the adjacent road in mid-winter. One result seems almost inevitable: the measurements into and out of a given intersection seldom agree, and therefore the map maker must use judgement in deciding what figures to use.

In many cases, a computer can help by doing the mass of calculations involved in looking at each major intersection in the city, figuring out the total number of vehicles measured as entering or leaving the intersection, adjusting the figures to make the inflow equal the outflow, and going on to do the same thing for the next intersection. The process of adjustment can keep on going until all of the intersections and roads seem to fit together as a single system. (These adjusted numbers can then be checked by comparing the number of residences with the number of jobs and stores in different parts of the city; see page 172 for a discussion of ways to analyze that kind of *spatial interaction*).

The third flow map is made by looking at the origins and destinations rather than the flows themselves. This technique is often used for maps that show migration or trade -- if you record the departures and arrivals, it is often possible to calculate the patterns of flow that would probably occur as a result. A flow map of this kind differs from one based on gauging stations or traffic counts in one important respect: the actual routes taken by the people or the products are of little concern. The map maker usually draws each presumed route as a sweeping curve or some other artistically pleasing shape. The alert map reader thus can look at the general shape of the flowlines and tell whether a particular flow map is based on simultaneous measurements, traffic counts at different times, or calculated connections between places.

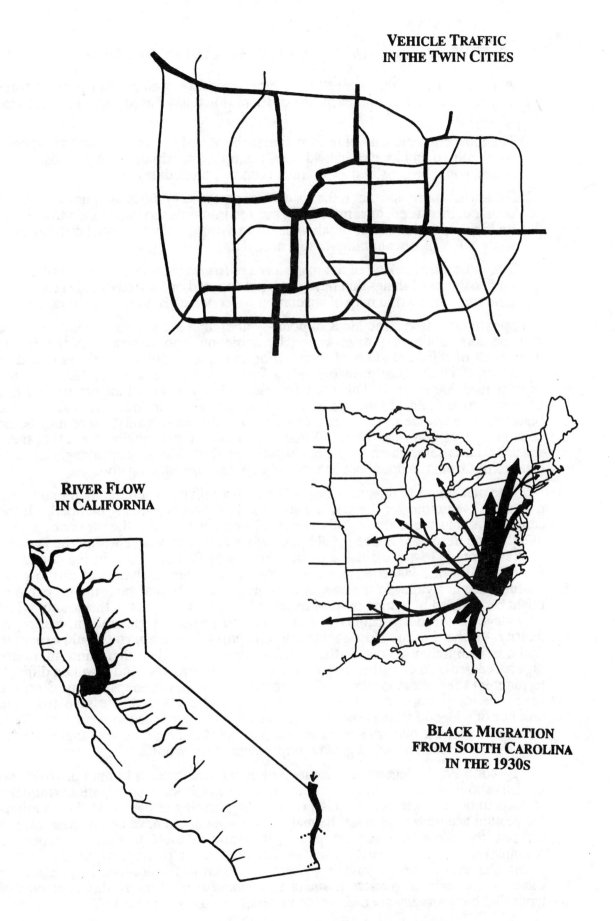

VEHICLE TRAFFIC
IN THE TWIN CITIES

RIVER FLOW
IN CALIFORNIA

BLACK MIGRATION
FROM SOUTH CAROLINA
IN THE 1930S

REPETITIVE-SYMBOL MAP -- AGRICULTURAL PRODUCTION

A map language that uses dots or other *repetitive* symbols can present three logically different ideas, and each one of them is actually based on a different kind of information:

1) The most concrete kind of information is the *actual positions* of things that can be identified and located individually (e.g. traffic deaths on county roads, which would be classified as discrete, nominal, point data)

2) Somewhat more abstract is the *spatial arrangements of things* that have been counted, measured, or sampled, but are too numerous to depict individually on the map (e.g. number of schoolchildren living in various school districts in a city, which is discontinuous, ratio, area data)

3) The most abstract kind of dot map shows *general impressions* of the number and positions of things that have not been counted or located exactly (e.g. pine trees on a world map of vegetation cover, which is nominal area data)

In appearance, these three kinds of point-symbol map are similar -- the differences may be too subtle to notice, except by someone who is aware of the innate limitations of different kinds of data. For example, a dot map of counted data (type 2 on the list) would probably have a legend that says something like: "one dot represents 5,000 cows." This does not mean that you would expect to find five thousand cows huddled together in a single herd if you went out and looked at the place marked by one of the dots on that map. On the contrary, there may be no cows in sight at that exact place. What the dot on the map really says is that there are 5,000 cows somewhere in an area around the dot. Roughly speaking, that area extends out from the dot about halfway to all of the surrounding dots.

The placement of dots on a map will be most reliable when the map maker has a good understanding of the actual distribution of the things being mapped. If the census says that there are 56,290 cows in a given county, then the maker of a map like the one described above should put eleven dots somewhere within the borders of the county (11 was calculated by dividing the 56,000-odd cows in the county by the map ratio of 5,000 cows per dot). Suppose, however, that most of the good pastures are in a valley to the west of the county seat. In that case, the map maker might be justified in putting most of the dots in the western part of the county. The advantage of the dot vocabulary is its ability to provide a general impression of density -- if the dots are close together in one part of the map, you would expect to find a large number of cows in that general area. If, on the other hand, there are big spaces between dots, then the area has relatively few cows and it will be difficult to pinpoint their exact locations. This same rule applies to maps of type 3 on the list above, only more so. The map reader should get a clear message from the absence of a legend saying how many cows each dot is supposed to represent. That message is that the map maker did not have detailed information, and therefore the map should be seen as only a general impression of the world.

By contrast, the legend of a dot map of actual occurrences (a map of type 1 on the list) should say something like "each dot shows the location of one earthquake of magnitude 6 or greater." This precision of phrasing implies that the locations are plotted accurately, because the map maker appears to have taken some care in defining the thing that was mapped. It is also possible to design symbols to communicate *kind* or *intensity* as well as simple *location*, perhaps by using different colors, shapes, or sizes of symbols. These variations of the dot-map language have some of the traits of *graduated-symbol* or *pictorial-symbol* maps, different symbol types that have already been discussed in detail on pages 118 and 114.

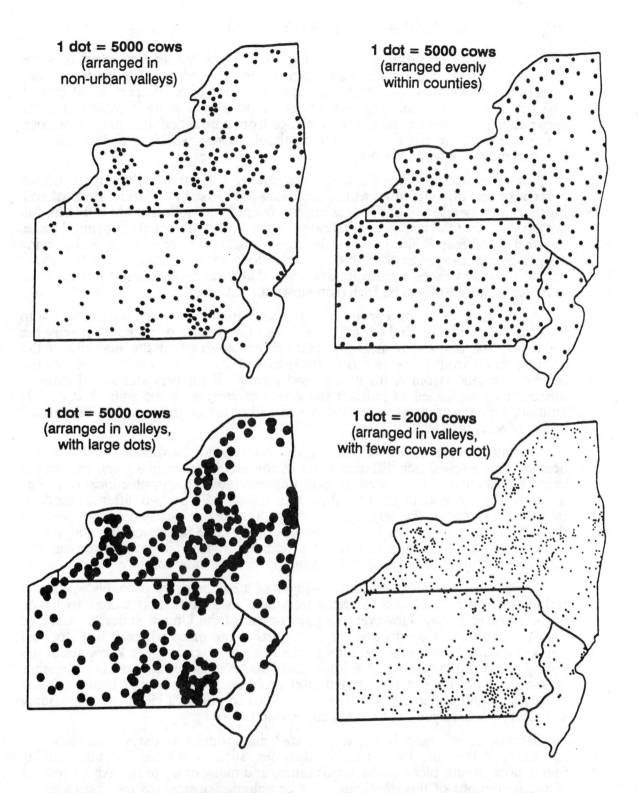

1 dot = 5000 cows
(arranged in
non-urban valleys)

1 dot = 5000 cows
(arranged evenly
within counties)

1 dot = 5000 cows
(arranged in valleys,
with large dots)

1 dot = 2000 cows
(arranged in valleys,
with fewer cows per dot)

These maps show the distribution of dairy cows in the Mid-Atlantic states. The maps differ in the sizes of the dots, the number of cows represented by a single dot, and the assumptions used in arranging the dots on the page. Data source: United States Census of Agriculture.

BOUNDED-AREA MAP -- SOIL SURVEY SHEET

The purpose of a bounded-area map is to show the *spatial extent* of some feature of interest. To make a soil map, a surveyor looks at the landscape and decides where to draw lines that will separate areas with different kinds of soil. The actual pattern of the phenomenon is almost always more complex than the map pattern. To get an undistorted message from a bounded-area map, therefore, the reader must already know something about the real world, or at least the way the map-maker viewed the world.

For example, the rules for a modern county soil survey allow up to fifteen percent of any bounded area to be "inclusions" of radically different kinds of soil. Furthermore, nearly half of the area can be covered with soils that are *similar to* but not *identical with* the kind of soil indicated by the letters and numbers printed there. In effect, a soil map is like a map of the ethnic neighborhoods of a city -- classifying a given part of Boston as an Irish community does not necessarily mean that every person who lives there is from Ireland, only that a randomly chosen person from that area is more likely to be Irish than any other nationality.

A soil surveyor prints a group of letters and numbers in each bounded area to indicate the dominant kind of soil there. The first letters or numbers specify the soil *series* (the one out of nearly 15,000 reference soils that the majority of the samples taken from the area most closely resemble). The next letter shows the *slope* of the land (from A for nearly level through F for very steep). Finally, a number may be added to indicate the *degree of erosion* of the soil: 1 is usually omitted, 2 means moderately eroded (about half of the original topsoil gone) and 3 means severely eroded.

Assigning a soil sample to its proper series is not as difficult as it sounds, because only a few dozen different kinds of soil are common in a given part of the country, and most of those tend to occur in predictable topographic locations (e.g., there may be three kinds of generally fertile soil on hilltops, two different kinds of thin and rocky soil on the slopes, and perhaps four or five clearly different types on the floodplain and terraces in the valley bottom). The processes that shape soils will change when you go into a different climatic region or geologic setting, and therefore each part of the country has a unique list of locally common soils.

If that were all there were to the subject of a soil map, we probably would not include an example of such a specialized map in a book that claims to be an introduction to maps. However, the government of the United States has decided that its collection of county soil survey reports is the place where it will store all kinds of detailed environmental information. Thus, if you want to know about the geology, natural vegetation, wildlife habitat, average and extreme weather conditions, landslide hazards, groundwater problems, or the proper kinds of forest trees, range grasses, crops, or ornamental plants to put on a given site, the county soil survey is where you can find that information.

Moreover, soil maps are often *recoded* and printed as maps that show the suitability of the land for particular purposes, such as wildlife habitat, building foundations, roads, picnic areas, septic tanks, and many other uses. An awareness of the limitations of this important class of bounded-area maps can therefore be very useful in interpreting what, at first glance, does not seem to be a soil map (e.g. a map of sites for a solid-waste disposal station, something that many people would prefer not have next door). Other uses for the bounded-area technique include land uses, vegetation types, language families, residential neighborhoods blighted areas in a city, and a host of other kinds of nominal area data.

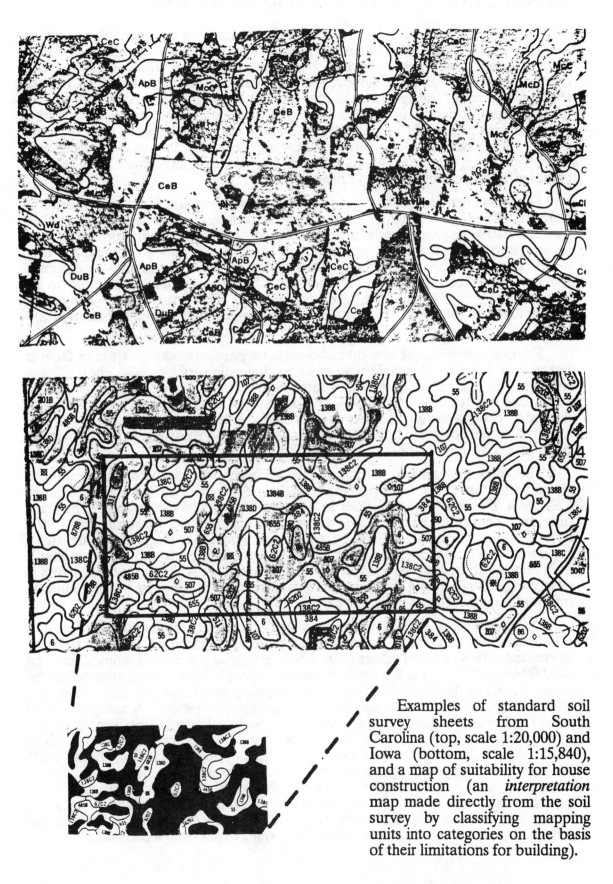

Examples of standard soil survey sheets from South Carolina (top, scale 1:20,000) and Iowa (bottom, scale 1:15,840), and a map of suitability for house construction (an *interpretation* map made directly from the soil survey by classifying mapping units into categories on the basis of their limitations for building).

CHOROPLETH MAP -- POPULATION CHARACTERISTICS

Data for this kind of map come from descriptions or counts of things within arbitrary spatial units (political areas, such as voting precincts, counties, or states, or designated counting areas such as *census tracts* or *minor civil divisions*). This graphic language is an honest portrayal of the data as they were acquired, but the shapes and sizes of the spatial units may have little or no relationship with what is being mapped. For that reason, a choropleth map is usually less accurate than a bounded-area map in showing something like the boundary between rich and poor areas. However, this disadvantage may be offset by the ease of making a choropleth map, because the map maker can use data that have already been gathered by an existing political infrastructure.

The choropleth vocabulary can be used to show many kinds of data -- individual states, counties, or other spatial units can be compared (nominal data), ranked (ordinal data), or given numbers that count or describe some feature within the areas (interval or ratio data -- see page 103). It is also easy to compare two or more choropleth maps, especially within a computer. The ability to compare different maps makes the use of choropleth maps especially vulnerable to an interpretation error known as the *ecological fallacy*. This error occurs when a map reader looks at the same area on two different maps and then assumes that any individual living in that area has the traits that are depicted on both maps.

For example, suppose one map shows that a particular census tract in Denver has a large number of people who work as domestic servants, and another map shows a high average income in that same census tract. After looking at the two maps, one might draw the perfectly reasonable but utterly wrong conclusion that domestic servants have a high average income. Keep in mind that we chose this example to be obvious; the ecological fallacy can be most dangerous when the relationship is subtle.

The sizes and shapes of map units can also pose problems in reading a choropleth map. For example, most of the people in San Bernardino County, California, live in a group of cities in one small corner of the county. The scale difference between the settled area and the political unit is the reason that 40,000 square kilometers of desert can be shown on a national map as an "industrial region" or "predominanty Republican area." Once alerted to this problem that is built into the choropleth language, most map readers are willing to forgive errors in describing *areas*, because they are aware that the map is designed to communicate information about the *people* in the region.

Finally, readers should remember that choropleth maps usually have a relatively small number of colors or line patterns. Each of those patterns is associated with a range of values (e.g., a light gray may represent incomes between $25,000 and $39,999), but the actual value for a specific area seldom appears on the map. Changing the "boundary" values that separate areas into different groups can have a dramatic effect on the appearance of a choropleth map. A concerned map maker will print the values or a graph of their statistical distribution directly on the map, so that the map reader can have some idea about the range of values shown by the same color or pattern on the map. The map reader, in turn, should study the legend carefully, to avoid seeing patterns that are not really there. With these caveats in mind, we remind you that the choropleth vocabulary can provide a powerful language for communicating many different kinds of data about small areas, and that includes precisely the kind of political, economic, and social information that a legislator or planner often wants to get from a census.

Foreign Born in Maine: Four Maps of the Same Data

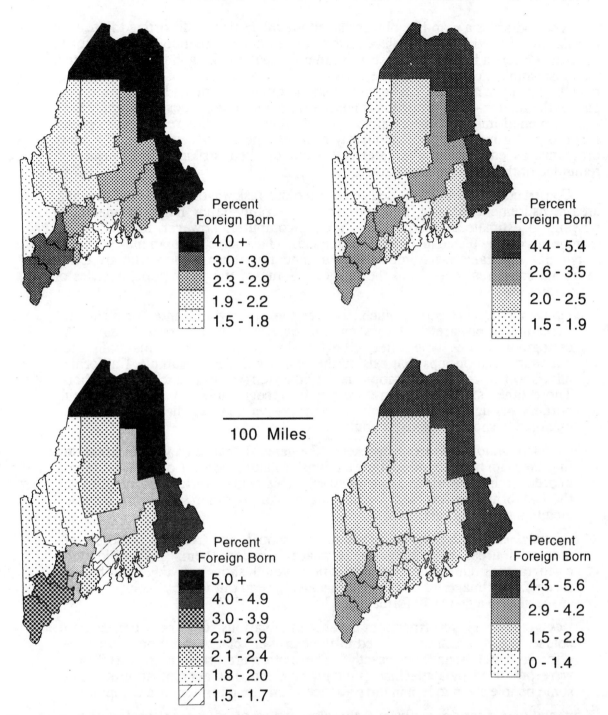

These four maps show the percentages of Maine residents who were born in another country. The maps differ in the number of visual groups and the logic used in deciding where to draw the boundaries between groups. The pattern would be quite different if the maps depicted the number of foreign-born people in each county, or the number per hundred square miles, or some other mathematical ratio. The exact wording of the legend is therefore more important for a choropleth map than for most other map types.

Data source: 1990 Census of Population.

CARTOGRAM -- ELECTION RESULTS, LAND OWNERSHIP

A cartogram is a map-like object that shows quantities by distorting the *sizes* of familiar areas. When done well, a cartogram can have tremendous visual impact, because it offers a form of visual surprise that is usually lacking in printed text (and, we must admit, in many of the less visually inspired dialects of the language of maps). At the same time, cartograms demand quite a bit of sophistication on the part of the reader -- size distortion is not really obvious if one does not already have a good mental image of the relative sizes of areas. For this reason, cartograms seem to go through cycles of popularity in newspapers, magazines, and TV news programs, as editors are alternately attracted by their striking appearance and reminded of their serious drawbacks.

Constructing a cartogram used to be a tedious task, involving a lot of drawing, area-measurement, erasing, and redrawing. Graph paper helps by making it possible to estimate areas quickly. With a computer, however, many kinds of cartograms can be tested in a matter of seconds. This helps the map maker choose a style that maintains visual impact without hindering those readers who are trying to obtain some real data from the image. Some of the most popular styles of cartograms are:

- *continuous-area cartograms*, which look like maps that were printed on a rubber sheet and then stretched to show the quantities in different areas. A cartogram of this type often mangles shapes in order to maintain the boundary relationships that exist in the real world. For example, California has almost twice as many people as the other ten western states put together. Those other states may therefore not be recognizable if you stretch their borders enough to keep them in their proper places when California is enlarged to show its relative population.

- *pseudo-continuous cartograms* preserve the general shapes of various areas so that they can be recognized, but relationships along borders often are altered in order to fit the various areas together. This kind of cartogram might solve the California size problem by stacking five or six other states in a column next to a tall California.

- *disjointed cartograms* try to preserve the shapes and relative positions of individual areas by adding empty space between them. A disjointed cartogram of United States population would show ten tiny and barely recognizable images of other western states spread out in a big block of blank space next to a giant California.

- *block-shape cartograms* transform the shapes of various states or countries into coarse blocks, which are printed in their proper relative positions with little effort to match boundaries exactly. These often are drawn to look as if they were produced by a machine (thus giving them that aura of accuracy that some people seem to feel in the presence of anything printed by a computer).

- *internal-image cartograms* have a shrunken image of each area located in the middle of its normal shape on an ordinary outline map. This method has less visual flair than other cartograms, but it can communicate proportions much more precisely. It is especially good for percentage data -- for example, on a map that shows the importance of Federal land ownership, the internal image of Nevada would be nearly as big as its "shell," because 87% of the property in the state belongs to the Federal government. Several eastern states, by contrast, would have only a tiny dot inside them, because nearly all of the land there is owned by private citizens, corporations, or local governments.

Change in Population, Predicted by the Year 2000

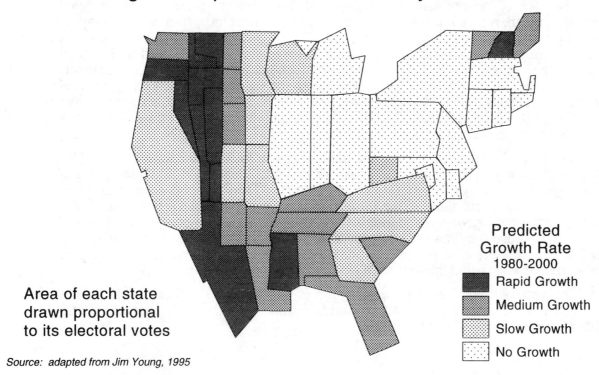

Area of each state
drawn proportional
to its electoral votes

Source: adapted from Jim Young, 1995

**Predicted
Growth Rate**
1980-2000
Rapid Growth
Medium Growth
Slow Growth
No Growth

Percentage of Land Under Federal Ownership

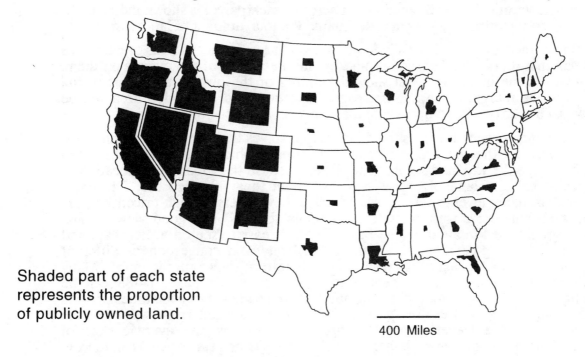

Shaded part of each state
represents the proportion
of publicly owned land.

400 Miles

Source: Statistical Abstract of the U.S., 1991; adapted from Argus, 1995

PLAT MAP -- PROPERTY OWNERSHIP

The idea of private land ownership is deeply rooted in the American legal system. It is therefore not surprising that one of the most important uses of maps is to show who owns certain parcels of land. These ownership maps are known as *cadastral maps*, *plat maps*, or *plat books*. The original is usually stored in the court house, where (as a public record) they are technically accessible but practically beyond the reach of most citizens. Because of the value of the plat maps for real estate people and planners, many towns and counties have hired companies like Rockford Map Publishers or The Title Atlas Company to print and sell a *county atlas* that contains copies of the plat maps.

"Only a fool would buy land on the basis of how it looks in a county atlas." Plat maps are not legally binding documents; only the original deed and survey in the county book of records has any standing in court. Thus the plat maps should be used only as a general guide to the pattern of land ownership in a local area. Even so, plat maps can provide useful insights into the economic and political workings of a region, because they can tell you what kinds of owners are important in a region. And, since a county atlas is usually updated every few years, it can be very helpful for someone who is studying trends in landownership or land use.

The symbolic vocabulary of a plat map is very simple. Where possible, the name of the owner of each parcel of land is printed directly on the parcel. Latin abbreviations show additional owners:

> *et al.* - and others
>
> *et ux.* - and spouse
>
> *et f.* - and children

Double-ended arrows (with a barb at each end) show that the land belonging to one owner extends across a map line to include land on the other side of a highway, railroad, or stream. In some cases the total acreage is listed beneath the name of the owner; in other cases the number of acres in each parcel is shown individually, and you must add these figures in order to find the total amount of land owned.

Some tracts of land, especially in recreational areas or near towns or cities, are so small that there is not enough room to write the names of the owners on them. In this case, the map might just show the initials of the owners and a list of full names in the margin or on another page. An even more crowded area will be shown by blocks or a dot pattern with the words "small tracts" printed on it.

"Reading between the lines" on a plat map involves that same kind of inference from experience that you use in interpreting a topographic map. In fact, it is often helpful to use the two kinds of maps together, because the topographic location of particular kinds of landholdings is one clue about their intended use. Farmers prefer reasonably level expanses of land, while developers of high-priced housing often seek hilly areas with lakes (or dammable streams) and good views. The survey system used in an area (see pages 77-80) is easy to see on a plat map, and one can infer a great deal about the accessibility and congestion of different neighborhoods by looking at the transportation pattern shown on the map. Many of the rural and urban settlement patterns described on pages 84-88 can be identified on plat maps; moreover, the names of the owners can sometimes provide useful clues about land use or speculative intent (e.g. Instant Homes, Inc., or the Twenty-Nine Mile Development Corporation). Finally, the average sizes of parcels (and the trend toward larger or smaller tracts from year to year) can tell you whether the local economy favors consolidation or splitting ownership.

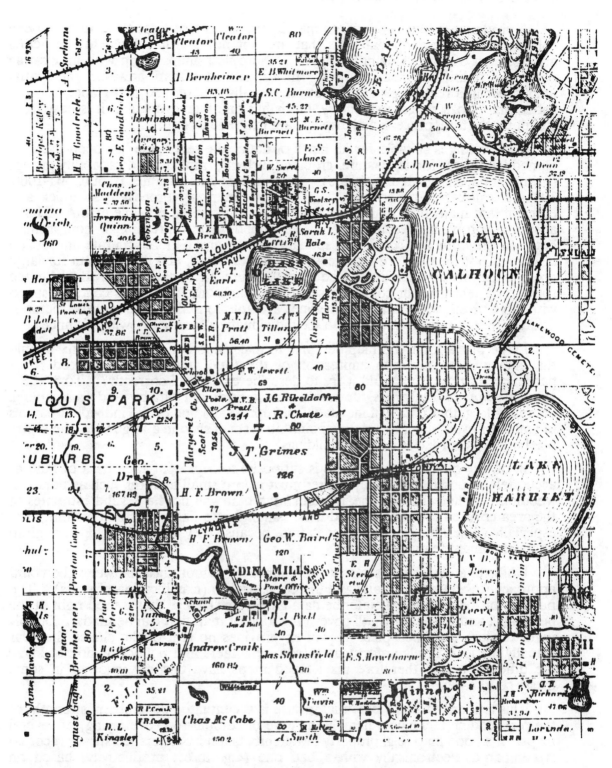

A portion of an 1887 Plat Map for Minneapolis; it shows a few farms, some subdivided country estates, a old mill, a newer railroad suburb, and several grid developments and upper-class tangletowns. All of this occurs within the confines of the Public Land Survey, although a few roads seem to follow an older system of trails, which may be of Native American origin.

PIXEL-CODED MAP -- LAND COVER

A pixel map is like a choropleth map in one important respect: data have been collected in arbitrary spatial units that are not necessarily related to the actual arrangement of what is being mapped. Choropleth maps begin with an existing pattern of political or census areas. In a pixel-coded map, however, the spatial units occur in a regular geometric pattern, usually square. At first glance, a pixel-coded map looks rough and clumsy, but it has one big advantage: it is easy for a computer to store, process, and display data in a regular grid.

Pixel-coding is suitable for all kinds of data; the technique has been used for named land uses (forest, pasture, cropland, urban), ranked land capability groups (prime, good, marginal, unsuitable), and numbered land values (0-500, 501-1000, 1001-2000 dollars per acre, etc.). The pixel mapping process is so quick and efficient that many map makers do not stop to think about possible errors. This is a serious problem, because every pixel-coded map represents a compromise between *resolution* and *cost*. Tiny spatial units can give a more accurate impression of shape, but the data are more costly to gather, store, and display than for large pixels (the word "pixel" is derived from "picture element," an individual lighted space on a television or computer screen; cheap computers have coarse displays with large pixels, whereas expensive ones are able to make more realistic pictures, because their pixels are too small to see individually at normal viewing distance).

Large pixels force the map designer to make another tough decision: should the map give an accurate impression of the total amount of area used for a particular purpose, or should it try to describe each pixel correctly? To make a good *inventory* of total areas, the map maker must obtain data by random sampling. Sampling to gather data will inevitably misrepresent some of the individual parcels of land; for example, if a sampling point hits a small shed in a large field, the entire pixel will be recorded as used for buildings.

If, on the other hand, the map is supposed to represent each tract of land as accurately as possible, the map maker must ignore small features such as ponds or woodlots. When that is done, the tabulated data will not have valid estimates of the area covered by different land uses; small things like ponds and buildings are especially vulnerable to misrepresentation, because they are seldom big enough to be the dominant feature in a pixel.

Unfortunately, there is almost no chance of compromise between the *count* approach (inventory of totals) and the *tag* approach (classification of parts). The purpose of the map will dictate the data gathering strategy that is used right at the beginning, and that in turn will govern the kind of map that can be made. Doubly unfortunately, a printed pixel map often provides no hint of the choice that was actually made. Triply unfortunately, some planners and politicians do not know the difference, and therefore pixel-coded maps have become involved in some messy court cases.

This tendency toward potential misuse is accentuated by another "strength" of the pixel-coding technique, namely the ease of comparison (overlaying) of several maps. If a good map (e.g. property ownership, taken from detailed survey records) is compared electronically with a bad one (e.g. forest productivity, based on measuring one tree every five square miles), the resulting combination map seldom has a chance to be more accurate than the bad input map. However, if the computer has access to some additional files, it is often possible to "improve" bad data by comparing with good files (e.g. by using a topographic map to help refine the locations of wet soils).

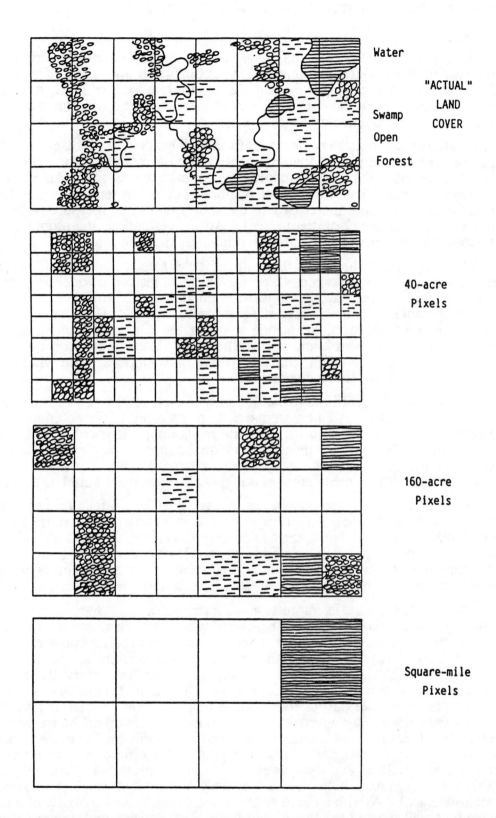

Water

"ACTUAL"
LAND
COVER

Swamp

Open

Forest

40-acre
Pixels

160-acre
Pixels

Square-mile
Pixels

A set of pixel-coded maps made by recoding a bounded-area map of land cover. Smaller pixels do a much better job of representing the pattern of land cover, but they are also much more expensive to enter, store, and manipulate in the computer.

SPECTRALLY CLASSIFIED IMAGE -- SURFACE FEATURES

Human eyesight is a remarkable process. The eye senses the intensity and wavelength of radiant energy and converts those sensations into electric impulses, which the mind translates into impressions of brightness and color. The sensitivity of the system is amazing: the eye can distinguish hundreds of levels of brightness and thousands of different colors for very tiny areas, and it can communicate that information to the brain many times a second.

A satellite has to make some tradeoffs in taking a picture of the earth. Assume (for the sake of illustration) that someone wanted a picture of the state of Iowa. The state has more than 56,000 square miles of corn, barns, roads, lakes, sailboats, and other features. That turns out to be about 145 billion sensory impressions at a *resolution* of one square meter (where the sensor takes one measure of brightness from every square meter of the surface). At that resolution, an automobile would be about a dozen squares with different brightness than the road.

The image might be easier to interpret if the satellite could "see" colors, but sensing the brightness of two or three wavelengths, instead of one, will double or triple the number of signals that must be communicated. Moreover, the resulting color of the squares is not necessarily the paint color of the car, because a given square meter of image might include some of the car roof, a bit of window, a roadmap on the dashboard, and part of the road. Each impression on a satellite image is the sum of the light from everything that happens to be within a given sensed area (*pixel*, as defined on page 132).

Suppose we increased the *resolution* so that each pixel is ten centimeters on a side (precise enough to tell a car from a pickup truck, but not good enough to "see" a license plate, let alone read it). At that resolution, a four-color image of Iowa would require 580 hundred thousand million brightness readings. And, if you shifted the image one centimeter sideways, a large number of those impressions would change, because the mixture of things within each pixel would be different.

Obviously, detailed resolution is not the only goal for a satellite sensor. In fact, it may be wise to choose a fairly coarse resolution, in order to get more colors and to minimize the cost of data transmission and processing. LANDSAT is a typical modern satellite: it passes over a given part of Iowa every 16 days, at exactly the same time of day, and it senses four "colors" (visible blue and green light, and two invisible *infrared* wavelengths). Its effective pixel is about the size of a softball field.

This satellite reports its impressions as a stream of radio signals, which can be displayed as a *false-color image* (with infrared wavelengths translated into colors the human eye can see). More often, a technician enters the coordinates of several *training fields* (areas of known land cover, such as cornfields, apartments, new construction, industrial smog, etc.). A computer then "interprets" the rest of the image, marking the places whose *spectral signatures* (intensities at different wavelengths) resemble one of the training fields. That process is fraught with chances for rather amusing errors. For example, a suburban house with a few trees, a garden, and a swimming pool, *taken as a unit*, might happen to reflect exactly the same wavelengths as a field of pinto beans after a rain, with some bare ground, a few puddles, and some weeds. Comparing pixels with their neighbors or with other maps can help, but a perfectly interpreted satellite image is an implausible goal. As with all map symbols, the communication ability of a satellite image falls well short of the "truth" that some laws, policies, and defense strategies seem to require. At the same time, a reasonably accurate and up-to-date image of a large area is a valuable resource for those who understand its limits.

A Ten-meter Pixel Image of a Suburban House

Each unit of data from a satellite sensor consists of its measurement of the *wavelength* and *intensity* of the light (or invisible radiation) from an area of fixed size and shape. In this example, a ten-meter grid placed over a house shows one pervasive source of confusion. A pixel that is half grass and half roof might reflect the same kind of energy as another pixel that is part car hood, part flower garden, and part oily driveway pavement. Careful selection of the wavelengths that are recorded by the sensor can reduce this difficulty. For example, healthy green vegetation tends to reflect a large fraction of a certain band of *infrared* energy. The engineers who designed the LANDSAT satellite chose to make it sensitive in this infrared "band." That sensitivity, in turn, makes the satellite useful for identifying things like rural drought problems and urban tree diseases before the symptoms are apparent to someone on the ground.

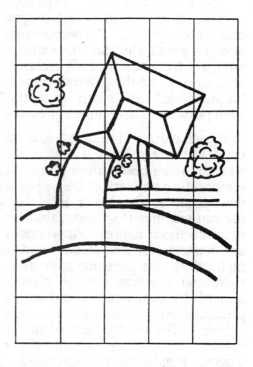

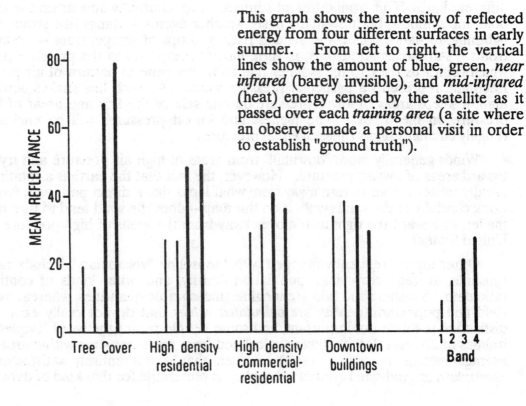

This graph shows the intensity of reflected energy from four different surfaces in early summer. From left to right, the vertical lines show the amount of blue, green, *near infrared* (barely invisible), and *mid-infrared* (heat) energy sensed by the satellite as it passed over each *training area* (a site where an observer made a personal visit in order to establish "ground truth").

ISOLINE MAP -- BAROMETRIC PRESSURE

An *isoline* map uses a set of roughly parallel lines to show the general pattern in a mass of information that originally came from a large number of individual observation points. A *contour* map (see Part B) is a kind of isoline map; it uses lines of equal elevation to show the general shape of the earth surface. To interpret the isolines of air pressure on a weather map, it often helps to view the lines as showing the general shape of a pressure "surface," with high "ridges," low "depressions," and steep or gentle "pressure gradients" or "slopes." In fact, it is even possible to draw an air-pressure "profile" between two points.

Each cluster of numbers and other symbols on a weather map is a coded record of the weather at an observation point. The present temperature appears at the upper left position; dew point at the lower left; a symbol for present weather (fog, snow, thunder, etc.) goes between those figures; cloud codes are put at mid-bottom (for low clouds) and mid-top (for high ones); air pressure appears at the upper right and pressure change directly below it; symbols for past weather and numbers for past precipitation (if any) are in the lower right corner. The shaded part of the central circle depicts the fraction of the sky covered by clouds. Finally, the line extending out from the center circle shows the direction from which the wind is blowing, and "flags" on that line indicate the speed of the wind.

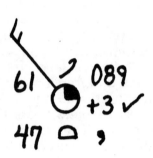

All of this information can help a weather analyst locate the *fronts* between different kinds of air from different sources. Fronts usually appear on the map as bold line symbols, because many nasty weather events -- things like strong winds, lightning, tornadoes, hail, and sudden rises or drops of temperature -- occur near fronts. Airmasses and fronts, in turn, move in response to the pressure pattern, which brings us back to the isolines that show the general pattern of air pressure. Each line represents a particular pressure value. As each line snakes across the map, it keeps areas of lower pressure on one side of the line and areas of higher pressure on the other. The highest and lowest pressures will be enclosed by roughly circular *isobars* (lines of equal pressure).

Winds generally move "downhill" from areas of high air pressure and try to go toward areas of low air pressure. However, the fact that the earth is a rotating ball usually causes the air to turn away from what looks like a direct path on a flat map. Look carefully at the wind symbols on this map -- does the wind tend to turn toward the left or toward the right as it moves away from the areas of high pressure in the United States?

Other topics frequently mapped with the isoline "vocabulary" include rainfall, sunshine, average crop yield, population density, and other kinds of continuous ratio data. Sunshine and rain are tangible, measurable quantities, whereas average yield and population density are *calculated values* that do not really exist. The distinction is subtle but important, and some people prefer the word "isopleth" for isolines of abstract data that were calculated from measurements within areas (e.g. average income in census tracts). Even that is not entirely satisfactory: a choropleth or graduated symbol vocabulary is preferable for that kind of data.

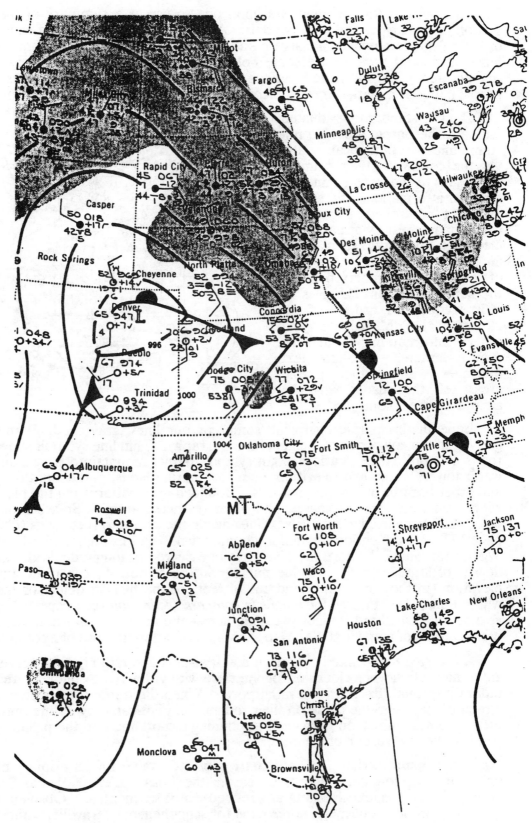

Source: United States Weather Bureau

MULTIPLE SYMBOLIC LANGUAGES -- AERONAUTICAL CHART

This popular kind of map is a good one to use as a summary of the entire section on data types and map symbols. An aeronautical chart uses a wide variety of symbols to communicate a large number of different kinds of information. The most prominent symbols are some bold purple circles (or, in some cases, odd-shaped areas) that show the locations and importance of various airports. Bold purple bands also mark some radio-controlled airways between major airports.

Unlike standard graduated symbols, the purple areas do not communicate numerical data. On the contrary, their primary purpose is to show some concrete nominal information: the spatial extent of "controlled airspace," in which pilots must fly at particular elevations and report regularly to air traffic controllers. A cluster of letters and numbers beneath the name of the airfield gives its radio frequencies, codes, and the elevation, length, lighting, and other information about the runways there. Short text messages within other purple areas tell the reader why the airspace there is controlled.

Beneath this purple overprint, some contour lines, gray shading, and pale green and tan colors depict the general topography. Thin line symbols show major roads and railroads. Various point symbols depict mountaintops, tall buildings, water towers, radio and television antennas, marine lights, parachute drop zones, and other hazards or navigational aids. Bounded-area patterns tell the pilot about wilderness zones, military bases, and other restricted areas. Splashes of yellow color mark urbanized areas. Black lines divide the area into rectangles (*pixels*; see page 132) with dimensions related to the map scale. For example, on a 1:1,000,000 World Aeronautical Chart, the pixels are one degree of longitude "wide" and one degree of latitude "tall." A blue number in the center of each pixel shows the elevation (in thousands and hundreds of feet) of the highest object or landform within that area. Finally, the *magnetic compass declination* (see page 16) appears as a set of dashed red isolines sweeping across the map. In short, an aero chart uses a variety of map vocabularies to show a lot of different kinds of information.

A *compass rose* printed over each major airport and radio beacon serves as an aid to navigation when clouds or fog interfere with visibility. A pilot can request a radar directional "fix" from several airports. When the traffic controllers tell what direction they "see" the plane on their radars, the pilot can draw a line outward in the appropriate direction from each responding airport and find the position of the plane at the intersection of the lines.

Like a nautical chart, an aero chart is of little value for its primary purpose unless it is up-to-date. For that reason, the Local (1:250,000) and Sectional (1:500,000) Aeronautical Charts are revised every six months. Obsolete charts, however, can be an inexpensive resource for schoolteachers, travellers, and people who need big pieces of interesting paper to cover ugly walls.

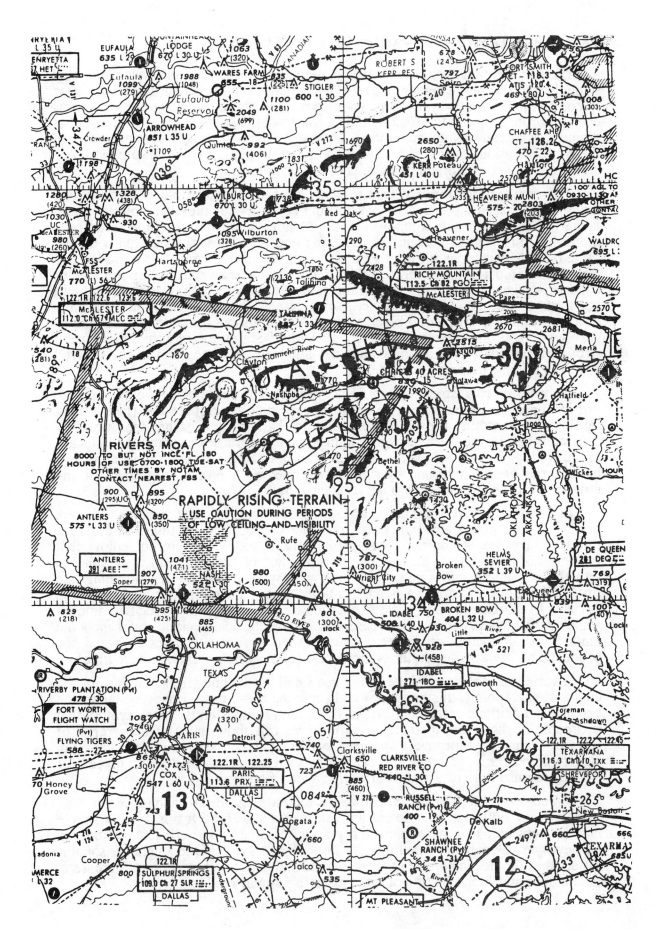

TEMPORAL-TREND MAP - CHANGE THROUGH TIME

Like an aeronautical chart, a trend map does not really introduce any new symbols into the map-language vocabulary. It does, however, use some familiar symbols in a different way, because its purpose is to show how geographic patterns change through time. In effect, it adds a fourth dimension -- time -- to the spatial dimensions already shown on a map. In order to depict this new dimension within the two dimensions of flat paper (or a computer screen), a trend map must make creative use of conventional point, line, or area symbols.

The most straightforward way to show change through time is to draw two maps (e.g. past and present, or present and future), put them side-by-side, and invite the map reader to compare them. A more sophisticated (and technically more difficult) way to accomplish the same end is to draft the two maps on the same base, with slightly different symbols to represent different time periods. For this kind of map, it is intuitively sensible (and therefore conventional) to use a paler color or weaker symbol to represent things in the past, as if they were fading into the mists of history. For example, a map of settlement might depict presently occupied buildings with solid black squares and abandoned buildings with hollow gray squares. "Photorevised" versions of United States topographic maps use a strong purple color to show new buildings and other changes that have occurred since the original map was printed.

An even more abstract way to depict change is to make time a data variable. For example, an isoline is able to show time as well as temperature (like a bank sign?); the "contours" represent areas that are early or late, rather than warm or cold, and the "degrees" are measured in days, years, centuries or whatever units are appropriate. This technique also works for topics like the spread of cities through history, the areas controlled by opposing armies as a battle progresses, or the movements of plant species through geologic time.

In a similar way, one might use an ordinal sequence of point symbols (e.g. red, orange, yellow, green, and blue dots) to depict the locations of things at different times. Likewise, a choropleth map might have states in different colors that represent of their date of admission into the Union or their amount of population growth between specified dates. To show growth or decline of something like production from a factory (a point location), a map maker might use graduated circles. In this case, a solid circle might indicate an increase of a specified amount while an open circle depicts a decrease. Alternatively, a solid circle could show the amount of production at present, while dashed or dotted circles depicted the production there at different times in the past (or at some predicted future time).

A variation of this technique would use small bar or line graphs in place of the circles at each point; this method would show the trend more precisely, but at the expense of additional visual clutter. In short, almost any standard map symbol that is capable of displaying quantitative differences can show dates of occurrence or rates of change. Moreover, any map symbol that can show nominal data can classify points, lines, or areas into categories such as growth or decline, present or past, or colonization (or withdrawal) within a specified time interval.

If budgets allow, a map maker might animate the entire sequence on film, videotape, or optical disk. Animation can take a variety of forms, from a simple fade-in transition to a new map or a gradual change in the sizes of symbols to Disney-style cartoon or a multi-media laser light show. One might reasonably expect that the declining cost of these new technologies will lead to an increase in the number and sophistication of trend maps in popular media.

LOCATION OF THE FRONTIER

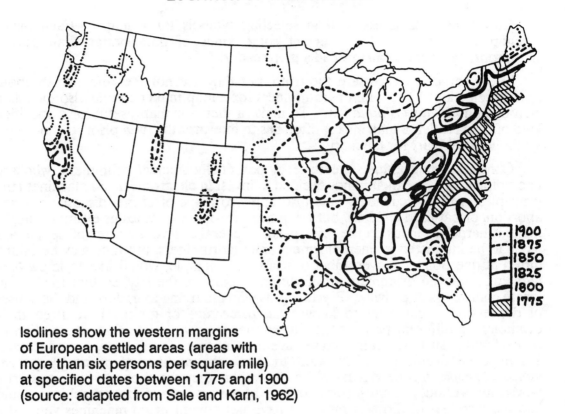

Isolines show the western margins
of European settled areas (areas with
more than six persons per square mile)
at specified dates between 1775 and 1900
(source: adapted from Sale and Karn, 1962)

CHANGE IN TONNAGE THROUGH MAJOR PORTS

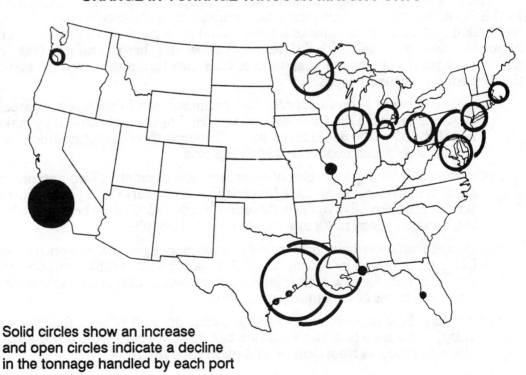

Solid circles show an increase
and open circles indicate a decline
in the tonnage handled by each port

DATA TRANSFORMATION

Classifying data is essential in selecting symbols for a map. Each major category of map symbol can depict some kinds of data better than others. Inappropriate symbols can mislead a map reader.

Those three sentences are the truth, but they are not the whole truth about symbol selection. The oath of truthfulness for a map maker should also include a clause about *data transformation*. To make a thematic map useful for a specified kind of map reader, a map maker often has to interpret the data prior to choosing a symbolic vocabulary for the map.

Consider, for example, the issue of potentially suicidal drummers, who are unemployed because their bands decided to invest in electronic drum machines (the principles in this discussion would also apply to maps of crime, disease, poverty, abortion, or battered children, but using headline-making issues as examples might make it harder to focus on the principles). Several different classes of people are likely to be interested in unemployment among drummers, but they may be asking different questions. Government officials, for example, would like to know *how many* unemployed drummers are in different parts of the city, so that they could locate counselors effectively. Psychologists who are trying to understand the causes of depression might want to know *what percentage* of groups have fired their drummers in different parts of the city, so that they can relate that information to other factors such as traffic noise, average income, family size, or education. Unemployed drummers might want to know the *number of music groups per thousand people* in various parts of the city, so that they can choose a place to start a new group without too much competition. Manufacturers of drum machines would like the *locations* of those groups that have not bought drum machines yet; the information would help them target their advertising. No single map could answer all of these questions, yet the same source of data (rock groups with and without drummers) is a good basis for the map that each interested party would like to see.

The process of tailoring data to answer a particular question has many names. In this book, we use the term *data transformation* to include a variety of ways of manipulating data in order to make it more useful for a particular purpose. A map of suicidal drummers will look different if it shows the basic numbers (the "raw" data) or the results of a common method of data transformation (ways of "cooking" the data for a particular purpose):

1) *absolute numbers* -- how many suicidal drummers are in each census area? Absolute numbers are the most concrete kind of data, because they make no effort to put the data into context. The next three transformations try to add background in order to clarify the data.

2) *percentages* -- what proportion of drummers are suicidal? Two potentially suicidal individuals in an area that has five drummers (40%) may show a serious problem; five out of a thousand bands (0.5%) may be about what you'd expect in any randomly chosen group of people.

3) *per capita values* -- how many suicidal drummers exist per person (or per hundred, thousand, or million people) in each tract? Unlike percentages that are based on a select group (drummers), per-capita values are figured in terms of the entire population.

4) *densities* -- how many suicidal drummers exist per unit of area (e.g. square mile)? If a map is drawn well, one can make a reasonable guess about absolute numbers from density symbols in each tract.

In addition to these four basic categories, there are four common ways of "cooking" data to clarify or emphasize a particular aspect of the information:

5) *proportions of some standard* -- how many suicidal drummers are there in a given area, expressed as a fraction of the number that occur in a specified reference area (e.g. the capital, the census tract nearest the center of the city, or some other area of interest)?

6) *deviations from average* -- how many suicidal drummers are in a given tract, compared with the average in the entire area? Deviations can be stated in absolute terms (e.g. five more than expected) or as a percentage or proportion (e.g. ten percent above average).

7) *percentiles* -- how many suicidal drummers are there in a given tract, expressed in terms of its position on a ranked list of tracts? Saying that a tract is in the "75th percentile" means that three fourths of the tracts have a smaller number (or proportion) of suicidal drummers than are found in this particular tract.

8) *Z-scores* -- how many suicidal drummers are there in a given tract, expressed in terms of its position on a normalized curve? Z-scores are widely used in various social sciences, where a phrase such as "1.7 standard deviations above the mean" allows statistically valid comparisons with other dissimilar groups.

Proportions, deviations, percentiles, or Z-scores can be calculated with any of the four basic kinds of data -- we can speak of a tract having 2.7 times the average number, proportion, density, or value per capita. Moreover, any basic number or complex transformation can also be compared across time (see page 140):

9) *trends* -- how many potentially suicidal drummers are in a given census tract, compared with the number (or density, percentile, deviation, etc) that were there at some other specified time? Moreover, trends can be expressed as deviations, percentiles, etc.

Translating from one data category to another is often a matter of simple division or multiplication. For example, a drummers' "union" might list the total number of drummers in each tract, while a survey might show how many drummers are unemployed. Dividing the survey number by the total on the list would give the percentage of unemployed drummers in the tract. Dividing that figure by the average unemployment percentage will give a deviation: drummer unemployment expressed in terms of how it compares with total unemployment. Written out in declarative sentences, this might seem rather elementary, but it is very easy for someone looking at a map to forget which term goes in the denominator and which one in the numerator of the division. If we are not sure about the basis for a given mapped value, can we expect to get the right meaning from the map as a whole?

Light at the end of the tunnel?

Nearly all of the maps you are likely to encounter will fit into one of the categories described above. In some specialized reports, you may run across maps with more complex data transformations: principal components, factor loadings, moving averages, minimax values, etc. It is impossible for one person to know all of the ways people can transform data, but a good map reader should at least be able to recognize an unfamiliar transformation and to exercise due caution in interpreting the resulting map. And a good map maker should clearly indicate what transformations have been used on a given map; if it is not clear, you might legitimately mistrust the rest of the map!

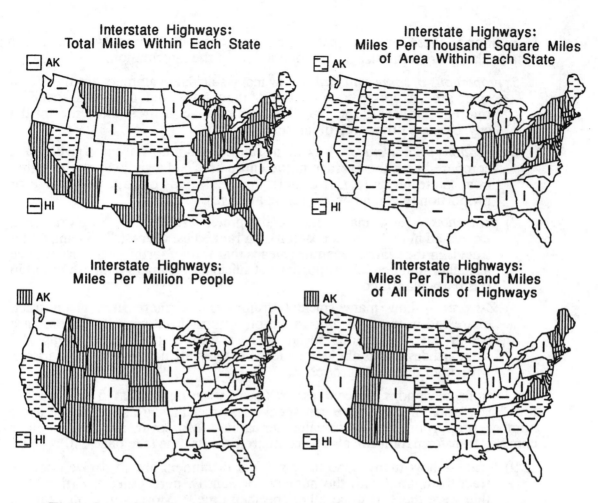

Interstate Highways:
Total Miles Within Each State

Interstate Highways:
Miles Per Thousand Square Miles
of Area Within Each State

Interstate Highways:
Miles Per Million People

Interstate Highways:
Miles Per Thousand Miles
of All Kinds of Highways

These four maps show the spatial patterns that occur when a single kind of data is transformed in several different ways. The phenomena (the Interstate highways of the United States) are *nominal discrete areas* (a given area is either road or not-road) at the scale of a human being. Drawing the routes of these roads on a national map has already transformed these long and thin areas into *nominal line data*. A cartographer then measured the total length of Interstate highways within each state and displayed those lengths on the map in the upper left corner of this page. The measurement is a *ratio number*, but the symbol is *ordinal choropleth* -- the map-maker first arranged the states in rank order from most to least highway mileage and then divided them into four equal groups. Parallel vertical lines show the top one-fourth of the states, a single vertical line marks those in the next quarter, a single horizontal line the third quarter, and horizontal dashes indicate the lowest one-fourth of the states.

The other maps use the same symbolic vocabulary to show how the same basic data (length of Interstate highways in each state) looks when the numbers are combined with other variables in order to make a specific point. A planner from a large Western state might cite the top right map in arguing for more highway funds to pay for roads across the mountains and desert. Someone from California or a densely populated Eastern state might point out that roads are used by people, not empty space, and therefore the funds should go to the states with relatively few miles of road per million people. Finally, a Midwestern politician might display the lower right-hand map as evidence that farm states have been discriminated against because they had already built themselves good roads, and therefore they did not get their fair share of the tax dollars for the Interstate system.

PART 5
SEARCHING FOR MEANING ON MAPS

Communication, as stated in the introduction to this book, is the multi-step process of transmitting some kind of message from one individual to another. The "message" or "meaning" of a thematic map is the spatial pattern that it depicts. For a map reader, that message is nothing more (and nothing less) than everything that can be learned by noting how much it resembles the patterns of other features that may be related in some way.

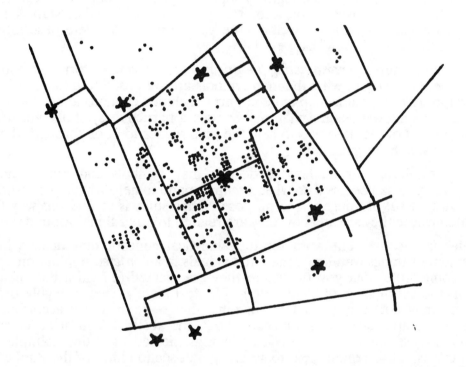

For example, this map is a simplified copy of one made by a doctor named Snow, who was searching for the causes of a London cholera epidemic. The dots represent deaths due to the disease in 1855; the stars mark the locations of public water pumps in a part of the city where indoor plumbing was almost nonexistent. A simple visual comparison of the patterns of dots and stars was enough to convince the doctor that the disease was somehow related to the water from the Broad Street Pump in the middle of the map.

CAUTION: once we see that two map patterns are similar, we still have with the problem of deciding what is cause and what is effect. Maps of crime, for example, show high murder rates in precisely those states that have strict capital punishment laws. Did people pass tough laws in response to a high rate of homicides? Or are the laws responsible for a climate of disrespect for life that leads to murders? Or, perhaps, both patterns are consequences of some as yet unknown cause (or they have no relationship except pure coincidence). Maps cannot answer those questions, but they can shed light on a related issue -- the similarity of the maps does make it hard to believe that capital punishment does a good job of deterring murder.

The purpose of this last part of the book is to explain some of the conventional ways of analyzing map patterns in a "scientific" way (i.e. an analysis that is capable of being duplicated by another person who looks at the same maps and uses the same methods). Once you have described a map pattern in an objective way, however, this book has done its job -- you are on your own in trying to explain the pattern. The ability to form or read a grammatically correct "sentence" in the language of maps is no guarantee that the sentence will communicate an idea worth knowing!

STEPS IN THE PROCESS OF MAP INTERPRETATION

The diagram on page 3 implied that the process of interpreting a map actually involves a number of related but logically separate steps. According to this model, the first phase is the visual process of *seeing the symbols*. This step is not as straightforward as it seems -- just ask three people for a complete description of some event that they all "saw" happen.

The second step is *reconstructing the original data*, trying to form a reasonably accurate mental image of what the map symbols are supposed to depict. Many of the descriptions of thematic map types in Part 4 included cautions about the ways in which data are altered when a map maker uses a particular symbolic vocabulary. The whole point of that Part was to help the map reader to "look through" the map symbols and see the original data.

Once you have learned how to decode map symbols and reconstruct the original data, you can begin to do what a map is made to help you do -- to study the *spatial arrangement* of things. The purpose of this study is to find out why things are located where they are and how they are related to other things around them.

Order is a convenient word for the analytical concept that deals with the arrangement of things within an area. Individuals in an *ordered* population appear to obey some "rule" that governs where they are located (e.g. in a line, near the shore, on the south sides of roads, etc.). Unfortunately, even a highly ordered population may not seem so, if the individual things are arranged according to a rule that the map reader does not see. Thus, the abstract idea of order cannot make much sense unless the rule is clearly communicated, as in this example: "The railroad tracks in this region seem to go along half-section lines of the Public Land Survey." The search for order, then, must begin with a systematic comparison of a map pattern with the patterns of other features on other maps, whether printed on paper, displayed on a computer screen, or stored in the memory of the map reader. The first step in that process, in turn, is a careful description of the spatial pattern on the map.

In the first five sections of this Part, we will look at a number of techniques for analyzing map patterns. It should come as no surprise that most of these analytical tools are related to the fundamental spatial ideas presented in Part 1. For that reason, we classify the tools into groups that focus on the analysis of location, distance, and direction, as they apply to mapped points, lines, and areas.

The next four sections will introduce several ways of comparing the patterns on different maps. This is followed by two sections on the connections and interactions among places on a map. The final section is a review of the ways in which the message of a map can be distorted -- the sources of "noise" that can obscure the "signal" a map is supposed to send. That section is extremely important, but it is also deceptively short, because it is really a capsule summary of the rest of the book.

GUT REACTIONS AND COOKBOOK ANALYSIS

The analytical techniques that are featured in this Part of the book can be presented and used on many different levels. Since this is an introductory book, we will not try to show how a given technique was derived, nor do we carry the measurements and calculations out to the level of statistical reliability that a professional journal would require. At the same time, it does not seem desirable to mask some of the complexities of the real world by using only simple techniques in map analysis. We have tried to seek a balance between these two extremes, but it is easy to fall off both sides of the bicycle: to miss important information by not being willing to apply some of the more sophisticated methods, and to let delight in the application of methods get in the way of actually seeing the map.

For these reasons, our treatment of a given map-analysis technique has four basic parts: a brief description of the purpose of a particular technique, a "cookbook" method of applying the technique, a few diagrams that show the typical patterns associated with different results, and a discussion of some advantages and limitations of the technique. These four topics have unequal length and emphasis for different techniques, partly because the techniques vary in their obviousness (and partly because the idea of a cookbook can also be carried too far, to the point of utter boredom from writer and reader alike).

The basic point of this introduction is that it is possible to use a given method of map analysis in several ways: *intuitively*, without consciously knowing we are applying a well-known method; *mechanically*, by following the cookbook rules; *visually*, by comparing a map pattern with the result diagrams; and *logically*, by thinking through the steps and making reasonable assumptions about the results. You might start by looking at the sample map below and writing down a few words or phrases that summarize the different ideas you see in it. Then, as you read through the next dozen pages, look back and see what else you could say about the pattern on this map.

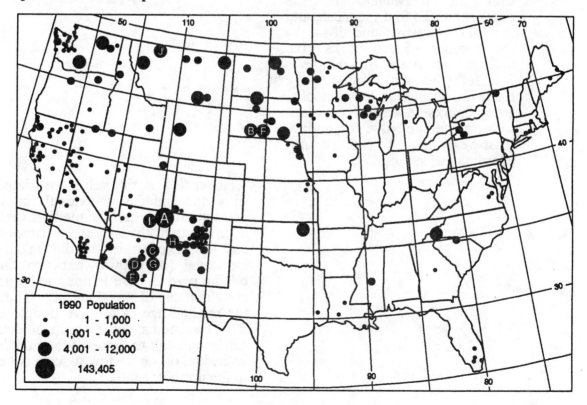

LOCATIONAL PATTERNS ON A MAP

Telling another person about a map is easier if you have the ability to make a brief but accurate description of the spatial arrangement of features on it. Trying to describe a locational pattern, however, is usually more difficult than talking about the location of one object. Adding objects to a map can multiply all of the circularities, ambiguities, and arbitrary aspects of the spatial language that was described in Part 1. Over the years, people have developed a number of conventional ways to analyze locational patterns and describe them to others. These are a big help, but all are not yet perfect; for example, the word "center" can mean several different things, and in fact there are four different ways of describing the "center" of a spatial pattern. For that reason, we'll begin with a loud

CAUTION: After using any method described in this section, take one more look at the map to see if the results make sense -- it is possible, intentionally or accidentally, to manipulate any analytical tool so that it says just about anything .)

With that in mind, let us look at **central tendency**, which is the major analytical idea based on location. The center is the spatial equivalent of three related (and often confused) mathematical ideas -- *mean*, *median*, and *mode*. In popular usage, the "average individual" in a group is roughly in the middle according to some measure of interest (e.g. age, height, annual income, musical ability, or speed in the 100-yard dash). Likewise, the center of a map pattern is the location that is in the middle of the pattern. Unfortunately, popular usage of the term "middle" tends to be quite vague, both mathematically and spatially. Depending on the context and the speaker, "middle" can imply at least four different ideas (which we will illustrate both mathematically, by looking at a group of five people with ages of 10, 10, 20, 40, and 80, and spatially, by looking at a simple dot map):

1) The *mean* is the mathematical average of the values associated with all individuals in the population. To find the mean, add the values together and divide by the number of individuals (the average age of the five people is 32: 160 (the sum) divided by 5). Likewise, the mean location of a group of dots on a map is the place with an average value for both X (east-west) and Y (north-south) coordinates (see page 7).

2) The *median* is the value associated with the middle individual in a population. To find the median, rank all of the individuals by some criterion and use the value of the middle individual (or midway between the middle pair, if there happen to be an even number of individuals). Thus, the median age of the five people is 20. The median of a group of dots can be difficult to figure, if the middle individual on an east-west scale is far to the north or south.

3) The *mode* is the most abundant value in the population. The modal age in the five-person group is 10. If the interests of the people do not overlap, a TV show aimed at 10-year olds would have the widest market. To find the mode of a population, make a *histogram*, a graph that shows how many individuals are associated with each range of values. The modal location on a dot map is the biggest clump of dots.

4) The *midpoint* is exactly halfway between the extreme values. To figure the midpoint, calculate the average of the lowest and highest value in a population. The midpoint age of the five people is 45, halfway between 10 and 80. Two measurements with a ruler can locate the midpoint of the group of locations. Or, find the average latitude of the places with the highest and lowest latitudes, and then do the same for longitude.

In spatial terms, the *mean center* is the point on which the population would exactly balance. This kind of information is useful to answer questions like "is the center of population in the United States moving westward faster now than during the 1800s?" The movement of a single individual can shift the mean center of a population, and therefore the mean center is a sensitive indicator of change through time.

The *midpoint*, by contrast, is a rather stable center -- only those individuals who are right at the edges of the pattern have any effect on the location of the midpoint. Individuals can move within the pattern without altering the midpoint. The idea of midpoint is useful in answering questions like "is this TV tower close to the middle of the population it is trying to serve?"

The *median location* tells us more about individual positions than the midpoint does, but the median does not over-react to the locations of a few extreme individuals. One hint of its usefulness is the fact that it is also called the *point of minimum total travel*, the place that can be reached from every other location in the pattern at the lowest total cost (assuming that the road network is complete enough to make transportation easy in all directions -- see pages 170-171). The idea of median is therefore important for someone who is trying to find a good site for a restaurant, shopping center, hospital, sports stadium, or other service.

Finally, you are most likely to encounter the idea of *mode* in New York City, although people there may not use the term. This city has the largest urban population on the continent, and some of the writers for the *New York Times* and the *New Yorker* seem to imply that Manhattan is the center of the universe, despite its obviously non-middle position by any other measure of central tendency. If current trends continue, however, the migration of one individual about forty years from now may shift the modal center of the United States to Los Angeles, all the way across the country in one day.

DISTANCE PATTERNS ON A MAP

The spatial patterns on two separate maps can be "centered" on the same place (see 148-149) and yet the arrangements of features can be very different. For example, the patterns of water wells and cholera deaths (page 145) have nearly the same center, but most of the dots are crowded much closer to the center than the stars are. The differences in spatial patterns are the result of differences in the *locations* of individual mapped features. However, describing a spatial pattern is usually faster and easier if we use the other basic spatial concepts, *distance* and *direction*, as key elements in our analysis. Of course, this means that the language of "high-level" pattern analysis will have some of the same logical "circularity" that occupied so much of our attention back on pages 5-20. The solution to the problem of logical circularity is still the same -- we just agree to use an arbitrary but generally useful term as a *convention*, a standard part of the language.

There are two conventional ways of using the idea of distance to help us describe a spatial pattern:

A) **Density** is the idea of spacing, crowding, or emptiness. Mathematically, it is the average number of things that occur in a specified area. Density is not related to the shape of the area, nor does it say anything about the arrangement of things within the area. For example, San Bernardino County, in sunny southern California, has an average population density of about 60 people per square mile (there are about a million people living on about 18,000 square miles of territory). However, most of those people live in an urban area that covers only a small corner of the map, while nearly all of the rest of the county is essentially uninhabited desert.

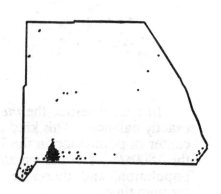

A map-maker could overcome this limitation by subdividing all large areas into smaller ones and figuring the density for each sub-area. Unfortunately, the data needed to do this are not always available. Despite this limitation, the concept of density has much value in comparing one area with another. In many situations, the density of something can communicate a message that would be hidden if all we have is information about absolute quantities.

For example, suppose someone told you about two urban areas, each with 20 abandoned buildings that appear to have been deliberately set on fire. Knowing these absolute quantities is not enough to allow us to speculate intelligently about whether arson is a problem for either part of the city. Adding the idea of density (bruned buildings per square mile) will help to put the total amount in perspective. If one part of the city had 10 burned buildings per square mile, and the other had an "arson density" of only one per square mile, we could be reasonably safe in assuming that a visitor to the second part of town probably would not see arson as a significant problem (more important, a banker look at that part of the town would be less reluctant to lend money to rebuild a burned building).

In general, it is safer to compare densities on a map with relatively small area units -- San Bernardino County is an analytical problem on some state or national maps precisely because it is one of the largest counties in the nation, and therefore it can have a lot of unevenness inside it.

A mapmaker can express the idea of density directly, by using the vocabulary of a choropleth or isoline map to show the number of something per unit of area in different places (see pages 126 and 136). A dot map, by contrast, is an indirect expression of density -- it just shows the general pattern and leaves the calculation of density up to the map reader. To describe the density of things in part of a dot or pictorial symbol map:

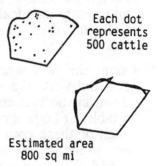

Each dot represents 500 cattle

Estimated area 800 sq mi

12,000/800

15 cattle per square mile

1) count (or estimate) the number of dots or symbols on the map.

2) figure out how many real-world individuals are represented by that number. Call that N.

3) review pages 19-24 on scale and area (if necessary) and figure out the size of the area (A).

4) divide N by A.

5) do whatever may be necessary to express the result in terms that are easy to comprehend.

B) **Cluster** analysis is a more refined analytical technique than density analysis. It provides a specific vocabulary for describing the spatial arrangements of things. In this language, a *dispersed* population is one that is scattered throughout its area. Individuals in a *clustered* population, on the other hand, tend to occur close to other individuals, although the groups (or clusters) may be separated by a lot of empty space. This pair of maps illustrates the two extremes with a historical example, as German immigrants moved to the Kansas frontier and changed from clustered villagers into dispersed farmers in one generation.

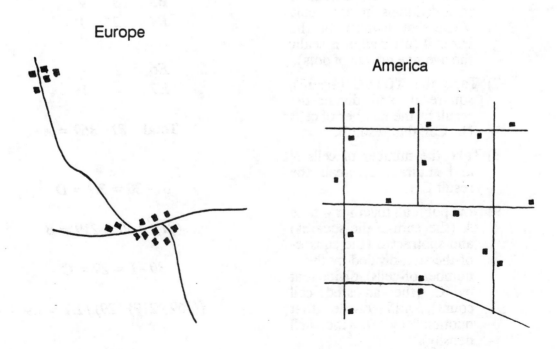

Europe

America

The *variance-mean ratio* is a measure of the degree of clustering of a map population. To calculate it for a dot map, follow these steps:

1) Divide the map area into about 30 sub-areas (called *cells* or *quadrats*). The cells should be similar in shape and nearly identical in size. Call the total number of cells N.

2) Count the dots within each cell and write the numbers down in the first column of a table. (To programmers: each of these counts might be elements of an array called **X** in a computer program to do the analysis (e.g., **X**(1), **X**(2), ... **X**(N)))

3) Add all the **X**'s together and call that sum the **TOTAL**.

4) Square each **X** and write the result down in another column on the table.

5) Add all of the squared numbers together and call that sum **A**.

6) Divide the **TOTAL** by the number of cells **N**. The result is the average number of individuals in each cell. Write that number by the letter **D** (after all, it is really the average *density* of dots).

7) Take the **TOTAL** (again!), square it, and divide the result by the number of cells **N**. Call that result **B**.

8) Take the number of cells **N** and subtract 1; call the result **C**.

9) Now put it all together -- take **A** (the sum-of-the-squares) and subtract **B** (the square-of-the-sum-divided-by-the-number-of-cells), divide that by **C** (the adjusted cell count), and divide that quotient by **D** (the cell density).

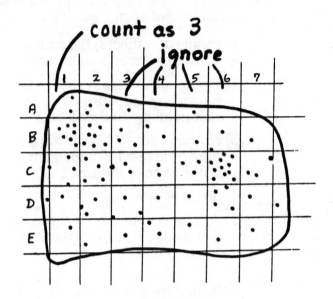

Cell	X	X^2
A1	3	9
A2	4	16
B1	7	49
B2	7	49
B3	3	9
B4	2	4
...		
E6	1	1
E7	1	1
Total	*81*	*369 = A*

$$81 / 30 = 2.7 = D$$

$$(81)^2 / 30 = 219 = B$$

$$30 - 1 = 29 = C$$

$$((369 - 219) / 29) / 2.7 = 1.9$$

The result of all these computations is called the *variance-mean ratio,* and it can be used to compare the clustering of one pattern with that of another. In general, the variance-mean ratio will be:

- near zero if the features of interest are *dispersed* evenly throughout a mapped area, as in the case of fire stations or schools in a metropolitan area. Many service industries tend to have dispersed patterns, because individual firms are often less profitable when located near potential competitors. For that reason, finding a dispersed pattern should make a map reader wonder about the possibility of competition or some other *push factor* among individuals.

- exactly one if the map pattern is *random* (a frequently misused word, which really means neither dispersed nor clustered). In general, a random pattern is the *null hypothesis* in many studies; we assume random spacing until proven otherwise.

- substantially more than one if the map features are *clustered,* as in the case of bait shops near the public access to a lake, fast-food restaurants near freeway intersections, or lawyers' offices near the courthouse. Clustered patterns almost always provoke questions about the *pull factors* that might be causing things to occur together.

Clustering can also be figured by measuring the average distance from each object to its nearest neighbor. *Nearest-neighbor analysis* is a tedious task when done by hand (in other words, you don't have to do it in this class), but computers are more than willing to take the UTM coordinates of a zillion objects and do the boring calculations all night long. When spacing is random (neither clustered nor evenly dispersed), the *expected average distance* between objects is equal to 0.5 divided by the square root of their density (another formula that computers can handle easily). An average distance that is less than random indicates clustering. Dispersed patterns, by contrast, have average distances that range up to double that of random patterns.

Unfortunately, nearest-neighbor analysis can produce spectacularly misleading results if individuals are arranged in pairs or trios, or if there is a gradual increase in density across the map. In those cases, one might repeat the test with the second and third nearest neighbors as well as the closest one. Even so, the results can still be weird for a particular arrangement of objects. We have said it before, but it is too important to take lightly -- it is possible, intentionally or accidentally, to manipulate any analytical tool to say just about anything about anything, including a pattern of dots on a map. The problem gets worse if the original data for a map are *continuous,* rather than *discrete* objects (see pages 102-103), and especially if they are *autocorrelated* (a condition in which both areas tend to be near other areas of similar value). On the other hand, autocorrelation (clear assocations of high and low values) is precisely what we often hope to find on a map, and it tends to be visually obvious even if the statistical tests are sometimes ambiguous.

DIRECTIONAL PATTERNS ON A MAP

As in the case of *locational* and *distance patterns*, there is a conventional language for describing *directional* patterns on a map. It has two major parts, one dealing with the directional *bias* of the pattern as a whole and the other related to the directional *alignment* of the individuals in the pattern:

A) **Bias** is a measure of the comparative number of things on each side of a line drawn through an area. A *balanced* map pattern has about the same number of individuals in any half of the area; a *biased* pattern has more individuals on the left, top, southeast, or some other easily-described part of the area. For example, the distribution of African-American people in Charlotte, North Carolina, is clearly biased toward the northwest; the map pattern of shopping centers, on the other hand, has a southeastward bias. To get a precise phrase for communicating the areal balance of the population shown on a dot map:

1) Draw a line that goes through the center of the area.

2) Count the dots on each side of the line.

3) Divide the larger of those two numbers by the total number of dots on the whole map.

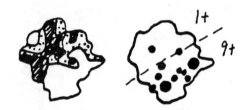

4) Multiply the quotient by 100. That product is a percentage index of left-right imbalance.

source:
J Clay

5) Try other lines with different angles and compare results. Your goal is to find the line angle that shows the most imbalance (highest percent of dots on one side of the line).

6) Describe that line in a way that is accurate and easy to communicate (e.g. 74% of the African-Americans in Charlotte live north of a line that cuts the city in half and is oriented 70 degrees to the right of true north)).

A more sophisticated version of the idea of balance would allow changes in the *absolute location* as well as the *directional orientation* of the line. The location of the line could be expressed in any of the dialects described in the first part of this book. For example, a police dispatch officer might use landmarks as reference points: "nearly all of the burglaries in the last three weeks were west of Decker Street." A group of foresters might choose to base their bias-description system on UTM coordinates or the Public Land Survey grid. This choice would yield statements like "63% of the harvestable trees in that township are northeast of a line that goes from the middle of Section 23 to the southwest corner of Section 5." Obviously, a simplified description of a spatial pattern almost always loses some of the detailed information on a map. This is yet another illustration of the inevitable tradeoff between efficiency and accuracy in communicating a complex idea.

B) **Alignment** is a measure of directional trends in a spatial pattern. Individuals in an *aligned* (or *oriented*) pattern tend to have neighbors that are much closer to them in one direction than in others. This map shows a suburb of Chicago in which the pattern of houses has an obvious north-south alignment, which is clearly related to the strong north-south pattern of streets and service alleys.

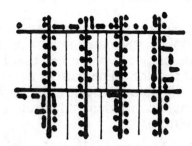

To get a general quantitative measure of the degree of orientation of symbols on a point-symbol or dot map:

N   NE   E   SE   S   SW ...

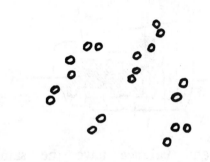

N	NE	E	SE	S	SW
I	II	I			II

N	NE	E	SE
S	SW	W	NW
3	11	4	2

1) Make a table with columns labeled for each cardinal direction (N, NE, E, etc., or, for more precision, use angle in degrees, e.g. 30, 60, 90, etc. or 20, 40, 60, 80, etc.).

2) Look at each symbol on the map (or take a sample of each fifth, tenth, or fiftieth one, if you are looking at a map with a lot of dots on it).

3) Measure the direction to the symbol that is nearest to the one you are examining.

4) Make a mark for that symbol in the appropriate column of the table.

5) Continue until you have tabulated the direction to the closest neighbor for each symbol in your sample.

6) Count the number of marks for each opposing pair of directions (e.g. NE/SW or 30/210). In most cases, the pair of directions with the most marks is the general orientation of the pattern (but always remember the caution and <u>look at the map</u> to see if the conclusion makes sense).

7) Take the number of marks that are within a specified angle (say 45 degrees) of that directional pair and divide it by the total number of marks; the result is a measure of the *significance* of the pattern orientation (on a 0-1 scale).

8) Express the result in a convenient way: "55% of the sinkholes appear to have a NE-SW orientation."

LINE PATTERNS ON A MAP

Line patterns on maps can be analyzed with modified versions of some of the same tools that we used in looking at point patterns. The purpose is the same -- to try to describe the pattern so that it can be compared with other kinds of patterns. A good test for a line pattern description is whether someone who can not see the map is still able to visualize the important facts about the pattern of lines on it. To make more convenient, it helps to use the same vocabulary as we used in describing point patterns:

A) Measuring **line density** on a map involves the same two actions as figuring point density: first define and measure an area on the map, then measure the length of all lines of interest within that area. For example, a traffic planner might define an area of 1000 square miles around a city and then measure the total miles of Interstate highways and other limited-access roads in that area. That information can tell us plenty about a city, both good and bad: a city with more freeway miles will probably have easier commuting, a more even pattern of land value, fewer large slums, more disrupted neighborhoods, more noise problems, and less success in getting mass transit systems built. Density measurements also work with other line patterns, such as stream systems; for example, one could calculate the density of the stream patterns described on pages 71-73.

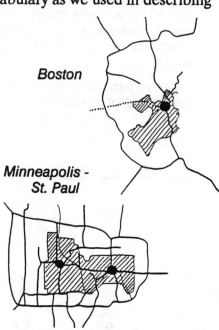

Boston

Minneapolis - St. Paul

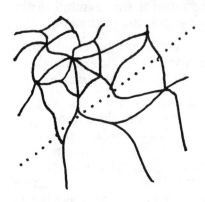

B) **Bias** and **balance** have the same meaning in a line pattern as with a point pattern: if more of the lines in an area are in one part of the area, the pattern has an obvious spatial imbalance. As in the case of point patterns, one good way to demonstrate imbalance is to cut the area in half, figure the line density in each half, and express the result as a ratio: "seven-tenths of the road mileage is in the northwestern half of the state." For even more precision, subdivide the whole area into a number of smaller areas, figure the line density in each subarea, and then make a map of the pattern of density.

C) Evaluating the directional **alignment** of a line pattern also uses the same technique as with a point pattern. The basic idea is to sample a reasonable number of line segments and see what direction they trend. Record the information on a table like the one on page 154, and express the results with a phrase such as "more than three quarters of the state highway miles in the ridge-and-valley area of Tennessee trend in a northeast-southwest direction."

D) Lines have length as well as position, and that fact makes it possible to analyze a line pattern in some ways that are not shared with point patterns. For example, one can put lines into categories according to several different criteria:

long as opposed to short

straight as opposed to curved

simple as opposed to overlapping

separate as opposed to crossing

E) Even with lines that are of similar length and shape, map analysts have found it useful to distinguish several ways in which lines can be arranged in space.

1) A **random** pattern occurs when there is no external force to impose order on the pattern of lines; random patterns are surprisingly rare in nature, and even more so in lines made by human activity, but the concept of randomness is useful as a benchmark against which to judge the degree of order.

2) Lines are **collinear** if one line begins where another ends and then continues in the same direction, like a dashed line to mark a state border. Collinear lines are rare in nature, which is why they are so useful on maps; they communicate a message about a whole line rather than individual parts.

3) Lines are arranged **en echelon** when they respond to forces that are not quite symmetrical. An example is a family of earthquake faults, where rocks slip as a result of directly opposing forces within the earth, but the line of the fault also must accommodate the curvature of the earth surface.

4) A **parallel** or **subparallel** pattern occurs when some kind of force pushes all lines in the same direction. Examples include lanes on a freeway, rows in an orchard, streams on a long slope, gouges made by a swarm of meteors, or routes taken by individual units in an advancing army.

5) **Radial** or **centripetal** patterns occur when forces act toward or away from a point in the center of the pattern. An **annular** or **concentric** pattern may be the result of similar forces, but the lines are oriented at right angles to the lines of force.

6) Finally, line patterns can fall into a number of categories that depend on the connections and overlap among various lines. You have already encountered a number of these terms, such as *braided, dendritic, grid,* or *weave*; in each case, the differences from a random pattern can provide clues about the forces that shaped the pattern.

F) Finally, line patterns can be analyzed in terms of their **connectivity**, the degree to which lines on a map are separate or connected into a system. This usually is done in order to see how well the line patterns are able to serve areas or connect points; this is a more sophisticated kind of analysis, which we will discuss in greater detail on pages 168-171.

AREA PATTERNS ON A MAP

The concepts of density, directional bias, and orientation are also valid for the analysis of area (two-dimensional) patterns, and the methods are similar:

A) Measuring area **density** on a map has the same two parts as figuring point or line density: first define and measure a study area on the map, then count the number of mapped areas within that study area. For example, a soil map of a 300-acre field might show fifteen subareas, classified into six different mapping units. If these had different fertilizer requirements, the farmer would need six different mixes and have to allow for fifteen different application areas. Likewise, a wildlife biologist might be curious about *habitat density*, the number of ecologically different areas within a specified larger area. A simple ecosystem, such as a pine plantation on a sand plain, would have a low habitat density; by contrast, a fairly accurate habitat map of a complex mixture of swamps and hills would have a large number of areas (a high density).

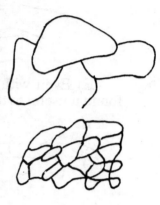

B) **Bias** and **balance** have the same meaning in an area pattern as with a point or line pattern: if more of the subareas in an area are in one part of the map, the pattern has an obvious spatial imbalance. The demonstration of area imbalance is also the same: subdivide the large area into smaller areas, figure the area density in each subarea, and then describe (or make a map of) the pattern of density.

C) Evaluating the directional **alignment** of an area pattern also uses the same techniques as with point and line patterns. Sample a reasonable number of areas and see whether they tend to be elongated in a given direction or closer to other areas in that direction. Record the information on a table like the one on page 154, and express the results with similar phrases (e.g. "more than nine-tenths of the swamps on the Carolina Coastal Plain are longer in a northwest-southeast direction than in any other cardinal direction.")

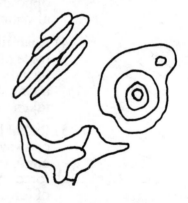

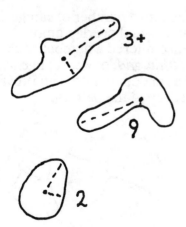

D) The two-dimensional nature of area patterns also allows us to analyze them in terms of their *compactness* or *complexity*. These ideas are easy to see visually, but the mathematical description of compactness is not always easy. A simple index might involve figuring the ratio between the longest and shortest radius from the center of the area (see pages 148-9 and 170 for a discussion of various meanings of the word "center"). Using more radii can produce a more refined index of compactness. This concept is not entirely academic -- a compact country is usually easier to govern than one with an irregular outline and complex shape.

E) Like lines, areas can overlap, and the analysis of areal overlap is one of the most important ways of using maps to solve real-world problems. For example, one might combine bounded-area maps of three kinds of information -- slope, vegetation, and soil -- to help choose a site for solid-waste disposal. The first step is to decide which traits on each map would pose problems for the waste site. Then, recode each map into a *binary* map of land suitablity (one with two categories: suitable and unsuitable; see page 125). Finally, combine those maps into a composite map by marking an area as unsuitable if it has any one of the critical traits: sandy or rocky soil, swamp vegetation, mature forest, or steep slope.

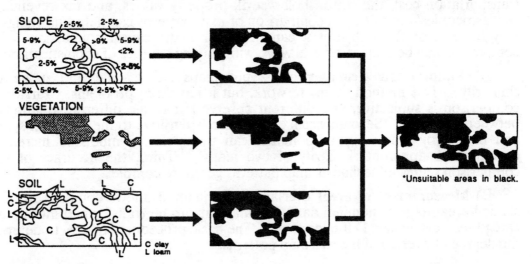

*Unsuitable areas in black.

This technique is called "overlaying" or "windowing," because it is like laying a set of partially painted windows on top of each other and seeing which parts of the stack you can still see through. A more elaborate method starts by devising a suitability index for each category on each input map. For example, the map maker might give a swamp or housing subdivision a value of 1 (least suitable for a waste site), dense forest 2, crops and pasture 3, and idle land 4 (most suitable). The next step is to add the numbers from each map and make a single map that shows the sum of all the input variables. Finally, one might set a threshold value of suitability (say 10 out of 12 for a sum map made from three maps with a maximum value of 4 on each map). This procedure is especially easy to do with computer pixel maps, because the area units on each input map are identical (see page 133). Faced with a neat computer printout, many people forget the weak links in the logical system: selecting input maps and assigning values to the variables on them.

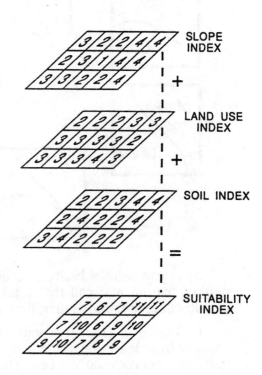

COMPARISON OF MAP PATTERNS

A major reason to use the language of maps is to compare the spatial patterns of features to see if they might be related. The relationship may be a simple cause-and-effect -- the map patterns of cornfields and hog feedlots are similar because hogs eat most of the corn grown in this country. More often, the connection is indirect, with both features linked to many others via a complex web of causes and effects. For example, the maps of inventions and welfare payments in various states are similar, but explanation of the patterns might involve Civil War damage, transportation cost, the cotton boll weevil, property values, and tax revenues, as well as peoples' attitudes. A comparison of map patterns can help find things that may be part of the web, but it cannot establish the causal connection. Map comparison can be done in several ways, with varying degrees of sophistication:

A) **Simple visual comparison** -- put maps side-by-side and judge their similarity. This method seems to work, but it has three problems. First, visual comparison is subjective, and different observers may see different relationships between two maps. Second, visual comparison is sensitive to the choice of symbols and map projections -- a map maker can manipulate symbols to increase or decrease the apparent similarity of two maps. Third, the accuracy of visual comparison seems to decline as map patterns get more complex.

B) **Measurement of areal overlap** -- this method allows comparison of two shaded-area maps of nominal data (or data that can be transformed into nominal categories; review part D if necessary). The basic procedure is to try to determine the degree of overlap of the two map patterns:

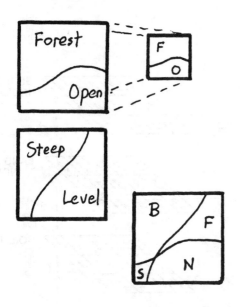

1) Redraw both map patterns on the same map base (in order to prevent problems that may arise as a result of differences in map scale or projection).

2) Use a planimeter or dot grid (pages 19-20) to measure the map areas that have <u>both</u> features (in this example, land that is both forested and steep). Call the total of these areas **B** (for both).

3) Measure the map areas covered by <u>one</u> of the features but not the other (e.g., forest land that is not steep). Add the areas and call the total **F** (for first).

4) Measure the areas covered by the <u>second</u> feature but not the first (in this case, steep but not forested land). Add them and call the total **S** (second).

5) If you want a built-in accuracy check, first measure the areas covered by <u>neither</u> feature and call that total **N**. Then, calculate the sum **B+F+S+N** -- it should equal the total area of the map.

6) Divide **B** (the area with both features) by the sum **B+F+S** (total area covered by at least one of the features) and multiply by 100. The result is called the *index of areal correspondence*. This index ranges from zero (for two map patterns that have nothing in common) to 100 (two spatial arrangements that coincide exactly with each other).

C) **Observed-minus-expected** -- This is a way to analyze the similarity of two maps of ordinal (ranked) data. The method will also work for some kinds of nominal data, especially if the maps have many categories. Finally, it can be used for interval or ratio data, if you are willing to give up some potentially valuable information by combining a range of values into a small number of groups. (Be warned, however: this process of combining data into categories is sure to look unfair to someone -- it's like putting all test scores from 60 to 100 into two letter grades, A and C, and expecting B-students not to notice.) The example compares a three-rank map (high/medium/low) with a two-rank one, and in this case there is little relationship between the two maps. The test has three steps:

1) Redraw both maps on the same base, as on the previous page.

2) Lay a dot grid over the map and count the number of dots that have each possible combination of traits (i.e. high on both maps, high on one and low on the other, etc.). Record those figures in a table or graph like this one.

2) Figure how much area "ought to" have each combination of traits if the two map patterns were not related at all. In this example, two-thirds of the total area (60 of 90 dots) has a high value on the first map. If the two map patterns were not related in any way, one might expect two-thirds of the area each category on the second map to have a high value on the first map. Two thirds of 42 is 28; two-thirds of 15 is 10; and so on. Record these estimates on the same kind of table or graph.

Observed value on first map

Observed value on second map		Hi	Lo	Total
	Hi	25	17	42
	Med	11	4	15
	Lo	24	9	33
	Total	60	30	90

Expected value on first map

Expected value on second map		Hi	Lo	Total
	Hi	28	14	42
	Med	10	5	15
	Lo	22	11	33
	Total	60	30	90

Map val 1st/2nd	Obs'd area	Exp'd area	Diff	Diff^2
Hi/Hi	25	28	-3	9
Hi/Med	11	10	1	1
Hi/Lo	24	22	2	4
Lo/Hi	17	14	3	9
Lo/Med	4	5	-1	1
Lo/Lo	9	11	-2	4
			TOTAL	28

3) Subtract the "observed" areas (the number of dots you counted in each category) from the "expected" areas (the number of dots that you would expect in each category if the patterns on the two maps are not related). Square each of those differences and add the results to get a total. If the total is large (many times the total number of dots), it is reasonable to conclude that the map patterns <u>are</u> related in some way. If it is small, you may conclude that the map patterns have little in common.

4) Consult a statistics book for the rules on doing a *chi-square* test if you want to determine the mathematical probability of getting a particular degree of relationship just by chance. This test is easy to use with data that have been arranged in columns of "observed" and "expected" quantities.

D) **Graphic correlation** -- This method is used to determine the degree of correspondence between the patterns on two interval or ratio maps; it will work with maps that use dots, graduated symbols, isolines, choropleth groups, or any other distinctly quantitative symbols. The procedure has five steps:

1) *Subdivide the maps.* Draw lines that divide the map into between 30 and 60 sub-areas that are about the same size in the real world. Then, put the same number of lines in the same places on the other map. *To maintain validity in the comparison, the lines on each map should be in <u>exactly</u> the same real-world locations.* For that reason, the sizes of sub-areas will be different on maps with different scales. The sub-areas may also have dissimilar shapes, if the maps were drawn with different projections. The important thing is to subdivide each map in an impartial way, so that the sub-areas on one map are directly comparable to those on the other. (Alternative procedure: if both maps are isoline or choropleth maps, put 30 to 60 dots in a regular or random pattern on one map, and then put the same number of dots in exactly the same real-world locations on the other map).

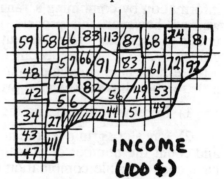

INCOME (100 $)

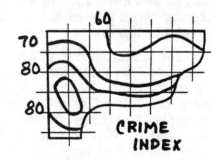

CRIME INDEX

2) *Tabulate the values.* Determine the mapped value for each sub-area on each map. On a dot map, count the dots in each sub-area. If a sub-area extends beyond the edge of the area (something that happens when a square grid is used to divide an irregular shape), you should adjust the count for that sub-area by estimating what it would be if the cell were full-size. You may choose to ignore sub-areas that are less than half the size of a full cell. On a choropleth or isoline map, determine the value in the center of each sub-area (or under each dot in your grid, if you used the alternative procedure). Record your data in a systematic way, so that the values for the same area on each map are easy to compare.

3) *Set up the graph axes.* Inspect your table of data in order to determine the largest and smallest value for each variable. Then, choose some convenient values to label the major lines of the graph. For example, suppose you first map showed average income per capita, with values ranging from $2,700 in the poorest sub-area to $11,300 in the richest one. In this case, the horizontal axis on the graph could represent "thousands of dollars" with divisions at 2, 4, 6, 8, 10, and 12, a set of six easy-to-remember round numbers (one for each vertical line) that extend from just below the smallest map value to just above the largest.

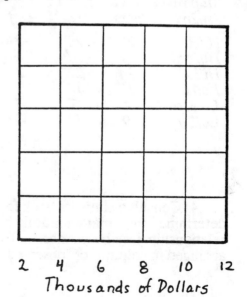

2   4   6   8   10   12
Thousands of Dollars

Now suppose that the second map in your comparison depicted crime rates, with a numerical index that ranged from 58 to 96 in different sub-areas of the map. In this case, the values of the horizontal lines (i.e. the vertical axis of the graph) might go in increments of 10 from 50 to 100 (50, 60, 70, 80, 90, and 100). Picking intervals in this way will ensure that the values for every sub-area on the maps will fit on the graph, and yet the graph can "spread" the sub-areas out for visual analysis. If we used a sequence from 0 to 100 for the axis on the crime graph, the dots would all be packed in one half of the graph, which would make it more difficult to see a relationship between the variables.

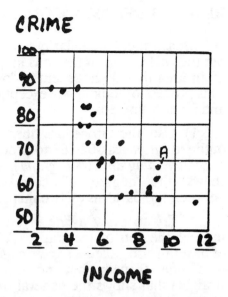

4) *Plot the values*. Put a dot on the graph to show the value of each sub-area on both maps. The A on the graph above represents a sub-area that has a mapped income of $9,200 and a crime rate of 63. When you have plotted all of the dots, count them to verify that you have graphed every sub-area on your data table.

5) *Interpret the graph*. The arrangement of the dots on the graph can give a good idea of the relationship between the two maps. A tight line of dots stretching upwards to the right indicates a strong *positive correlation* between the maps. A positive correlation means that a high value on one is associated with a high value on the other (as with corn and hogs, for example). A line sloping downward from left to right indicates a *negative correlation* -- high values on one map are associated with low values on the other (e.g., educational levels and unemployment rates). Loose bands of dots indicate weak relationships. Finally, a random scatter of dots all over the graph is evidence that there is no relationship between the maps.

Degree of Correlation

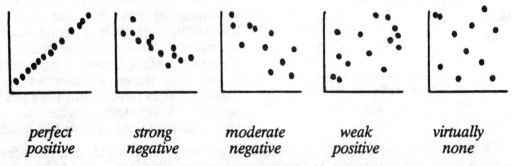

| *perfect positive* | *strong negative* | *moderate negative* | *weak positive* | *virtually none* |

CAUTION: A high correlation does not necessarily prove that the feature on one map is the *cause* of the feature on the other. To use a slightly ridiculous example to make a point that can be quite subtle, map comparison could "demonstrate" that the patterns of hospitals and deaths are positively correlated. Graphic correlation clearly shows that many people die in the city blocks that have hospitals in them, and few people die in blocks without hospitals. This being the case, is it fair to jump to the conclusion that hospitals *cause* people to die?

RESIDUALS FROM A MAP COMPARISON

Measuring the similarity between map patterns can be interesting all by itself, but the real payoff of rigorous map analysis often comes when we identify the parts of an area that do not seem to "obey" the apparent order that we have identified. This process of looking for exceptions to the rule is known as *mapping the residuals*, and it has four steps:

1) Use the procedure that was outlined on pages 162-163 to produce a *scatter diagram* (*dot graph*) that shows the degree of correlation between the patterns on two maps.

2) Try to draw a *line of best fit* through the dots on the graph. A line of best fit (also called a *regression line*) is a line (usually but not always straight) that shows the general trend of the dots and is positioned so that about half of the dots are above the line and half below it.

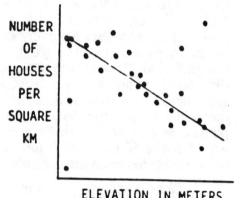

Statisticians have developed methods for positioning a regression line very accurately (and for substituting a mathematical curve for the straight line if the presumed relationship is complex). If you have access to a computer, these methods can work well. However, a high degree of mathematical sophistication is usually unnecessary if the map patterns of two phenomena are well correlated. And, it's fair to note that when a correlation is weak or non-existent, the residuals usually have little meaning anyway!

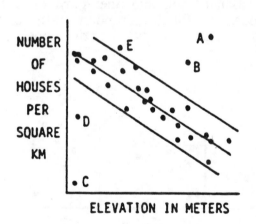

3) Draw two parallel lines a short distance on either side of your line of best fit. Dots that lie beyond those "fences" (i.e. far from the line) are *residuals from the regression* (usually called just *residuals*). They represent places where, for some reason, the "normal" relationship between what's shown on the maps does not occur. In this example, there is a strong negative correlation between house density and elevation. Most houses seem to be in valleys (or, stated another way, low-elevation sites have a lot of houses per square kilometer), whereas the mountaintops tend to have few houses.

Dot **A** on the graph obviously deviates from the general trend, and therefore it represents a place that might be worth investigating. Perhaps it is a hilltop resort that has more houses than you would expect at such a high elevation. Dot **B** is a less significant residual, one that is not as far from the "rule." Dot **C** could be an undrained valley swamp with fewer houses than expected at that level. Dot **D** is another negative residual; Dot **E** a barely significant positive one (where "significance" is defined in terms of the arbitrary lines we drew; there are statistical tests to determine significance).

4) *Map the residuals*. After identifying the residuals from a correlation of map patterns, it is often useful to make a map of them. Copy the original basemap and put choropleth symbols (see page 126) in those areas that have much more or less of one of the phenomena than expected. A residual map of this kind may tell you even more if you analyze its pattern. For example, you might see whether the residuals are *clustered* or have a noticeable *bias*. You can even make a map of the residuals you get by correlating a map of residuals with the map some factor that you think may be a cause or effect (and so on, until your computer runs out of electricity).

CAUTION: analyzing a map of residuals can be misleading if you are not careful to distinguish cause and effect -- dot **A** on the previous graph can be interpreted in two ways: as a hilltop with an unexpectedly large number of houses on it, _or_ as a group of houses with an oddly high elevation. The residuals graph tells you only that the area represented by dot **A** is "out of line;" you have to try to figure out what is unusual about it.

ANOTHER CAUTION: analysis of the residuals from a comparison of map patterns can give different results with different sizes of areas or different numbers of sample points. For example, a large area can include quite a range of densities of things within it (e.g. the San Bernardino County situation described on page 150). At the other extreme, tiny sample areas in an area of regularly spaced towns can have low densities, if they fall into gaps between towns, or high densities, due to the presence of clusters within them.

The only really safe way to avoid problems is to repeat the analysis using a large number of different sample areas or numbers. This, of course, usually means *work*; it is therefore worthwhile to cultivate a good "eye for reasonableness." In effect, you should learn to recognize inappropriate inferences from map evidence, just as a good lawyer is able to recognize what kinds of verbal or written testimony are credible and which ones should be dismissed as hearsay or the result of "badgering the witness."

RESIDUALS -- PRACTICE

On the next pages are a table of data, some blank maps, and a form for a correlation graph. This exercise will illustrate several different ways to approach the idea of residuals. Follow these steps:

1) The first column of data shows *population* (in millions). On the first map, shade the twelve states with the largest populations.

2) Draw a pattern of horizontal lines (like minus signs) through the twelve states with the fewest people.

3) The second column shows *industrial output* (in billions of dollars). On the second blank map, use the same symbols to distinguish the dozen states with the greatest and the dozen with the least industrial production.

4) Make a visual comparison of the map patterns of population and industrial production -- what relationship do you see?

5) The third column of data shows the amount of *industrial production per person*, calculated by dividing the industrial output of each state by the population of that state. Use the same *choropleth vocabulary* to put those data on the third map, which will have shading for the top twelve states and lines for the lowest dozen.

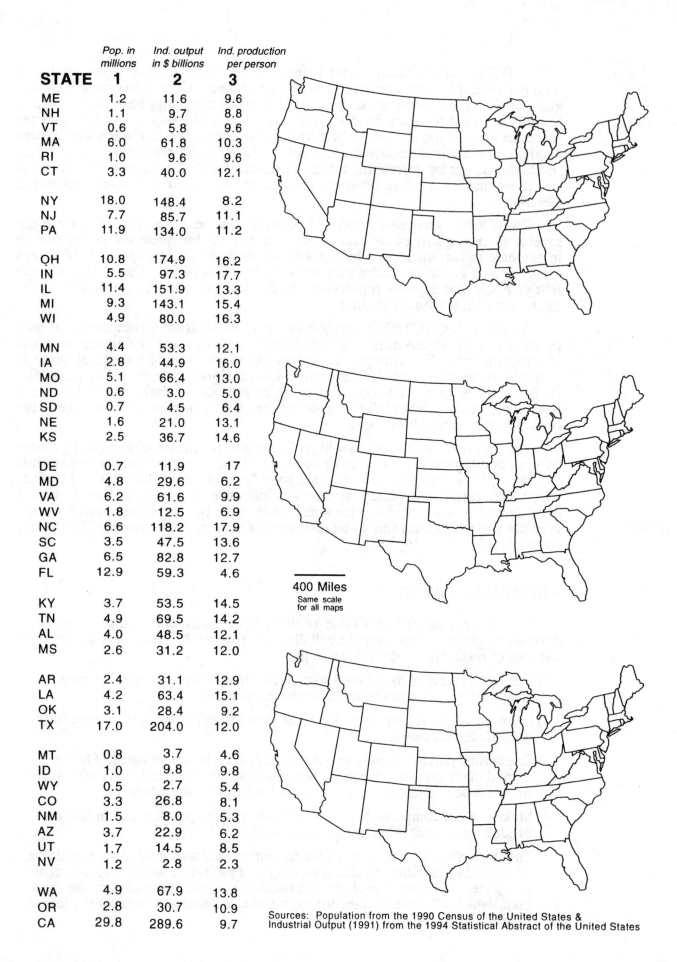

STATE	Pop. in millions 1	Ind. output in $ billions 2	Ind. production per person 3
ME	1.2	11.6	9.6
NH	1.1	9.7	8.8
VT	0.6	5.8	9.6
MA	6.0	61.8	10.3
RI	1.0	9.6	9.6
CT	3.3	40.0	12.1
NY	18.0	148.4	8.2
NJ	7.7	85.7	11.1
PA	11.9	134.0	11.2
OH	10.8	174.9	16.2
IN	5.5	97.3	17.7
IL	11.4	151.9	13.3
MI	9.3	143.1	15.4
WI	4.9	80.0	16.3
MN	4.4	53.3	12.1
IA	2.8	44.9	16.0
MO	5.1	66.4	13.0
ND	0.6	3.0	5.0
SD	0.7	4.5	6.4
NE	1.6	21.0	13.1
KS	2.5	36.7	14.6
DE	0.7	11.9	17
MD	4.8	29.6	6.2
VA	6.2	61.6	9.9
WV	1.8	12.5	6.9
NC	6.6	118.2	17.9
SC	3.5	47.5	13.6
GA	6.5	82.8	12.7
FL	12.9	59.3	4.6
KY	3.7	53.5	14.5
TN	4.9	69.5	14.2
AL	4.0	48.5	12.1
MS	2.6	31.2	12.0
AR	2.4	31.1	12.9
LA	4.2	63.4	15.1
OK	3.1	28.4	9.2
TX	17.0	204.0	12.0
MT	0.8	3.7	4.6
ID	1.0	9.8	9.8
WY	0.5	2.7	5.4
CO	3.3	26.8	8.1
NM	1.5	8.0	5.3
AZ	3.7	22.9	6.2
UT	1.7	14.5	8.5
NV	1.2	2.8	2.3
WA	4.9	67.9	13.8
OR	2.8	30.7	10.9
CA	29.8	289.6	9.7

400 Miles
Same scale
for all maps

Sources: Population from the 1990 Census of the United States &
Industrial Output (1991) from the 1994 Statistical Abstract of the United States

6) On the graph form below, make a dot graph (*scatter diagram*) of the correlation between population and industrial output (it will have 48 dots, one for each state).

7) Identify 9 to 12 *positive residuals* (states that are farthest above the line of best fit) and the same number of *negative residuals*

8) On the blank map, shade the positive residuals and put the horizontal line pattern through the negative residuals.

9) Compare this map with the map of output per capita.

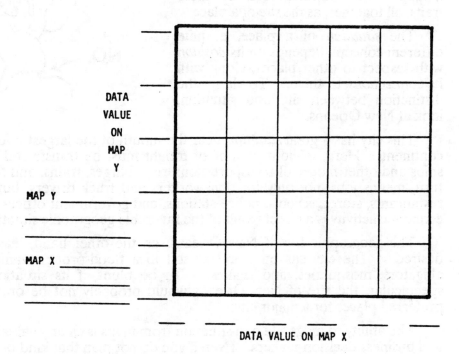

DATA VALUE ON MAP Y

MAP Y _____

_____

MAP X _____

_____

DATA VALUE ON MAP X

CONNECTIONS AMONG PLACES ON A MAP

The economic importance of a place depends on more than just the characteristics of the place itself (such as its elevation, climate, mineral resources, slope, soil fertility, industrial activity, the average family income or educational achievement of its inhabitants, and other things we can learn from thematic maps). Geographers refer to these traits, all together, as the *site* of a place.

The *situation* of a place, a quite different concept, depends on its *position* with respect to other places, along with its *connections* to them. To clarify the distinction between site and situation, look at New Orleans.

This city has a great *situation* near the mouth of the largest river system on the continent. Here, millions of tons of freight must be transferred between ocean ships and other modes of transportation: river barges, trains, and trucks. That, in turn, means jobs, not only for dockworkers and truck drivers, but also in hotels, restaurants, stores, schools, police stations, and government offices. Much of that economic activity is a direct result of the favorable geographic situation of the city.

The geographic *site* of New Orleans, on the other hand, leaves much to be desired. The city sits on a mucky soil in a flood-prone swamp infested with alligators, mosquitoes, and snakes. To be blunt, if its situation were not so spectacular, the site of New Orleans would probably not be on anyone's list of preferred places for a major city.

The ability to judge site and situation from maps is clearly valuable for planners and business decision-makers. Even if you do not plan that kind of career, the skill can still be a useful thing to get out of a required class. It can help you evaluate places in terms of their job prospects, residential desirability, or vacation potential. In making these evaluations, one must remember that both site and situation depend partly on the general culture of a region. To note two rather obvious examples: a deposit of iron ore is a resource only if people have the technology to use iron, and a great harbor has little value for people who produce diamond rings, a tiny but valuable product that they can afford to airmail to their customers.

Large-scale topographic and thematic maps can provide information about the site of a city. Analyzing the situation of a city is easier on medium-scale topographic and planimetric maps; the analysis involves several related processes:

A) **Describing the hinterland.** The *hinterland* (or *trade area* or *service area*) of a city includes all of the people that think of it as "their" place to shop, get financial, governmental, or medical services, or be entertained. This idea would be simple if all services were similar to each other, but in the real world, a person who lives in southeastern Mississippi might drive east to Maxie to buy groceries, south to get clothes in Wiggins, and north to visit a shopping center in Hattiesburg (which is farther but bigger, and therefore it has some things that are not available in Maxie and Wiggins). Moreover, people from all these places might occasionally go southwest to New Orleans to get things they cannot find any closer. The rule is simple: if people need something often, they can probably find it in lots of places.

To get a tentative idea of the hinterland of a town on a map, put a mark midway between it and all nearby towns of the same size or larger. Connect those marks with a smooth curve. The result is a map of the presumed service area of the town, although the term strictly applies only to those things that cannot be found in smaller towns within the area. In other words, to get a true picture of the economic role and prospects of a town, we also need to see how it fits into the *hierarchy* of towns in an area.

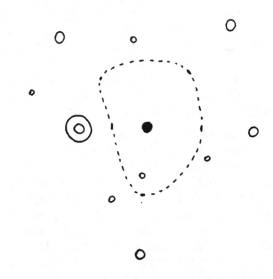

B) **Establishing a hierarchy**. All towns within a region are part of a *ranked set* of service areas that range in size from national down to local. A map can help us judge the rank of a given town within that hierarchy. We can do the analysis by noting a number of different clues (and, since each method has some uncertainty, it is often useful to do it several ways and then compare the results in order to get a composite picture):

- *Areas*. Delimit the hinterlands served by different towns, and then use one of the area-measurement techniques described on pages 19-20 to estimate the comparative sizes of the service areas of each town.

- *Populations*. Find a census map or data table and calculate the total population within the service area of each town. Settle for a reasonable estimate for comparison -- after all, if we cannot measure areas exactly, it makes little sense to carry any of the other calculations out to the third or fourth decimal place.

- *Smaller towns*. Count and compare the number of smaller towns within the service area of each town.

- *Town order*. Compute the *order* of each town -- a first-order village has no smaller settlements within its hinterland, whereas a second-order town has some first-order villages in its service area, a third-order town serves some second-order ones, and so on. By some rankings, New York is a ninth-order city; Chicago and Los Angeles are in the eighth order.

- *Transportation connections*. Rank the towns by noting the number and size of the highways and railroads that meet in each one.

- *Political significance*. Evaluate the comparative importance of the towns in the local political scene. Some maps will use different symbols for town centers, county seats, and state capitals. It is true that the most important town is not always the political center of a region, but political importance can and often does generate jobs, population, and transportation connections that may increase the rank of a town in the regional hierarchy.

C) **Evaluating centrality**. If a mapped area has no transport facilities, then the *central place* is usually easy to find -- it is the one that is closest to the geometric center of the area (i.e., place **C** on the top map). When a canal, road, or other transport facility is built in the area, however, the resulting increase in speed (or decrease in cost) of movement along the new transport lines can change the economic "center" of the area. The bottom map shows the same region after a system of roads was built to connect a coastal port to the other cities. In an economic sense, place **B** has become the "center" of the region.

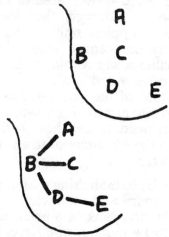

To test the comparative centrality of places on a map, just calculate (or let your computer count) the total number of miles of travel needed to get from each place to every other one in the region. The place with the shortest total connect distance is usually the economic center. In this example, if each road is ten miles long, the total distance from **B** to every other place is 50 miles, but it would take 80 miles of travel to bring a representative of every other town to place **C**.

___ Is place **A** more or less central than **E**?

___ Is place **C** more or less central than **D**?

A map reader can also use the idea of centrality within an urban area, to help evaluate the efficiency of the locations of such things as schools, fire stations, police precincts, hospitals, and other services. To make the analysis even more valid, find a topographic map and look for barriers (such as cliffs, freeways, railroad yards, large industrial areas, etc.) that divide the metropolitan region into sub-areas with few easy ways of getting from one to the others. Then, note the locations of service facilities within each of those sub-areas.

D) **Measuring connectivity**. A road network like the one in the lower sketch map is typical of a *colonial situation* (America in the 1600's, Africa two centuries later, some farm areas and mining regions today). A classic colonial situation is one in which a "foreign" power builds the roads it needs to get troops into and goods out of the country easily. The location of an economic center near the edge of a region is a key element of the colonial strategy, but the narrow focus of the transportation network is equally important. When a nation achieves independence, it usually builds a more complete transport network, and the center of economic activity often shifts toward the middle of the country. The same can be said for areas within a city -- a district may have good connections into or outside of the area but poor links within it, and the inferior quality of the internal network is a hindrance to economic development there.

Two good measures of the usefulness of a transportation network are its *density* (the total length of road per unit of area) and its *connectivity index* (the number of actual links between places, expressed as a percentage of the number of links there would be if every place were connected to every other one). Fortunately for map readers who dislike routine math, geographers already know the maximum possible number of links for *linear modes* (surface roads, where each junction "creates" a new "place") and *leapfrog modes* (like airline or interstate routes, which can cross each other without making a new place):

THEORETICAL MAXIMUM NUMBER OF TRANSPORT LINKS

Number of places	2	3	4	5	6	7	8	9
Two-way surface roads	1	3	6	9	12	15	18	21
One-way surface roads	2	6	12	18	24	30	36	42
Two-way airline routes	1	3	6	10	15	21	28	36
One-way airline routes	2	6	12	20	30	42	56	72

In evaluating the connectivity of the road network sketched on the previous page, begin by counting the cities (five). Look on the table above, and note that the maximum possible number of two-way surface links among five places is nine. Then, count the actual number of roads in the area (only four). Finally, calculate the connectivity percentage, which in this case turns out to be 44 (four divided by nine and multiplied by 100). Planners often use the ideas of connectivity and total travel time to decide which additional streets would have high priority. In this example, which two cities should be connected in order to improve the total travel time the most? With similar logic, architects often use a modified form of connectivity analysis to evaluate the size and spacing of emergency exits from a building.

CENTRALITY AND CONNECTIVITY -- PRACTICE

The maps to the right show the actual (top) and idealized (bottom) connections between buildings in an areas. The idealized map is a form of cartogram, in which the map maker has chosen to "sacrifice" accurate depiction of the distance and directional relationships between places in order to focus attention on the transportation links between them (see page 120). For one-way roads, the allowable direction of movement is shown by an arrow; two-headed arrows indicate two-way streets.

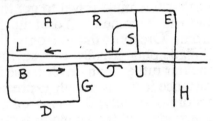

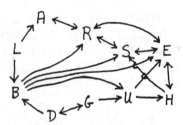

_____ What is the connectivity index of the network?

_____ Which place is farthest from the hospital (H)?

_____ Which place is most central for trips *toward* the place (i.e., has the lowest total number of links to get from all other places to it)?

_____ Which place is most central for trips *away from* the place (i.e., has the lowest total number of links to get to all other places from it)?

_____ Which place would be most central if all of the roads had two-way traffic?

_____ Which road should be made two-way in order to make the biggest improvement in connectivity to the hospital?

INTERACTION AMONG PLACES ON A MAP

The *gravity model* is an abstract but useful way to predict movement of things among places shown on a map. The theory gets its name from its similarity to Newton's description of gravity. As applied in map analysis, the gravity model makes the controversial assumption that human beings, *en masse*, behave like objects in a gravitational field; their attraction to a place is related *directly* to the size of the place (they're *more* likely to go to big places) and *inversely* to the distance to the place (they're *less* likely to go to distant places). Despite the crudeness of the assumption, the gravity model seems to work for some purposes, and it is widely used in planning highway systems, telephone connections, shopping centers, bus routes, and many public facilities. Most versions of the gravity model have between three and seven subparts, which we will illustrate by describing a hypothetical highway project:

1) **Size of the origin.** One of the most obvious things that can affect the traffic on a road is the number of people living at one end of it. This population at the origin (usually called P_O) can be estimated from a map by measuring area, counting houses, or interpreting census data.

2) **Attractiveness of the destination.** The number of people that are likely to travel on a particular road also depends on the size of the destination; a larger population there can provide a greater variety of things to do, see, or buy. This factor, P_D, can be calculated in the same way as P_O (though for some purposes, such as predicting rush-hour commuting, it is better to figure P_O in terms of residents and P_D on the basis of job opportunities).

3) **Distance from origin to destination.** The farther one must travel to get to a place, the less likely the trip becomes. Yosemite Park has more visitors from Oregon than from Indiana; people in Philadelphia usually choose to go to a local movie theater rather than drive to one in New York. The

$$\frac{P_O \times P_D}{D^2}$$

distance factor is usually expressed as **D** raised to some power (in Newton's original theory of gravity, **D** is squared because the area of a "circle of influence" increases fourfold when the diameter is doubled).

4) **Cost of travel.** The distance factor is more realistic if one figures it in terms of travel time, money, and scenery as well as simple distance. A well-studied topographic map can tell much about the nature of the terrain, the curviness of the road, and the apparent speed limit along the route. The cost of distance can be expressed as A_{O-D}, a number that is used to adjust the distance on each route to some comparable measure of travel effort or cost.

$$\frac{P_O \times (P_D - R)}{D_{O-D}^2 \times A_{O-D}}$$

5) **Intervening opportunities.** People are less likely to travel to a given destination if they can get what they want at another place that is not so far away. This simple idea, of course, can get very complicated if the brand of the product is not the same, or the price is different, or people are planning to visit an aunt in the town anyway. Nevertheless, we can improve the gravity model by taking P_D and subtracting **R**, which is basically an estimate of the number of "redundant" providers of things that are available closer to home. The sizes and locations of these *intervening opportunities* may be apparent on a good map (see the discussion of service hierarchies on pages 168-169.

6) **Propensity to travel.** An unmarried 30-year-old freelance writer is more likely to travel than a steelworker with two grade-school children and a part-time job on weekends. The gravity model can include differences in travel behavior due to age, occupation, and income; simply multiply P_O (the population of the origin) by T (a measure of travel propensity, estimated on a 0-1 scale). In a formal traffic analysis, this factor will usually be determined on the basis of a questionnaire study, but you can make a reasonably good guess by looking at map traits such as street networks, house sizes, and industrial patterns.

7) **Congestion.** If predicted traffic exceeds the capacity of a road, speeds will decrease, travel times will increase, and people will be less likely to use the road. In that case, we should adjust the travel time by a congestion factor, C_{O-D}, and try the model again.

$$\frac{(P_0 \cdot T) \times (P_D - R)}{D_{O-D}^2 \times A_{O-D} \times C_{O-D}}$$

To use the gravity model, divide the map into reasonable origin and destination areas. Make other assumptions as reasonably as possible, then do the formula for each origin-destination pair. The result is an *index of potential interaction* along each link in a transportation system. These indices have no absolute meaning all by themselves -- they predict the comparative amount of traffic on different roads, not the actual amount on a given road. A few actual traffic counts can allow us to calibrate the model for present traffic patterns, and it can then be used to predict future traffic on roads that have not been built and in areas that have not yet been developed (and even to improve maps of traffic -- see pages 120-121).

INTERACTION -- PRACTICE

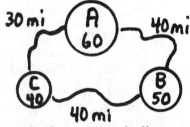

A counter has recorded 300 vehicles per day on the road between **A** and **B** on this map. Using the simple form of the gravity model ($(P_A \times P_B) / D$), we get an interaction index of 75 (60 times 50 divided by 40) for the A-to-B route. The actual count is four times the index, and therefore the calibration factor is four (if we had measured distance in kilometers or population in families, the calibration factor would be different, but the model would still give the same <u>comparative</u> results).

_____ 1) What is the traffic index for the road from **B** to **C**?

_____ 2) Multiply that by the calibration factor (4) to get the estimated traffic on that road (in vehicles per day).

_____ 3) Suppose the population of place **C** doubles. How much traffic would the model predict on the **B**-to-**C** road then?

_____ 4) Suppose the road from **B** to **C** were rebuilt with an average speed of 45 miles per hour instead of 30 mph. What would be the new traffic estimate?

Have you become uncomfortable with the original calibration factor (4) after these two changes? If so, you have discovered the major problem with the gravity model of spatial interaction -- it can be calibrated to "explain" traffic flows or telephone calls as they exist now, but its validity as a tool for predicting future traffic is uncertain, because an accurate calibration of the model depends on real-world measurements (and by then it may be too late).

ACCESSIBILITY, BUFFER ZONES, AND AT-RISK POPULATION

A whole group of map-analysis techniques is based on the idea of *buffer zones* around map features. These analytical tools have one idea in common: they divide space into subareas on the basis of accessibility to particular points, lines, and/or areas. For example, one might map all areas that are within twenty miles of an interstate highway. That map would interest someone who has to decide where to locate a factory that depends on timely receipt of supplies or shipment of products. A similar logic can divide a city into zones of varying distance from police stations, fire stations, schools, or hospitals. This kind of information is widely used in figuring out how much to charge people for fire insurance or ambulance service.

All by itself, a simple measurement of distance on a map is neither difficult nor particularly realistic. It can be a good first guess, but the analysis has to include more factors to be really useful. One of the most promising additions is based on the ideas of connectivity and congestion. To include these factors, the map reader should adjust the distance to the feature of interest (i. e., the width of the buffer zone) by considering the nature of the affected population, the terrain and land cover, and the locations of streams and highways (which can extend the range of possible impact as well as provide avenues for evacuation).

This advanced form of buffer-zone analysis is especially useful in one common form of emergency planning, the identification of the *at-risk population* for a natural hazard or an event such as a nuclear accident or toxic waste spill. This analysis has five steps:

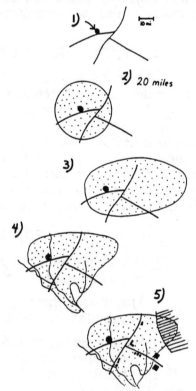

1) identify the location of a toxic waste spill or other hazard (or a possible one, for planning purposes),

2) determine how far away from that point the hazard might have an impact under normal circumstances,

3) adjust that distance to account for the effects of big forces, such as a prevailing wind that is likely to extend the impact farther in one direction than in another,

4) adjust the distances again to account for rivers, road networks, and other landscape features that can alter how far the waste may spread and thus affect the shape of the impact zone, and

5) get information from other maps in order to describe the traits of the population in the area that has been identified as being at risk from the accident.

One final complication: a simple division of a map area into two zones -- at-risk and safe -- is not necessarily the most useful way to provide information for emergency planners. For this reason, a map maker might choose to use a more elaborate map vocabulary, such as an isoline of risk (isorisk?), to define areas that have different degrees of hazard (e.g., critical, severe, moderate, slight, and none).

DISTORTION OF A MAP MESSAGE

Recognizing *distortion* in the message of a map (whether due to accidental confusion or deliberate intent) is the most abstract and yet the most important skill of map analysis. The analysis of distortion builds on ideas presented throughout this book -- we have repeatedly said that spatial patterns are a unique kind of information, and that the communication of spatial information requires a specialized vocabulary and grammar. Like any other spoken or written language, the language of maps has many ways in which a message can be distorted. A skillful map reader is aware of the processes that can introduce distortion ("noise") into the message (the "signal"). That awareness, in turn, allows the map interpreter to filter out the noise and thus get a fairly clean message, even from a badly designed map. For several common sources of map distortion, here is a brief description of their cause, some typical examples, and a prescription for remedial action:

A) **Projection distortion.** Geometric alteration of reality occurs when a map maker tries to fit the irregular surface of a three-dimensional earth onto a flat page or video screen. All such attempts are at best compromises, which must sacrifice some important information in order to preserve other parts of the message. For example, a *cylindrical* projection is able to show compass direction well, but it will inevitably distort distance or area; an *equal-area* projection can show sizes accurately, but it distorts distance and position. Prescription: be able to identify each major type of map projection, and know the nature and spatial arrangement of the distortion introduced by it. Pages 30-31 included examples and descriptions of some common map projections. The sketches below show how North America looks on four common world map projections; each one was traced from a textbook or atlas that was on the market in 1990 (and this set doesn't even include an example of an ultra-simplified "children's" map, or a geometrified depiction of the world as a set of simple squares and triangles, or one of those dreadful "renderings," in which an lazy cartographer draws a general impression of what the continent feels like on a given day. All of those communicate an idea about the spatial characteristics of the continent; the question is: what message?)

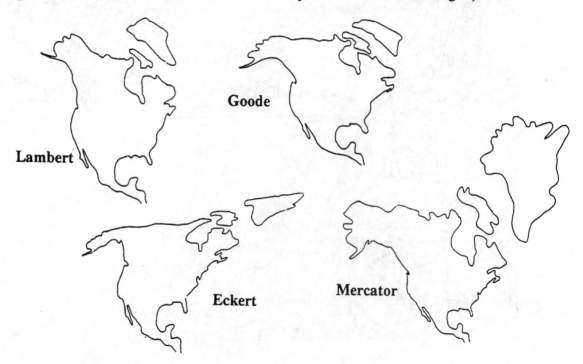

B) **Reduction distortion.** Selective enlargement of features is necessary in order to keep them visible while a whole landscape is reduced to fit on a printed page. That enlargement, in turn, means that the features are no longer accurately shown at the scale of the map (see pages 21-24). Examples: streets often are drawn nearly as wide as city blocks on a road map of a city; "raised relief" maps or globes tend to exaggerate the heights of mountains to make them noticeable (the height of Mount Everest should actually be about a quarter of a millimeter (a hundredth of an inch) on a standard 16-inch classroom globe). Prescription: know the scale of a map and mentally figure how big things like roads or houses really should be.

C) **Simplification distortion.** A map must omit or minimize some features in order to show the positions or relationships of other features. Small clearings, swamps, and patches of forest are usually ignored in making a generalized vegetation map. Side roads and minor curves are not shown on a highway map, even though they can affect speed and travel time. Prescription: stay aware of how much may be missing from a map. Try to identify the *threshold* size or importance that the map maker used in deciding whether to include or omit a particular feature. Remember: a full understanding of the patterns on a map may involve factors that are <u>not</u> visible on the map.

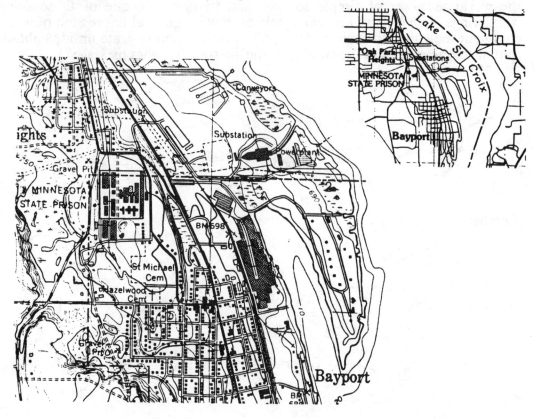

D) **Sampling distortion.**
Early in the process of gathering data, a map maker must decide whether the purpose of the map is to describe every small area accurately (the *tag* approach) or to show general patterns and quantities in an entire region (the *count* approach; see pages 132-135). The first goal requires some kind of *importance evaluation* in each sub-area, so that the map can show what are really the most important features there. The second goal demands some kind of statistically valid *sampling*. Unfortunately, that will inevitably misclassify some small areas in the interests of "capturing" those features that are small but present all through the region and therefore ought to be included in a valid inventory of the area. Prescription: try to figure out whether the purpose of the map maker was to *tag* each subarea or to *count* features in the entire region. Do not expect one kind of map to provide valid answers to the other kind of question.

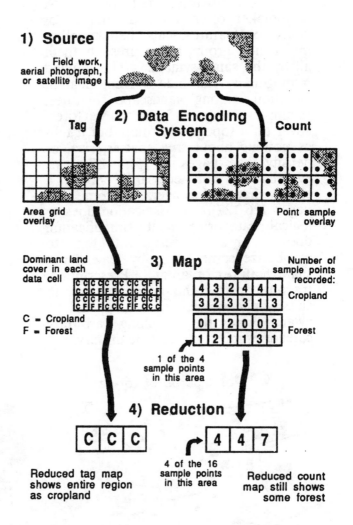

1) Source
Field work, aerial photograph, or satellite image

2) Data Encoding System
Tag — Count

Area grid overlay — Point sample overlay

Dominant land cover in each data cell — **3) Map** — Number of sample points recorded:

C = Cropland
F = Forest

| 4 | 3 | 2 | 4 | 4 | 1 | Cropland |
| 3 | 2 | 3 | 3 | 1 | 3 | |

| 0 | 1 | 2 | 0 | 0 | 3 | Forest |
| 1 | 2 | 1 | 1 | 3 | 1 | |

1 of the 4 sample points in this area

4) Reduction

C C C — 4 4 7

Reduced tag map shows entire region as cropland

4 of the 16 sample points in this area

Reduced count map still shows some forest

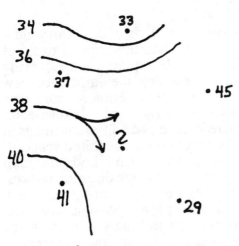

E) **Extrapolation distortion.** Map-makers do not usually have enough time to measure everything they put on a map; they take what they hope is a representative sample of reality and then extend the results of those observations to fill in all of the "empty" areas on the map. This is especially true in the case of isoline maps, which make the assumption that the data are *continuous* (exist everywhere on the map, even between sample points, and change gradually from one place to another; see pages 102-104 and 136-137). Examples: weather information is usually measured at an airport and assumed to apply to a nearby city; a census table shows how many people live in an area, but it does not indicate exactly where in that area they live. Prescription: try to find out the source for the data on a map, in order to determine what parts of the map are reliable.

F) **Classification distortion.** A map-maker often takes a number of landscape features, puts them together in a logical group, and represents them all by the same symbol. The implied homogeneity can hide a great deal of variation among landscape features. Examples: a green color shows forest cover on a topographic map, but it tells us nothing about tree species, size, or density (see pages 74-76). Likewise, everybody is not necessarily poor in a county that has low average income (see pages 126-127). Classification does to logical categories what simplification does to physical sizes: both tend to emphasize some things by leaving out small features or areas. Prescription: try to reconstruct the procedures used to classify phenomena for a map, and be aware how the resulting arbitrary categories might mislead the unwary.

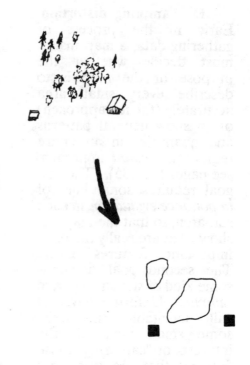

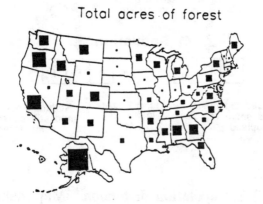

Total acres of forest

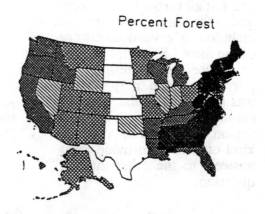

Percent Forest

G) **Manipulation distortion.** Combining two or more kinds of data can yield a third kind that is more meaningful and thus more useful than the original two, but the result can also be misleading (see pages 142-144). Examples: a map showing percentage of population growth can be useful in assessing the impact of new residents. However, a 50% increase in population will require many more new houses in a city of a million people than in a town of a few hundred. Likewise, an average population density of ten people per square mile implies different things in a rural county full of family farms than in a desert county with uninhabited space all around a few big towns. Prescription: try to figure out what methods the map maker used to figure the densities, averages, growth rates, localization indices, factor scores, or other mathematical and/or logical expressions that appear on a given map. That is undoubtedly a lot of work, but it is simply not possible to get the correct message from a map if you do not understand its vocabulary. It also helps to have some mental maps of things like area, climate, population, energy reserves, and income to use as a basis for comparison.

H) **Perception distortion.** A "normal" human eye perceives some shapes, colors, sizes, and orientations of symbols as larger, more prominent, or more intense than a "scientifically" measured comparison would seem to justify. Examples: a circle with about three times the area of another one appears to be only twice as big to most people (see pages 118-119); red areas seem larger than blue ones of the same size; apparent lengths of lines can be altered by other lines around them. Prescription: check the legend of a map carefully to see whether the cartographer has made allowance for some of the common perceptual "distortions."

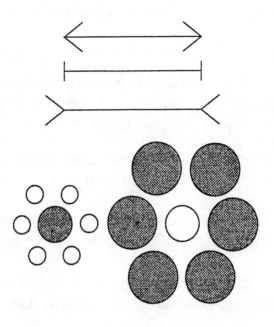

I) **Propaganda distortion.** It is a sad fact that some people simply do not want to tell the truth. Some of these people know the ways in which a map reader can get the wrong message from a printed map. indeed, they may be even more aware of the possible sources of distortion than the average map maker, because they often deliberately use inappropriate projections, sampling strategies, or symbols to mislead the reader. The prescription for protecting yourself against map liars is the same as for any kind of liar: know the person who is speaking, or know enough to recognize falsehood when you see it.

SUMMARY. A map can show a world of information, but one fact stands out: a map reader has to know much in order to get the message straight.

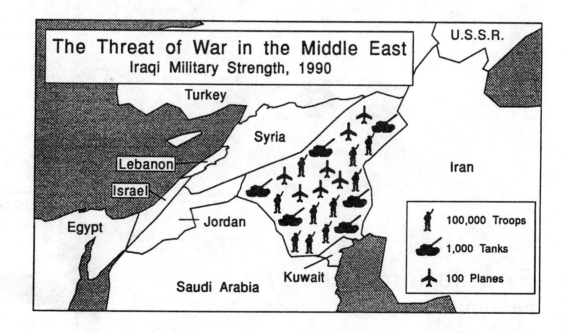

SAMPLE QUIZ QUESTIONS -- THEMATIC MAP ANALYSIS

You will be given a copy of a thematic map.

1) Briefly describe the original phenomenon the map-maker observed before making this map -- comment about their original dimensionality, presence, continuity, scaling, temporality, etc.

2) Briefly describe the transformations the map-maker made to these data before displaying them on the map.

3) Briefly describe the symbolic language used on this map. Is this kind of symbol appropriate for the data being mapped? Why or why not?

4) Briefly desribe the spatial pattern (order, bias, etc.) of the data on this map. Use standard terms and analytical tools to support your observations.

5) Briefly describe the possible sources of distortion on this map. Cite specific map locations as examples where appropriate.

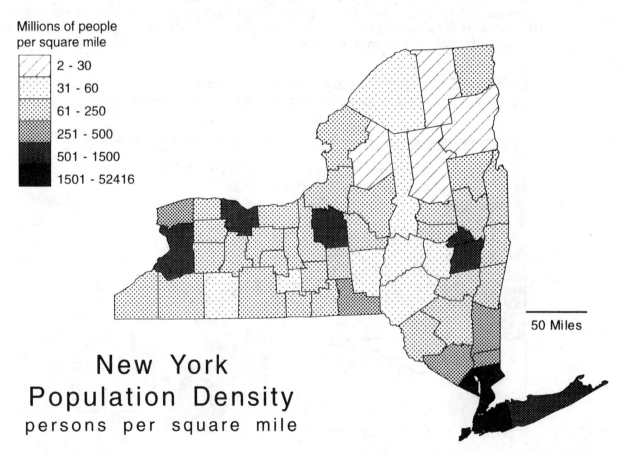

Millions of people per square mile

- 2 - 30
- 31 - 60
- 61 - 250
- 251 - 500
- 501 - 1500
- 1501 - 52416

50 Miles

New York
Population Density
persons per square mile

Source: U.S. Bureau of the Census, 1990

METRIC-ENGLISH CONVERSIONS

Slowly but surely, map making in the United Staes is shifting toward the metric system, with its computationally simple use of powers of ten for the primary units of mass, length, area, and volume.

nanometer ---------- one billionth of a meter
micrometer --------- one millionth of a meter

millimeter ---------- one thousandth of a meter
centimeter ---------- one hundredth of a meter
decimeter ---------- one tenth of a meter

meter ----------------- the standard unit of length

dekameter ---------- ten meters
hectometer --------- one hundred meters
kilometer ------------ one thousand meters

megameter ---------- one million meters
gigameter ----------- one billion meters

The Universal Transverse Mercator grid, long used by the military, is a metric location system (see pages 33-35). The new series of 1:100,000 topographic maps and the digital data files of the Census Bureau use metric units. Legal descriptions of property, however, are still recorded in English units, and the cost of conversion from metes-and-bounds (see pages 77-78) or Public Land Survey sections (pages 38-41 and 79-80) is quite high. For the next few decades, therefore, a map reader must be able to use both systems of measurement. The table below lists some approximate (rule-of-thumb) conversions; it is usually easier to memorize some common objects (the width of your hand, the length of your stride, the size of your city block, the weight of your bicycle, etc.)

1 kilogram is about 2.2 pounds
   1 pound is about 0.45 kilograms

1 centimeter is about 0.4 inches
   1 inch is about 2.5 centimeters

1 meter is about 3.3 feet
   1 foot is about 0.3 meters

1 kilometer is about 0.6 miles
   1 mile is about 1.6 kilometers

1 square centimeter is about 0.16 square inches
   1 square inch is about 6.5 square centimeters

1 square meter is about 10.8 square feet
   1 square foot is about 0.09 square meters

Degrees Fahrenheit	Degrees Celsius
-40	-40
-22	-30
-4	-20
14	-10
32	0
50	10
68	20
86	30
104	40

1 hectare is about 2.5 acres
   1 acre is about 0.4 hectares

1 square kilometer is about 0.4 square miles
   1 square miles is about 2.6 square kilometers

1 cubic meter is about 35 cubic feet
   1 cubic foot is about 0.03 cubic meters

1 meter per second is about 2.2 miles per hour
   1 mile per hour is about 0.45 meters per second

100 bushels per acre are about 6 tons per hectare
1000 millibars are about 15 pounds per square inch

SOURCES OF MAPS

The State Cartographer. Some states have a government official whose job is to keep a record of all maps produced for the state as a whole or for various counties or regions within it. Check under State Government in the telephone directory for the state capital.

The *National Cartographic Information Center.* NCIC publishes a number of catalogs of maps (and digital data bases that can be used to make maps); address your request to the National Cartographic Information Center, 507 National Center, Reston, VA 22092 or to the Mid-Continent Mapping Center, 1400 Independence Road, Rolla, MO 65401.

World crises are the concern of the Central Intelligence Agency; its maps and atlases are often available at surprisingly low cost from the Superintendent of Documents, United States Government Printing Office, Washington, DC 20402.

The International Bank for Reconstruction and Development publishes the *World Bank Atlas* and other maps. Write to the Information and Public Affairs Department, 1818 H Street, NW, Washington, DC 20433

Graphic summaries of the Census contain maps of population, housing, business, industry, retail and wholesale trade, transportation, and other topics -- write to Customer Services Branch, Data User Services Division, Bureau of the Census, Washington, DC 20233.

Public, Newspaper, and University Libraries. Most libraries have a few basic globes and atlases. Many have a selection of thematic atlases and reference maps. Some have special rooms for historical and modern map collections.

The local *Chamber of Commerce, Tourist Bureau,* or a municipal agency with a title like *Economic Development Commission* produce unpredictable but often large collections of city road maps, zoning maps, economic development plans, environmental impact statements, and tourist maps of all kinds.

Plat books (with maps of property ownership) are available for inspection and often for sale in the office of the county tax assessor; many real-estate agencies also have copies of plat maps.

Bookstores. Most bookstores have maps for sale: general-purpose atlases, in the *Reference* section; tourist maps, in the *Travel* section; and local street maps and state thematic atlases, (published in about 40 states so far) in a section called something like *Local Interest* or *Regional.*

Map and globe publishers, such as American Eagle, Cram, DeLorme, Hammond, Hubbard, Oxford, Prentice-Hall, Rand-McNally, Replogle, and others. Ask in your library for a recent listing of publishers' addresses and specialties.

Detailed road maps are sold or given away by the county or state highway department, which has the responsibility of keeping them up-to-date. The American Automobile Association, 8111 Gatehouse Road, Falls Church, VA 22047 publishes good maps free for their members.

Sanford insurance maps show the patterns of land use in a city at selected times in the past. Ask in the public or university library, or write Chadwyck-Healey Inc., 623 Martense Avenue, Teaneck, NJ 07666 for microfilm versions; also check *Historic Urban Plans,* Box 276, Ithaca, NY 14850.

Local and regional *histories* can have all kinds of maps of local interest. Start with your local library; if you don't find what you want there, try the archives in the county courthouse or the county or state historical society.

For *topographic maps*, look in camping or fishing stores, your State Geological Survey, or write to the Map Distribution Center, U.S. Geological Survey, Federal Center, Denver, CO 80225, and ask for the index map for the states of interest.

Aeronautical Charts are for sale at most airports; ask for an agency with a name like "Pilot Services," or look in the Yellow Pages under something like "airplane rental and leasing" or "flying instruction."

Nautical charts are available from the Physical Science Service Branch, National Ocean Survey, NOAA, Rockville, MD 20852, but it is usually quicker to phone some boat rental places or fishing outfitters in your favorite port.

Weather maps are sent electronically from a national center to airports and television stations all over the country. These people often give away copies of out-of-date weather maps. Or, write the National Climate Data Center, U. S. Department of Commerce, Federal Building, Asheville, NC 28801

National forest maps are available from the Forest Service (listed under United States Government, Department of Agriculture).

Hunting maps and *Lake maps* are usually sold by the state office of the Department of Natural Resources (or whatever it may be called in your state).

Soil surveys and maps of prime farmland, land capability, wildlife habitat, building limitations are available in the county office of the Soil Conservation Service (listed under United States Government, Department of Agriculture).

Geologic maps come from both public and private sources: most states have a Geological Survey which often cooperates with private organizations such as the American Association of Petroleum Geologists.

Environment Impact Statements often contain maps of general environmental and economic conditions. Depending on the region and the project in question, go to the area office of the Bureau of Land Management, Bureau of Reclamation, National Park Service, Forest Service, Federal Energy Administration, or Army Corps of Engineers (all listed under United States Government in the telephone directory); many states have equivalent governmental departments.

Zoning maps are the responsibility of the city or county zoning office (it may be called a planning board, resource agency, land management office, or some other similar name, but people in the courthouse can direct you to it).

Many government agencies make *Land Use Maps*; ask in the courthouse. Some areas have "umbrella" agencies with names like Southeast Michigan Council of Governments (SEMCOG) or San Diego Area Governments (SANDAG).

Aerial photographs are abundant, but it can sometimes be difficult to find the one that covers a particular area. In most eastern and some western states, start with the county office of the Agricultural Stabilization and Conservation Service (listed in the phone directory under United States Government, Department of Agriculture); in many parts of the West, go to the regional office of the Bureau of Land Management (listed under United States Government, Department of the Interior); and in the Appalachians, try the Tennessee Valley Authority.

Satellite images come from EOSAT, 4300 Forbes Boulevard, Lanham, MD 20706, or SPOT Image Corporation, 1897 Preston White Drive, Reston, Va 22091

Finally, if you really have money to spend, travel to the *Geography and Map Division*, Library of Congress, Washington, DC 20540, the *National Archives*, Pennsylvania Avenue at 8th St, NW, Washington, DC 20408, or the *American Geographical Society Map Collection*, P.O.Box 399, University of Wisconsin-Milwaukee, Milwaukee, WI 53201

GLOSSARY AND INDEX

(Italicized words are also defined separately in this glossary)

ANSWERS TO PRACTICE EXERCISES AND QUIZZES

Page 12:

DISTANCE:	A	B	C	D	E	F
EXPRESSION						
meters	1000	1609	2400	*6970*	*27200*	*25*
kilometers	1	1.6	2.4	*6.97*	*27.2*	*.025*
miles	0.62	1	1.5	*4.4*	17	*.016*
feet	3281	5280	*7920*	23,000	*89760*	83
time at 30 mph	75 sec	2 min	3 min+	*8.7 min*	*34 min*	*1.9 sec*

Page 13: 72 miles, 66 miles, 70 miles, 46 minutes, Claude, A3

Page 17:

DIRECTION	A	B	C	D	E
EXPRESSION					
Cardinal name	east	southwest	*NW*	east northeast	*SSE*
Points	8	*20*	28	*6*	14
Azimuth degrees	*90*	225	315	*67+*	*157+*
Mils	1600	4000	*5600*	*1200*	2800
Bearing	N90°E	S45°W	*N45°W*	N67°E	*S22.5°E*
Backsight	S90°W	*N45°E*	S45°E	S67°W	*N22.5°W*

22.5, 199, 107, 162, G, D

Page 24:

MAP	A	B	C	D	E	F
verbal phrase	1 inch = 1 mile	1 inch = 4 miles	4 cm = 1 km	*1 cm = 10 km*	*1 cm = 38 m*	*1 in = 28 mi*
representative fraction	1: 63,360	1: 250,000	1: 25,000	1: 1,000,000	*1: 3840*	*1: 1,774,080*
centimeters on map	10	*20*	5	14	50	*10*
inches on map	4	8	2	*5.5*	20	4
kilometers in real world	6.3	*51*	*1.2*	*140*	1.92	*179*
miles in real world	4	32	*0.8*	87	*1.2*	112

1:380,160, 960 m, 10.2 km^2, 3.3 miles, 1:124,500, 3.7 km.

Page 26: TFF, TFF, TTF, TFT, FT, TTF, TTF, FTFTFF

Page 29:

PLACE	1	2	3	4	5	6	7
Hemisphere	N	N	S	N	S	N	N
Latitude degrees	30	56	49	20	85	28	42
Date	Oct 24	July 4	Feb 12	Sep 23	Dec 1	Feb/Oct 22	Apr 23
Degrees up from horizon	47	56	55	70	27	52	60
Degrees down from zenith	43	34	35	20	63	38	30

Moscow, 34OS and 151^OE, 12,400 km, 265°, 4 a.m., 45^OE, 3900 miles, 8 hrs, 34°

Page 35: 342,390m, 5,728,650m, 343,090m, 5,728,260m, 190m, 900m, 920m, 700m, -390m, about 800m

Page 37: 617,290m, G, 4,305,180m, 617,510m, 616,950m, 4,304,380m

Page 40: J. Smithson
should be N 1/2 and SW 1/4
S 1/2 and NE 1/4 of the SE 1/4 plus SE 1/4 of the NE 1/4 of Sec 10
N1/2 of the S1/2 of the SW1/4 of the SW1/4 of Sec 1

Page 41: 18ha; NW 1/4 of the SE 1/4 of Sec 20, R3W, T?N;
S 1/2 of the SW 1/4 of Sec 17 plus NW 1/4 of the NW 1/4 of Sec 20;
120 acres, 120 acres

Page 64: 40', 4,999', 4860', 1080', 19°, 37%
177°, 61%, G, 4980', No

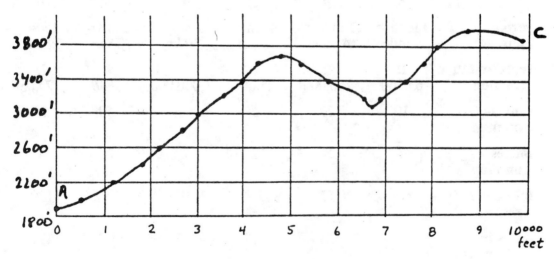

Page 66: C, H, E, B, A, G, D, F